Police Innovation
and
Control of the Police

David Weisburd   Craig Uchida
Editors
with Lorraine Green

Police Innovation and Control of the Police

Problems of Law, Order, and Community

Springer-Verlag
New York Berlin Heidelberg London Paris
Tokyo Hong Kong Barcelona Budapest

David Weisburd, Ph.D.
Director
Center for Crime Prevention Studies
Rutgers University
15 Washington Street
Newark, NJ 07102, USA
and Associate Professor
Institute of Criminology
Hebrew University Law School
Jerusalem, Israel

Craig Uchida, Ph.D.
Deputy Director
National Institute of Justice
633 Indiana Avenue, N.W.
Washington, DC 20531, USA

Library of Congress Cataloging-in-Publication Data
Police innovation and control of the police : problems of law, order,
  and community / David Weisburd, Craig Uchida, editors.
      p. cm.
    Includes bibliographical references.
    ISBN 0-387-94013-8 (New York). — ISBN 3-540-94013-8 (Berlin)
    1. Community policing — United States.   2. Public relations —
Police — United States.   I. Weisburd, David.   II. Uchida, Craig D.
HV7936.C83P65 1993
363.2'0973 — dc20   92-45633

Printed on acid-free paper.

Production coordinated by Chernow Editorial Services, Inc. and managed by
  Christin R. Ciresi; manufacturing supervised by Vinnie Scelta.
Typeset by Best-set Typesetter Ltd., Hong Kong.
Printed and bound by Edwards Brothers, Ann Arbor, MI, USA.
Printed in the United States of America.

9 8 7 6 5 4 3 2 1

ISBN 0-387-94013-8 Springer-Verlag New York Berlin Heidelberg
ISBN 3-540-94013-8 Springer-Verlag Berlin Heidelberg New York

Contents

Part V Crime Control and Police Control:
Future Trends and Problems

Contributors

Michael E. Buerger, Ph.D., Assistant Professor, Department of Public Affairs, University of Wisconsin, Oshkosh, WI 54901, USA

John Eck, M.A., Associate Director, Police Executive Research Forum, Washington, DC 20037, USA

Lorraine Green, Ph.D., Assistant Professor, Northeastern University, Boston, MA 02115, USA; Senior Research Associate, Center for Crime Prevention Studies, Rutgers University, Newark, NJ 07102, USA

Jack Greene, Ph.D., Professor, Center for Public Policy, Temple University, Philadelphia, PA 19122, USA

Stephen Mastrofski, Ph.D., Associate Professor, Administration of Justice, Pennsylvania State University, University Park, PA 16802, USA

William McDonald, Ph.D., Associate Professor, Department of Sociology and Institute of Criminal Law and Procedure, Georgetown University Law Center, Washington, DC 20001, USA

Louise Shelley, Ph.D., Professor, Department of Justice, Law and Society, The American University, Washington, DC 20016, USA

Lawrence Sherman, Ph.D., Professor, Department of Criminology and Criminal Justice, University of Maryland, College Park, MD 20742, USA; President, Crime Control Institute, Washington, DC 20007, USA

Jerome H. Skolnick, Ph.D., Claire Clements Dean's Professor of Law, University of California at Berkeley, Berkeley, CA 94220, USA

Craig Uchida, Ph.D., Deputy Director, National Institute of Justice, Washington, DC 20531, USA

Samuel Walker, Ph.D., Professor, Department of Criminal Justice, University of Nebraska at Omaha, Omaha, NE 68182, USA

David Weisburd, Ph.D., Director, Center for Crime Prevention Studies, Rutgers University, Newark, NJ 07102, USA; Associate Professor, Institute of Criminology, Hebrew University Law School, Jerusalem, Israel

Part I
Introduction

1
Raising Questions of Law and Order

David Weisburd and Craig Uchida with Lorraine Green

> The police in democratic society are required to maintain order and to do so under the rule of law. As functionaries charged with maintaining order, they are part of the bureaucracy. The ideology of democratic bureaucracy emphasizes initiative rather than disciplined adherence to rules and regulations. By contrast, the rule of law emphasizes the rights of individual citizens and constraints upon the initiative of legal officials. This tension between the operational consequences of ideas of order, efficiency, and initiative, on the one hand, and legality on the other, constitutes the principle problem of police as a democratic legal organization. (Skolnick, 1966:6)

In the 1960s Jerome Skolnick described the main problem of police in democratic society as one of effectively maintaining order while adhering to legal norms that emphasize constraint on the initiative of police authority. Contrary to what was and continues to be a common theme in American images of justice, that law and order are complementary, Skolnick argued that one necessarily is in conflict with the other. To emphasize the rule of law was to place the rights of citizens to be free from undue interference of public officials above society's right to maintain order. To emphasize order was to place society's need to be free from crime problems above the rights of individual citizens.

The problem that Skolnick raised was particularly important in the decade in which he wrote. Although the police were not the cause of the unrest of the 1960s, which clearly lay in problems of race and poverty as well as opposition to the Vietnam War, they were often the flash point around which violence would develop. For example, the Watts riots followed an arrest made by white officers. The police, who were caricatured by students as "pigs," featured prominently in the violence surrounding the 1968 Democratic National Convention in Chicago. The notion that the police were "part of the problem" rather than the "solution" was not an uncommon one two and a half decades ago (see Crawford, 1973; Groves and Rossi, 1970; Lohman and Misner, 1966; National Advisory Commission on Civil Disorders, 1968; President's Commission on Law Enforcement and Administration of Criminal Justice, 1967a, 1967b).

Skolnick's recognition of a tension in the police role in modern society fit easily into the realities of that time.

Concern about the limits of police authority were being raised not only in the streets, but also in the courts (see Chapter 3) and among police professionals themselves who sought to find effective ways of curbing police abuse and corruption (Chevigny, 1969; Culver, 1975; Dempsey, 1972, 1973; Goldstein, 1975; The Knapp Commission, 1973). It was clear to most scholars and lay people that major changes would have to be made if the police were to regain the confidence of large sectors of the populations they served. Programs that sought to reach out to minority communities and the young were common at this juncture (see, for example, Brown, 1971; Cizanckas and Purviance, 1973; Hale, 1974), as were innovations that sought to limit the potential for unlawful intrusions by police into the lives of citizens (see, for example, American Bar Association, 1973; Brown, 1972; Goldstein, 1975; Jolin and Gibbons, 1984; Pennsylvania Crime Commission, 1974). Looking back on many of the changes that came to major American police departments during this time, one is struck by the extent to which the police began to place the problem of law above that of order. Indeed in many of America's most populous cities, the emphasis on control of the police, as reflected in new rules of conduct or in the development of internal affairs units, brought many line officers to complain that the departments they worked for were more concerned with police control than with crime control (Cape, 1971; Goldstein, 1977; *New York Times*, September 3, 1971, p. 1, col. 2).

The 1980s raised a new set of challenges for police administrators and scholars. The decay in many inner cities and a sense among citizenry that the streets had been lost to vagrants and criminals led to a call for a different type of policing that would focus on returning the community back to its law-abiding members (see, for example, Goldstein, 1979, 1987; Skolnick and Bayley, 1986; Wilson and Kelling, 1982). Armed with research that detailed the "failures" of technological policing such as rapid patrol response (Kansas City Police Department, 1978; Spelman and Brown, 1984), scholars and practitioners sought to define new strategies that would team the police and the public together in an effort to control crime and disorder (Eck and Spelman, 1987; Farrell, 1988; Greene, 1987; Greene and Taylor, 1988; Kelling, 1987; Oettmeier and Brown, 1988). Police administrators in the 1980s were faced with a public that wanted them to do much more to aid communities in their fight against urban decay and crime. It was no longer enough merely to respond to calls for help by citizens; the police were expected to become partners in efforts to rehabilitate urban communities.

In some sense, this call of citizens was a reflection of the success of police in reforming their image in the 1970s. But it also meant that the balance between police control and crime control was to shift. Many of those who have been central in creating the crime control policies of the last decade also played a role in analyzing the problems of police in the 1960s. Thus it is not surprising that major innovations in policing were now intricately linked to the communities in which they developed. Both scholars and police professionals came to argue that effective crime and disorder control could not be achieved without the cooperation of the public (see, for example, Brown, 1985; Feins, 1983; Goldstein, 1987; Greene and Mastrofski, 1988). And the understanding that police resources were limited, and thus must be carefully focused, made it essential that the police turn to the community for direction not only in fighting crime but also in prioritizing crime and disorder problems. With few exceptions, however, it was problems of efficiency and crime control that police addressed, usually giving brief comment to the impact of such policies on police abuse and corruption.

It was against this backdrop that the idea for this book was developed. In a decade that saw the adoption of a series of thoughtful and popular police innovations, there appeared little discussion of the debate that Jerome Skolnick had raised some two decades earlier. Although new programs focused on order, and many called for police to extend the scope of their authority, practitioners often assumed that they would derive both increased crime control and police control from the innovations they developed. In part it was that most of the new innovations had some connection to what had come to be called "community policing" (see Oettmeier and Bieck, 1986; Skolnick and Bayley, 1986; Trojanowicz and Bucqueroux, 1990; Trojanowicz and Carter, 1988). Many of the problems that police encountered in the 1960s developed from their alienation from minorities and the poor. For the most part the new innovations called for the police to be partners with those communities as they sought to free themselves from crime and disorder problems. This involvement with the community was seen to provide a barrier to problems of corruption and abuse (see Weisburd, McElroy, and Hardyman, 1988). But we suspect as well that many of those responsible for the new innovations simply assumed that the mechanisms of police control had become so well entrenched that they did not need special mention in the development of new strategies or programs.

We did not assume that the tension between the rule of law and crime control Skolnick raised was exacerbated by the new innovations that had come to policing in the 1980s. We were, however, disturbed at how little attention was being given to this issue in the rush to ameliorate crime and disorder problems. For example, in a review of more than fifty recent drug enforcement programs Hanrahan and Green (1991; see also Hanrahan, 1990) did not find one that evaluated the impact of new strategies on the risks of police corruption or excessive use of force, and only a handful raised such concerns even in theory. We wanted to bring together scholars who were intimately involved with recent trends in policing to examine how the development of new crime control strategies had impacted on problems of law, order, and community.

The two chapters that follow provide a background for the questions we raise. In Chapter 2, we draw from Jerome Skolnick's volume, *Justice Without Trial*. In Chapter 3, Samuel Walker provides a historical overview of the development of legal control of the police. We believe that even those familiar with Skolnick's ground-breaking book will benefit from reacquaintance with his basic thesis. Walker's historical overview places problems of law, order, and community in perspective. It also suggests that the trend toward greater control of the police is likely to continue, even though legal and scholarly focus has shifted to problems of crime control.

In Chapters 4 through 6, we provide three essays that examine how recent innovations such as problem-oriented or community policing challenge traditional mechanisms for maintaining control of the police. Each chapter addresses directly the tensions that have been created by the crime and disorder control emphasis of recent programs, as well as the confusion raised when police departments seek to define ambiguous concepts such as community. The fact that aligning with the "community" does not necessarily insulate new programs from the risk of abuse is very much evident here, though as John Eck argues the implications of this new involvement with community for the rule of law are neither clear nor unambiguous. Stephen Mastrofski and Jack Greene contrast the possibilities that recent innovation in community policing have raised for redefining the relationship between Police and Community with the practical difficulties of achieving real change in police practices and organization. Michael Buerger suggests that such change is unlikely given the culture of street policing.

Two essays that take a comparative perspective follow these reviews of recent American trends. Chapter 7, by Louise Shelley, documents the development of the rule of law in the Gorbachev era in the Soviet Union. Her essay is in sharp contrast to the trends noted in the earlier chapters, providing a view of the difficulties encountered in a totalitarian society when police begin to shift toward emphasis on law rather than order. Chapter 8, by William McDonald, attempts to place the community policing movement in America in context by drawing from European law enforcement history. The focus in this chapter is on the dangers that recent American trends present to the rule of law, and the choice made in European countries to place greater authority for crime control in the hands of prosecutors rather than the police.

The concluding chapters reflect our desire to encourage debate rather than to come to any specific conclusions about problems of law, order, and community in recent police innovations. In Chapter 9, Lawrence Sherman provides a well-reasoned defense for policies of crime control.

We believe the reader will find his contention that such policies need not be seen as reactionary nor be placed in a context outside the rule of law both interesting and thought provoking. The final chapter is by Jerome Skolnick, who reassesses his original thesis in *Justice Without Trial* in the context of drug enforcement. Here he documents how the police are being pushed into areas that cannot but exacerbate the tensions he identified in the 1960s.

These essays together provide a broad overview of how recent policies of crime and disorder control impact on problems of police abuse and corruption. Many had assumed that such concerns were no longer relevant in the context of communities that feel overrun by crime problems and police departments that have adopted in great measure the rhetoric of legal control of the police. Events in the Spring of 1992 suggest that this assumption is wrong and that scholars and practitioners need to give more attention to the debates this book addresses. Certainly, the riots that occurred in Los Angeles and other American cities in 1992, like those of the 1960s, cannot be blamed primarily on the police. Their cause, as that of earlier disturbances, lies in deeper American social problems. But once again the police have become the flash point, and the tensions between law and order that Skolnick raised almost thirty years ago must be brought from the periphery to the center of evaluation and discussion of police innovation.

References

American Bar Association. (1973). *Standards Relating to the Urban Police Function*. Washington, DC.

Brown, L. (1971). A Typology of Police-Community Relations Programs. *The Police Chief 38*, No. 3, March:16–21.

Brown, L. (1985). Police-Community Power Sharing. In Geller W.A. (Ed.), *Police Leadership in America: Crisis and Opportunity*. New York: Praeger.

Brown, W. (1972). A Study of the New York City Police Department Anti-corruption Campaign State University of New York; NY.

Cape, W.H. (1971). Policemen, Dissenters and Law-Abiding Citizens. *The Police Chief 38*, No. 11, November:45–53.

Chevigny, P. (1969). *Police Power: Police Abuses in New York City*. New York: Pantheon Books.

Cizanckas, V. and C.W. Purviance. (1973). Changing Attitudes of Black Youths. *The Police Chief 40*, No. 3, March.

Crawford, T. (1973). Police Over-perception of Ghetto Hostility. *Journal of Police Science and Administration 1*, No. 2, June:168–174.

Culver, J.H. (1975). Policing the Police: Problems and Perspectives. *Journal of Police Science and Administration 3*, No. 2, June:125–135.

Dempsey, L.J. (1972). The Knapp Commission and You. *The Police Chief 39*, No. 11.

Dempsey, L.J. (1973). The Knapp Commission and You. *The Police Chief* *40*, No. 1.

Eck, J. and W. Spelman. (1987). Who Ya Gonna Call? The Police as Problem Busters. *Crime and Delinquency 33*:1.

Farrell, M. (1988). The Development of the Community Patrol Officer Program: Community-Oriented Policing in the New York City Police Department. In Greene, J. and S. Mastrofski (Eds.), *Community Policing: Rhetoric or Reality*. New York: Praeger.

Feins, J.D. (1983). *Partnership for Neighborhood Crime Prevention*. Washington, DC: National Institute of Justice.

Goldstein, H. (1975). *Police Corruption: A Perspective on its Nature and Control*. Washington, DC: Police Foundation.

Goldstein, H. (1977). *Policing A Free Society*. Cambridge, MA: Ballinger.

Goldstein, H. (1979). Improving Police: A Problem-Oriented Approach. *Crime and Delinquency 25*, April:236–258.

Goldstein, H. (1987). Toward Community-Oriented Policing: Potential, Basic Requirements and Threshold Questions. *Crime and Delinquency 33*, No. 1:6–30.

Greene, J. (1987). Foot Patrol and Community Policing: Past Practices and Future Prospects. *American Journal of Police 6*, No. 1:1–15.

Greene, J. and S. Mastrofski. (Eds.) (1988). *Community Policing: Rhetoric or Reality*. New York: Praeger.

Greene, J. and R. Taylor. (1988). Community-Based Policing and Foot Patrol: Issues of Theory and Evaluation. In Greene, J. and S. Mastrofski (Eds.), *Community Policing: Rhetoric or Reality*. New York: Praeger.

Groves W.E. and P.H. Rossi. (1970). Police Perceptions of a Hostile Ghetto: Realism or Projection. *American Behavioral Scientist 13*, No. 5 and 6:727–743.

Hale, C. (1974). *Police Community Relations*. Albany, NY: Delmar.

Hanrahan, K. (1990). A Literature Review of Local Level Law Enforcement Strategies. *Center for Crime Prevention Studies: Report Number 1*. Newark, NJ Rutgers University.

Hanrahan, K. and L. Green. (1991). A Review of Local Level Law Enforcement Strategies: Crime Control vs Police Control. *Center for Crime Prevention Studies*. Internal correspondence, Rutgers University, Newark, NJ.

Jolin, A. and D.C. Gibbons. (1984). Policing the Police, The Portland Experience. *Journal of Police Science and Administration 12*, No. 3 September:315–322.

Kansas City Police Department. (1978). *Response Time Analysis: Executive Summary*. Washington, DC: National Institute of Justice. U.S. Government Printing Office.

Kelling, G.L. (1987). Acquiring a Taste for Order: The Community and Police. *Crime and Delinquency 33*, No. 1:90–102.

The Knapp Commission. (1973). *The Knapp Commission Report on Police Corruption*. New York: George Braziller.

Lohman, J.D. and G.G.E. Misner. (1966). *The Police and the Community: The Dynamics of Their Relationship in a Changing Society*. A report prepared for the President's Commission on Law Enforcement and Administration of Justice, Vol. II. Washington, DC: U.S. Government Printing Office.

National Advisory Commission on Civil Disorders. (March 1968). *Report of the National Advisory Commission on Civil Disorders*. Washington, DC: U.S. Government Printing Office.

Oettmeier, T.N. and L. Brown. (1988). Developing a Neighborhood-Oriented Policing Style. In Greene, J. and S. Mastrofski (Eds.), *Community Policing: Rhetoric or Reality*. New York: Praeger.

Oettmeier, T.N. and W.H. Bieck. (1986). *Developing A Policing Style for Neighborhood Oriented Policing: Executive Session No. 1*. Houston, TX: The Houston Police Department.

Pennsylvania Crime Commission. (1974). *Report on Police Corruption and the Quality of Law Enforcement in Philadelphia*. Saint Davids, PA: Pennsylvania Crime Commission.

President's Commission on Law Enforcement and Administration of Criminal Justice. (1967a). *The Challenge of Crime in a Free Society*. Washington, DC: U.S. Government Printing Office.

President's Commission on Law Enforcement and Administration of Criminal Justice. (1967b). *Task Force Report: The Police*. Washington, DC: U.S. Government Printing Office.

Skolnick, J. (1966). *Justice Without Trial: Law Enforcement in a Democratic Society*. New York: John Wiley and Sons.

Skolnick, J. and D.H. Bayley. (1986). *The New Blue Line: Police Innovation in Six American Cities*. New York: The Free Press.

Spelman, W. and D.K. Brown. (1984). *Calling the Police: Citizen Reporting of Serious Crime*. Washington, DC: Department of Justice, National Institute of Justice.

Trojanowicz, R. and B. Bucqueroux. (1990). *Community Policing: A Contemporary Perspective*. Cincinnati, OH: Anderson.

Trojanowicz, R. and D. Carter. (1988). *The Philosophy and Role of Community Policing*. Flint, MI: National Neighborhood Foot Patrol Center.

Weisburd, D., J. McElroy and P. Hardyman. (1988). Challenges to Supervision in Community Policing: Observations on a Pilot Project. *American Journal of Police 7*, No. 2:29–50.

Wilson, J.Q. and G.L. Kelling. (1982). Broken Windows. *The Atlantic Monthly*, March:29–38.

Part II
The Development of Legal Control of the Police

2
Justice Without Trial

JEROME H. SKOLNICK

For what social purpose do police exist? What values do police serve in a democratic society? Are the police to be principally an agency of social control, with their chief value the efficient enforcement of the prohibitive norms of substantive criminal law? Or are the police to be an institution falling under the hegemony of the legal system, with a basic commitment to the rule of law, even if this obligation may result in a reduction of social order? How does this dilemma of democratic society hamper the capacity of the police, institutionally and individually, to respond to legal standards of law enforcement?

Such questions have posed a predicament since the introduction of the London metropolitan police in 1829. Reith, in his book *The Police Idea* (1938), describes the hostility of early nineteenth-century England even to the idea of developing a metropolitan police force out of fear that the notorious activities of the prerevolutionary French police would be duplicated. He cites a parliamentary report of 1818 that considered the police idea and recommended against the establishment of a police force:

The police of a free country is to be found in rational and humane laws—in an effective and enlightened magistracy—and in the judicious and proper selection of those officers of justice, in whose hands, as conservators of the peace, executive duties are legally placed, but above all, in the moral habits and opinions of the people; and in proportion as these approximate towards a state of perfection, so that people may rest in security; and though their property may occasionally be invaded or their lives endangered by the hands of wicked and desperate individuals, yet the institutions of the country being sound, its laws well adjusted, and justice executed against offenders, no greater safeguard can be obtained without sacrificing all those rights which society was instituted to preserve. (Reith, 1938:188)

Reith, who is propolice and pro-Peel, may exaggerate somewhat the degree of opposition to the police. Other authors also interpret the period as one of considerable hostility to a formal institutionalization of police. Mather (1959), for example, points out that historians, like Whigs, are fundamentally antipolice. Given such opposition, therefore, before introducing his "Bill for Improving Police in and Near the Metropolis" in 1829, Peel laid a formidable groundwork.

Peel, with his usual caution, brooded for years over the problem before he undertook to solve it. In 1826 he began to collect evidence for the purpose of comparing crime with population. In 1828 he secured the appointment of a Parliamentary Committee to investigate the subject—the last of four successive Committees in the past twenty-five years, but the first to do valuable work. He had at first intended a measure which should create a police force throughout the kingdom: he ended with a modest scheme, whose operation was confined to London, and at first to a limited number of parishes. (Ramsay, 1938:88)

To buttress his argument for the necessity of a police force, Peel based his claims on the need for public order. Citing population statistics from London and Middlesex, he argued that crime was dramatically increasing in this early period of the Industrial Revolution, and increasing at a faster rate than population. In the period from 1821 to 1828, population had increased 15.5 percent, whereas criminal committals had risen by 41 percent. Deploring the existence of an army of "trained and hardened criminals" in London and Middlesex, Peel announced that "not less than one person in every three hundred and eighty-three had been convicted for some crime or other in 1828" (Ramsay, 1938:250), without mentioning, although he was fully aware of the fact, that the number of acts considered criminal was so large and the conditions of the working classes so onerous that the figures he cited were hardly shocking.

In making this appeal for more efficient controls over crime, Peel was quick to add that he was confident they would be able to dispense with the necessity of a military force in London for the preservation of the tranquility of the metropolis (Ramsay, 1938), an assurance he could hardly dispense with considering the strength of his opposition. The early conception of police accountability to the rule of law is a tradition that has continued to the present day. Maitland reaffirmed it in 1885 when he wrote in a book entitled *Justice and Police*:

There is a large body of rules defining crimes and the punishment of those who commit them, rights and the remedies of those who are wronged, but there is also a body of rules defining how and by whom, and when and where, rules of the former kind can be put in force. . . . It will little avail us that our law about rights and remedies, crimes and punishments, is as good as may be, if the law of civil and criminal procedure is clumsy and inefficient. (Maitland, 1885:1–2)

This same tradition of the hegemony of the rule of law is eloquently stated in the 1962 Royal Commission Report in a refutation of the argument that a national police force would lead to the development of a "police state" in Great Britain. The commission argues:

British liberty does not depend, and never has depended, upon any particular form of police organization. It depends upon the supremacy of Parliament and on the rule of law. We do not accept that the criterion of a police state is whether a country's police force is national rather than local—if that were the test, Belgium, Denmark and Sweden should be described as police states. The proper criterion is whether the police are answerable to the law and, ultimately, to a democratically elected Parliament. It is here, in our view, that the distinction is to be found between a free and a totalitarian state. In the countries to which the term police state is applied opprobriously, police power is controlled by the government; but they are so called not because the police are nationally organized, but because the government acknowledges no accountability to a democratically elected parliament, and the citizen cannot rely on the courts to protect him. Thus in such countries the foundations upon which British liberty rests do not exist. (Royal Commission on the Police Cmnd., 1962:45)

The theory of the police in the United States mirrors the conflict between order and legality found in English conceptions of the police, but characteristically American features add complexity. In reading about the American police, especially through the period of the 1930s, one feels that constitutional issues of legality have been almost too remote to be of immediate concern. Not that American police conformed to the rule of law. Rather, they seemed so far out of line that a writer summarizing a major American study of police practices entitled his book *Our Lawless Police*. The study, completed in 1931 by the National Committee of Law Observance and Enforcement (1930–1931) (the Wickersham Commission), found practices so appalling and sadistic as to pose no intellectual issue for civilized people. It is one thing to talk quietly to a suspect without his counsel and artfully, perhaps by deceit, persuade him to incriminate himself; it is quite another to hang a suspect out of a window by his heels from a great height, or to beat a confession out of him by putting a telephone book on his head and pounding the book with a blackjack so it does not leave marks. Both techniques may be illegal, but responsible police officials would not publicly support blackjack interrogation. On the other hand, interrogation of suspects without the presence of counsel and even deceptive interrogation are standard "professional" police techniques.[1]

For many municipal police forces in the United States, the observer's question is, therefore, not whether police operate under the constraints of due process of law, but whether they operate within bounds of civilized conduct. In the old-fashioned police department, riddled with political appointees and working hand in hand with the rackets, a reformer is not concerned primarily with the niceties of constitutional rights. When the citizenry is facing the arbitrary use of "club, blackjack, and gun,"[2] the

---

[1] See, for example, Inbau and Reid (1962:20–115); O'Hara (1956:95–114); and Kidd (1940:124–125, 133–186).
[2] For a summarization of the Wickersham Commission Report, see Hopkins (1931, index reference to "National Commission on Law Observance and Enforcement").

police reformer's problem is to reduce gross brutality, which seems traditionally to have been associated with corruption. Given this situation, it
is not surprising that the solution to the "police problem" in America has
been frequently conceived as changing the quality of people, rather than
the philosophies of policing. Fosdick wrote in 1920, in a characteristically
American passage on police reform:

We are concerned with facts and conditions and not with theories or labels. It is
not a matter of democracy, of caste, or birth, or position, or anything else. It is
solely a matter of finding the best possible brains to handle a most difficult public
task. (Fosdick, 1920:221)

Police reform means finding a new source of police, and police control
is a matter of having the "right" sort of people in control. "Reform" of
police means increasing the efficiency of police personnel. It is rarely
recognized that the conduct of police may be related in a fundamental
way to the character and goals of the institution itself—the duties police
are called on to perform, associated with the assumptions of the system of
legal justice—and that it may not be people who are good or bad,
so much as the premises and design of the system in which they find
themselves. For example, V.A. Leonard, a specialist in police administration, indicates how the conception of punishment as the basis of order
invites objectionable side effects:

A system of legal justice based upon the thesis of punishment has exerted a
tremendously negative effect on the professionalization of police service. As a
corollary the low quality of personnel required to exercise the police power under
these conditions was not conducive to good public relations, with the result that a
negative public opinion had been created. The withdrawal of public interest and
support, together with public apathy and indifference, has further served to retard
the advance toward professionalization. No less important has been the fact that a
substandard personnel became easy prey for corrupt political figures and others in
the community who profit when the risks associated with vice operations are
reduced. The highly lucrative enterprises of prostitution, gambling, and narcotics
enjoyed a field day during this period of American police history. (Leonard,
1951:6)

Leonard, however, does not raise the basic issue of the meaning of the
"professionalization of police service." Clearly such a notion suggests that
police must be honest and capable. But is this enough? This question is
what the concept of "professionalization" suggests to police in a society
committed to the rule of law.

With the concern for reform of police practices in America, a growing
and responsible debate over the theory of the police in America may be
anticipated. There are those police officials and other spokesmen for law
enforcement who emphasize the importance of social order. They are not
unconcerned about the arbitrary use of police authority, but feel that that
answer lies in the continued improvement of internal police administra-

tion. By raising the standards for admission to the police force and by making efficiency a goal and personal honesty a requisite, the quality of police work will be raised and police work will become akin to a "science" (Parker, 1957; Wilson, 1962).[3]

At the same time, there has always been a considerable body of opinion, usually outside police circles—among defense attorneys, law professors, and judges—demanding that police adhere strictly to the rules governing the legal system, that they ultimately be accountable to the legal order irrespective of their "practical" needs as law enforcement officials. This position was summarized in the landmark case of *Escobedo v. Illinois*, the U.S. Supreme Court overturning a conviction when the police refused to honor the request of a suspect to have a lawyer present at his interrogation. Justice Goldberg, for the majority, wrote:

We have . . . learned the . . . lesson of history that no system of criminal justice can, or should, survive if it comes to depend for its continued effectiveness on the citizens' abdication through unawareness of their constitutional rights. No system worth preserving should have to *fear* that if an accused is permitted to consult with a lawyer, he will become aware of, and exercise, these rights. If the exercise of constitutional rights will thwart the effectiveness of a system of law enforcement, then there is something very wrong with that system. (*Escobedo v. Illinois*, 378 U.S. 478, 490 (1964))

The purpose of this study (see Skolnick, 1966) is to show, through empirical investigation of police, how value conflicts of democratic society create conditions undermining the capacity of police to respond to the rule of law. Its chief conclusion (and orienting hypothesis), may be summarized:

The police in democratic society are required to maintain order and to do so under the rule of law. As functionaries charged with maintaining order, they are part of the bureaucracy. The ideology of democratic bureaucracy emphasizes initiative rather than disciplined adherence to rules and regulations. By contrast, the rule of law emphasizes the rights of individual citizens and constraints upon the initiative of legal officials. This tension between the operational consequences of ideas of order, efficiency, and initiative, on the one hand, and legality, on the other, constitutes the principle problem of police as a democratic legal organization. (Skolnick, 1966:6)

The work attempts to analyze, through empirical investigation of police, how conceptions associated with order and interpretations regarding legality develop within a professionalized police department, and to study the processes through which these conceptions and interpretations come to be associated with certain patterns and practices of policing.

---

[3] Also see two police journals, *The Police Chief* (pub. Chicago) and *Police* (pub. Springfield, IL), for ongoing discussions about professionalization of the police occupation.

Law and Order: The Source of the Dilemma

If the police could maintain order without regard to legality, their short-run difficulties would be considerably diminished; however, they are inevitably concerned with interpreting legality because of their use of *law* as instrument of order. The criminal law contains a set of rules for the maintenance of social order. This arsenal comprises the substantive part of the criminal law, that is, the elements of crime, the principles under which the accused is to be held accountable for alleged crime, the principles justifying the enactment of specific prohibitions, and the crimes themselves. Sociologists usually concentrate here, asking how well this control system operates, analyzing the conditions under which it achieves intended goals and the circumstances rendering it least efficient.[4]

Another part of the criminal law, however, regulates the conduct of state officials charged with processing citizens who are suspected, accused, or found guilty of crime.[5] Involved here are such matters as the law of search, the law of arrest, the elements and degree of proof, the right to counsel, the nature of a lawful accusation of crime, and the fairness of trial. The procedures of the criminal law, therefore, stress protection of individual liberties within a system of social order.[6]

This dichotomy suggests that the common juxtaposition of "law and order" is an oversimplification. Law is not merely an instrument of order, but may frequently be its adversary (Barth, 1963). There are communities that appear disorderly to some (such as bohemian communities valuing diversity), but that nevertheless maintain a substantial degree of legality. The contrary may also be found: a situation where order is well maintained, but where the policy and practice of legality is not evident. The totalitarian social system, whether in a nation or an institution, is a situation of order without rule of law. Such a situation is probably best illustrated by martial rule, where military authority may claim and exercise the power of amnesty and detention without warrant. If, in addition, the writ of habeas corpus, the right to inquire into these acts, is suspended, as it typically is under martial rule, the executive can exercise arbitrary powers.[7] Such a system of social control is efficient, but does not conform

---

[4] See, for example, Barnes and Teeters (1951); Glueck (1952); Korn and McCorkle (1959); Morris (1951); Roucek (1961); Reckless (1961); and Sutherland and Cressey (1960). One exception is the text of Tappan (1960), which emphasizes criminal procedure in great detail. Tappan, it should be noted, however, was also trained as a lawyer.

[5] Thus, a leading casebook in criminal law devotes its final sections to problems in the administration of criminal law. See Paulsen and Kadish (1962).

[6] See, for example, Rubin, Wiehofen, Edwards, and Rosenzweig (1963); Tappan (1960); and Orfield (1947). An excellent discussion of problems of criminal procedure is found in Goldstein (1960).

[7] See Fairman (1943), especially Chapter 3.

to generally held notions about the "rule of law" (Selznick, 1961; Report and Recommendations, 1962).[8]

Although there is no precise definition of the rule of law, or its synonym, the principle of legality, its essential element, is the reduction of arbitrariness by officials—for example, constraints on the activities of the police—and of arbitrariness in positive law by the application of "rational principles of civic order" (Selznick, 1961). A statement expressive of the rule of law is found in a report on police arrests for "investigations." The authors, who are lawyers, write "Anglo-American law has a tradition of antipathy to the imprisonment of a citizen at the will of executive officers" (Report and Recommendations, 1962). A more explicit definition of the rule of law in the administration of criminal law has been presented as follows:

The principle of *nulla poena sine lege* imposes formidable restraints upon the definition of criminal conduct. Standards of conduct must meet stringent tests of specificity and clarity, may act only prospectively, and must be strictly construed in favor of the accused. Further, the definition of criminal conduct has largely come to be regarded as a legislative function, thereby precluding the judiciary from devising new crimes. The public-mischief doctrine and the sometimes overgeneralized "ends" of criminal conspiracy are usually regarded as anomalous departures from the mainstream. The cognate principle of procedural regularity and fairness, in short, due process of law, commands that the legal standard be applied to the individual with scrupulous fairness in order to minimize the chances of convicting the innocent, protect against abuse of official power, and generate an atmosphere of impartial justice. As a consequence, a complex network of procedural requirements embodied variously in constitutional, statutory, or judge-made law is imposed upon the criminal adjudicatory process—public trial, unbiased tribunal, legal representation, open hearing, confrontation, and related concomitants of procedural justice. (Kadish, 1962)

Thus, when law is used as the instrument of social order, it necessarily poses a dilemma. The phrase "law and order" is misleading because it draws attention away from the substantial incompatibilities existing between the two ideas. Order under law suggests procedures different from achievement of "social control" through threat of coercion and summary judgment. Order under law is concerned not merely with the achievement of regularized social activity but with the means used to come by peaceable behavior, certainly with procedure, but also with positive law. It would surely be a violation of the rule of law for a legislature to make epilepsy a crime, even though a public "seizure" typically disturbs order in the community. Although most law enforcement officials regard drug addicts as menacing to the community, a law making it a crime to be an addict has been declared unconstitutional

---

[8] See footnote 12.

(*United States* v. *Robinson* 361, U.S. 220 (1959)).[9] This example, pur-
posely selected from substantive criminal law, indicatcs that conceptions
of legality apply here as well as in the more traditional realm of criminal
procedure. In short, "law" and "order" are frequently found to be in
opposition, because law implies rational restraint on the rules and procedures used to achieve order. Order under law, therefore, subordinates
the ideal of conformity to the ideal of legality.

Conceptions and Applications: The Dilemma Complicated

The actual requirement of maintaining social order under the principle of
legality places an unceasing burden on the police as a social institution.
Indeed, the police is the institution best exemplifying the strain between
the two ideas. The 1962 Royal Commission on the Police Cmnd. states
the law enforcement dilemma as follows:

The police systems in England, Scotland and Wales are the products of a series of
compromises between conflicting principles or ideas. Consequently, in contrast to
other public services such as health and education, the rationale of the police
service does not rest upon any single and definite concept of the public good.
Thus, it is to the public good that the police should be strong and effective in
preserving law and order and preventing crime; but is equally to the public
good that police power should be controlled and confined so as not to interfere
arbitrarily with personal freedom. The result is compromise. The police should be
powerful but not oppressive; they should be efficient but not officious; they
should form an impartial force in the body politic, and yet be subject to a degree
of control by persons who are not required to be impartial and who are themselves
liable to police supervision. (Royal Commission on the Police, Cmnd. 1962:9)

The law enforcement dilemma, however, is more complex than suggested by the Royal Commission. Not only are the police in a democracy
the product of a series of compromises between conflicting principles or
ideas, but the ideas themselves are not as clear as they (and we) have so

---

[9] Fuller (1964) criticizes the grounds of the decision. The court held in this case
that the statute violated the Eighth Amendment by imposing a "cruel and unusual
punishment" for an "illness." Professor Fuller argues that the statute should have
been overturned on grounds that it is both ex post facto and vague. My own
position is inbetween, as I do not conceive of an addict as one who necessarily
had the intent of becoming one when she or he began using drugs. Therefore, I
find the ex post facto objection less than compelling. On whatever grounds,
however, the case stands as a good example of positive law in violation of the rule
of law.

far suggested. If "law and order" is a misleading cliche, then a gross conception of order may be even more misleading. Depending on the institution or community, there may be quite different conceptions of order, some more permissive, others less. A traditional martial conception of order, for example, abhors individual differences. The soldier whose bearing or uniform sets him off from his comrades in arms is an abomination to his commanding officer. Even the slightest deviation, such as wearing gloves on a cold day, is forbidden as an expression of differences in individual feelings. In any given military unit, either all the soldiers wear gloves, or none do. The hands of some soldiers will perspire, others will be numb with cold, but all soldiers will act alike.

Other institutions or portions of society are traditionally more yielding. The area surrounding the University of Paris is noted for its emphasis on individuality. Students, artists, and writers may be dressed elegantly or poorly, raffishly or provocatively, the mode being considered an extension of the ego, an expression of personality, or perhaps merely an attempt to experiment with novelty. The idea of order in this setting is surely a more permissive conception than the standard military notion. Our conclusion is that conceptions of order seem to be variable and tend to correspond to the requirements of different communities or institutions.

Conceptions of order also seem to be associated with conceptions of appropriate modes of achieving it. The response of a soldier needs to be quick and unquestioning, as failure to respond instantaneously may result in severe damage to himself and to his comrades-in-arms. The socialization of the soldier therefore emphasizes unquestioning obedience. A trained soldier is a person who responds unthinkingly to command, and the norm of command is sharp command. Failure to respond is met with punishment, seemingly severe to those who receive it. Its justification, however, is located not in the precipitating act itself, but in the implications of nonobedience for the combat situation. The basic trainee whose inspected boot has been found to have a relatively low gloss may lose a weekend's liberty not because a less than sparkling boot is intrinsically important, but because it presumably signifies future sloth.

By contrast, an institution expressive of liberal and humanistic values, such as a university, will usually emphasize persuasion through reason as the instrument for the achievement of order. Because its institutional goal is scholarship, it is traditionally tolerant of behavioral and attitudinal variations, stressing contemplation and dialogue over obedience to rules, and persuasion rather than force as the instrument of an order predicated on diversity. University police, for example, are far more permissive than local urban police forces. Varying social conditions—the nature of the criminal law, the presence of danger in the community, the political complexion of the community, the social dissimilarity of the population being policed—all contribute to the conception of order held by the police.

The organizational model of the police also influences their conception of order. To the degree that police are organized on a military model, there is also likely to be generated a martial conception of order. Internal regulations based on martial principles suggest external cognition based on similar principles. The presence of an explicit hierarchy, with an associated chain of command and a strong sense of obedience, is therefore likely to induce an attachment to social uniformity and routine and a somewhat rigid conception of order. Such a conception of order is probably increasingly at variance with segments of the community where police, perceiving themselves as "workers" who should exercise initiative, are coming to be concentrated. As this process occurs, police are more likely to lean toward the arbitrary invocation of authority to achieve what they perceive to be the aims of substantive criminal law. Along with these effects is an elevation of crime control to a position where it is valued more than the principle of accountability to the rule of law.

Aiding this process is ambiguity about the application of the rule of law. In the abstract, the rule of law embodies rational restraints on authority as it defines criminal conduct. There must be specificity, clarity, prospectivity, and strict construction in favor of the accused. There must be procedural regularity and fairness, and so forth. In practice, however, such standards may not be clear. The principle of procedural regularity and fairness commanding that the legal standards be applied so as to minimize the chances of convicting the innocent, protect against the abuse of official power, and generate an atmosphere of impartial justice (Kadish, 1962) is, for example, subject to varying interpretation by the police and the courts. One year illegally seized evidence may be admitted into evidence under a legal system subscribing to the rule of law, and the next year it may not. A confession may be admitted into evidence at one point in time whether or not the suspect was informed of his or her right to counsel; at a slightly later point in time such a confession is found to violate constitutional protections. Thus, although certain fundamental and relatively changeless principles on the rule of law are specifiable, the practical constraints on official conduct derived from these principles are always in a degree of flux. A legal order is never a fixed body of rules, but, as Fuller (1964) suggests, an "enterprise" of governance by rule.

It may also be suggested that whenever rules of constraint are ambiguous, they strengthen the very conduct they are intended to restrain. Thus, the policeofficer already committed to a conception of law as an instrument of order rather than as an end in itself is likely to use the ambiguity of the rules of restraint as a justification for testing or even violating them. By such a process, the practical ambiguity of the rule of law may serve to undermine its salience as a value. In sum, the actual enterprise of maintaining order by rule of law serves to complicate the conflict of these principles inherent in a democratic society.

The Seclusion of Administration: The Dilemma's Setting

Perhaps, if the administration of criminal law conformed to its popular image, study of the police would be less important. Popularly, even though the police are an object of much romanticized attention, the trial is perceived as the culmination of the process of administering criminal law.[10] Trials are dramatic spectacles, and folklore surrounding prominent criminal trial attorneys has had a profound impact on the general public. In fact, the typical method of conviction is by the accused's plea of guilty, with no trial required. In the federal courts, the guilty plea receives the heaviest use, 86 percent in the fiscal years 1960 through 1963, whereas in the state courts, the use of the plea trails by 5 to 10 percent (U.S. Administrative Office of the Courts, 1963:132). Mostly, therefore, the system of administering criminal justice in the United States is a system of justice *without* trial.[11]

The plea of guilty is often seen by criminal law personnel as a means of coping with the problem of limited court facilities. In partial justification for a heavier sentence on the one of five defendants who refused to plead guilty, a federal judge opined: "if in one year, 248 judges are to deal with 35,517 defendants, the district courts must encourage pleas of guilty. One way to encourage pleas of guilty is to establish or announce a policy that, in the ordinary case, leniency will not be granted to a defendant who stands trial" (*United States v. Wiley* 184, F. Supp. 679 (N.D. Ill., 1960); Vetri, 1964). Not only is the plea of guilty recognized as playing an integral role in the criminal process, it is also evident that the necessity for frequent invocation of the plea is a key institutional factor in shaping the position of the defendant vis-à-vis the State.

The statistical pattern of guilty pleas and the reasons for this pattern are interesting themselves, but not so interesting as their implication that routine decision making in the administration of criminal justice is hidden from public view. When a plea of guilty is entered, encounters between prosecutor and defense attorney, defense attorney and client, prosecutor and police officer, and police officer and suspect are never brought to public attention, and in the nature of the situation cannot be. The case is often "tried" in an informal setting, perhaps over a cup of coffee or in the corridor behind the courtroom.

---

[10] Thus, a recent television program called *Arrest and Trial* implied by its title that the latter inevitably follows the former. The tendency to make the implication is understandable.

[11] Some important work on the plea of guilty has been conducted by Newman (1962a, 1962b). An able review of the subject is to be found in a paper prepared by Vetri (1964). Also, some interesting materials on the guilty plea are to be found in Trebach (1964).

The frequency and seclusion of the plea of guilty raise far-reaching questions in legal theory: (1) To the extent that courts seek to control the behavior of police in such areas as searches and seizures, eavesdropping, and confessions, does the frequent invocation of the plea of guilty serve to shield from public view the patterned occurrence of violations of criminal law by police? (2) At every other level of the system are there systematic practices that rarely or never come to light because the guilty plea "covers up" whatever took place before it occurred? (3) What factors influence agreement to a plea of guilty, and what is the relationship of these factors to what would be countenanced in the formal system of appellate decisions? (4) Finally, how does heavy dependence on the plea of guilty affect the accomplishment of the goals of the legal system?[12]

Police work constitutes the most secluded part of an already secluded system and therefore offers the greatest opportunity for arbitrary behavior. As invokers of the criminal law, the police frequently act in practice as its chief interpreter. Thus, they are necessarily called on to test the limits of their legal authority. In so doing, they also define the operative legality of the system of administering criminal law. That is, if the criminal law is especially salient to a population that has more or less recurrent interactions with the police, it is the police who define the system of order to this population. This work of interpretation, this "notice-giving" function of police, is a crucial consideration in assessing the degree to which legality penetrates a system of criminal justice.

Whenever a system of justice takes on an insular character, a question is raised as to the degree of justice such a system is capable of generating. Lon L. Fuller, a legal philosopher, has suggested the broadest significance of the seclusion of criminal law administration when he discusses the affinity between legality and justice. He asserts that both share a common quality, as they act by known rule. Fuller discusses the significance of public scrutiny as follows:

The internal morality of the law demands that there be rules, that they be made known, and that they be observed in practice by those charged with their administration. These demands may seem ethically neutral so far as the external aims of law are concerned. Yet, just as law is a precondition for good law, so acting by known rule is a precondition for any meaningful appraisal of the justice of law. "A lawless unlimited power" expressing itself solely in unpredictable and patternless interventions in human affairs could be said to be unjust only in the sense that it does not act by known rule. *It would be hard to call it unjust in any more specific sense until one discovered what hidden principle, if any, guided its interventions.* It

---

[12] Newman (1962a) points out that the effect of informal conviction methods ("bargain justice") on selection for probation is to make placement on probation dependent on the skill of the defendant or his or her lawyer rather than on factors thought to have relevance for rehabilitation through probationary treatment.

is the virtue of a legal order conscientiously constructed and administered that it exposes to public scrutiny the rules by which it acts. (Fuller, 1964:157–158)[13]

The system of justice without trial is not a system of "unpredictable and patternless interventions." Rather, it is one that operates against a background of known rules, but that also, especially in the instance of the police, develops a set of informal norms or "hidden principles" in response to the formal rules. These, in turn, are influential in determining how the formal rules actually operate.

Law as an Enterprise

That law is an enterprise summons us to its empirical study. It reminds us that highly general propositions about law may be either circular or premature. Consider the following propositions: the economic structure of society affects law; the power structure affects law; public opinion affects law; the Protestant ethic affects law. All such statements are but a beginning, as is a statement that law is "integrative" or that law affects the economy. Whether law is seen as an independent or dependent variable, the important work is the specification of those processes intervening between the two. Thus, from the perspective of law as an enterprise, what needs to be specified is how economy affects law, how politics affects law, and the kind of legal order enhancing types of social integration. The development of a sociology of law depends on detailed analysis of the social foundations of legality and of empirical elaborations of processes through which relations among variables result in determinate outcomes.

It may be instructive to draw an analogy to the sociology of bureaucracy, where scholars have taken a similar view. They have not tried to spell out the "functions" of bureaucracy in society, but rather have concentrated on case studies investigating problems associated with certain forms of organized cooperation. Neither have they primarily attempted to be managerial experts who would improve the efficiency of this system. They have been concerned, to be sure, with the effects of different forms of organized cooperation on the satisfactions of human existence; but as scholars, they have sought first of all to understand the conditions under which these forms result in varying outcomes. Their approach has been to consider what Crozier (1964) has termed "the bureaucratic phenomenon."

Crozier sees this as the indispensable "exploratory" phase of scientific development, a phase that elaborates the problem by the generation of descriptive hypotheses. Such hypotheses serve only as examples, to be sure, and are valid only for the case at hand. Crozier adds, however, that,

---

[13] Italics added.

limited as such examples may seem initially, they are capable of yielding more information about the functioning of social systems of the same order, and even of larger systems, than studies insisting on a "premature rigor." He concludes:

To resolve upon a clinical approach may seem regressive after certain earlier ambitions of the social sciences. However, this seems to us indispensable for all those problems which touch upon the sociology of institutions and the sociology of action. There are no shortcuts possible. General statistical relations, which can be perceived at the opinion level, are fragmentary and undifferentiated; they can testify to accomplished changes, but not to the process of change, nor to the laws of action, nor even to the general direction of the evolution. Only models of functioning at an operational level can help us progress. This is what a clinical approach can offer us. (Crozier, 1964:4–5)

Crozier's examination of French bureaucracy also indicated to him that understanding the dynamics of bureaucracy is not possible unless its operation is examined within the setting of a culture. Although there are similarities, under close empirical examination the dynamics of bureaucracy in France and in Germany are distinguishable. Crozier asserts that the "study of the bureaucratic phenomenon permits a new breakthrough at this more 'operational' level" (Crozier, 1964:8). Similarly, Blau found that certain features of the bureaucratic model were not equally applicable in different cultures. He argues that in the Germany of Max Weber, strict hierarchical control may have constituted the most efficient method of management, but that in an American culture valuing social equality, "permitting junior officials considerable discretion in discharging their responsibilities may be a more efficient system of administration" (Blau, 1955:202–203). Such findings and others as well (Bendix, 1963; Clark, 1960; Gouldner, 1954; Selznick, 1949) suggest that the operation of social organizations will always reflect the cultural, political, social, and economic contexts in which they are located. The important task is to specify the role of culture and ideology in determining the conduct of people and their social organizations.

Law Enforcement in Democratic Society

The police in this study are considered as a class of authorities facing the problem of managing divergent expectations of conduct. Democracy's ideological conflict between the norms governing the work of maintaining order and the principle of accountability to the rule of law provides the justification for various demands on the police. They may be expected to be rule enforcer, parent, friend, social servant, moralist, streetfighter, marksman, and officer of the law. The problem of organizing and defining such demands furnishes the basis for the institutional analysis of police.

The problem itself suggests the situational difficulties affecting the police's capacity to be responsible law enforcement officials who enforce order under the rule of law.

The dilemma of the police is further complicated. It is possible in practice for applications of the rule of law as well as conceptions of order to vary. Standards for applying the rule of law are developed by the courts in the setting of specific police practices. Standards governing search and seizure practices, for example, are usually developed in narcotics cases, whereas standards of the legality of procedures for obtaining confessions typically arise in cases in which there is an element of assault. Similarly, conceptions of order are subject to varying interpretations and tend to influence and be influenced by conditions prevailing in police work. General statements about the police conception of order and its sources can be made, but it is also possible to show how the generalized conception is modified by the perceived requirements of various police assignments. When the informer system is discussed, for example, it becomes clear that the meaning of criminal conduct is differently evaluated depending on how the perceived criminality fits in with procedures characteristically used to enforce specific categories of the law.

The division of labor within the police department (burglary, vice control, traffic control, patrol) supplies a methodological framework for observing and comparing the assumptions and outcomes of police practices in democratic society. Policing specialties generate distinctive patterns for the invocation and enforcement of the law of crimes: who first sees a criminal act, how it is reported, how apprehension takes place. In gathering participant-observational data, then, the division of police labor sets the background for the working hypothesis of the study (see Skolnick, 1966): *The characteristic pattern of enforcement, with its special arrangements for gathering information, processing offenders, and evaluating the competence of personnel, all under rule of law, determines operational law enforcement.* The idea of operational law enforcement should suggest both the attitudes and the behavior of police responding to judicial rulings and interpersonal relations with the accused, the prosecutor, the defense attorney, the judge, and, whenever applicable, the general public.

Underlying this working question is a more general and fundamental issue growing out of the concept of law enforcement. This issue is the meaning and purpose of law in democratic society. The idea of law enforcement in such a society, taken seriously, suggests that legally constituted institutions such as the police exist not only to preserve order, but to serve the rule of law as an end in itself. On the other hand, the circumstances of the occupational environment, with its associated requirements that the police maintain order, might develop a very different conception of law in police, a conception without articulation or explicit philosophical justification, but existing nevertheless. Such a conception might perceive law not primarily as an instrument for guaranteeing individual freedom but, as in the Soviet Union, an instrument of education, as a father is a teacher of children. Harold Berman describes the paternalistic character of Soviet legality and its consequences as follows:

Soviet law cannot be understood unless it is recognized that the whole Soviet society is itself conceived to be a single great family, a gigantic school, a church, a labor union, a business enterprise. The state stands at its head, as the parent, the teacher, the priest, the chairman, the director. As the state, it acts officially through the legal system, but its purpose in so acting is to make its citizens into obedient children, good students, ardent believers, hard workers, successful managers.

This, indeed, is the essential characteristic of the law of a total state.

We have seen that legal consequences follow from this conception of the role of law. Court procedure is informal and speedy; the judge protects the litigants against the consequences of their ignorance, and clarifies to them the nature of their rights and duties; there is elaborate pre-trial procedure directed toward uncovering the whole history of the situation. The rule: "Let the punishment fit the crime" is supplemented (though not supplanted) by the rule: "Let the punishment fit the man." (Berman, 1963:366)

The conception of law as a teacher is closely connected to the idea that law is primarily an instrument for achieving social order. Thus, the Soviet regime (and the Chinese Communist as well) adopted a secret police almost immediately on coming into existence. The Soviet secret police, the Cheka, was given broad powers, although it was not until 1924 that even a document was published explaining its existence and purposes. Under this statutory authorization, the main task of the secret police was to act as the investigative and punitive arm of the dictatorship, hunting out and liquidating "counterrevolutionary . . . attempts and actions throughout Russia, no matter what their origin" (*Pravda*, December 18, 1927, p. 2: see Wolin and Slusser, 1957:4). The Cheka was answerable only to the top leadership of the Party and government, although experience was to demonstrate that whatever actions the Cheka considered necessary to defend the dictatorship (of the proletariat), including arrest, imprisonment, and even execution, would be approved by the Party leadership, notwithstanding any formal or legal limitations on its power.

As a system based on law as the instrument for imposing a "necessary" social order, the Cheka became the object of wide-ranging criticism, not only among its opponents, but within the ranks of the Party itself. Its own *Yezhenedel'nik* [*Cheka Weekly*] (No. 2, September 29, 1918, p. 11: see Wolin and Slusser, 1957:6) acknowledged these complaints, noting that "reports are coming in from all sides that not only unworthy but outright criminal individuals are trying to penetrate the . . . Chekas." But in reply to such criticisms, Lenin defended the secret police on grounds that the arbitrary use of authority was permissible in the cause of achieving a society ordered on proletarian principles. He said to a conference of

Cheka representatives in November 1918 that despite the presence of "strange elements" in its ranks, the Cheka was "putting into practice the dictatorship of the proletariat, and in this respect its role is invaluable; there is no other path to the freeing of the masses than the suppression of the exploiters by force. The Cheka is engaged in this, and in this consists its service to the proletariat" (Lenin, 1926–1932).

The meaning of law in a society is ultimately dependent on its political and social philosophy. When law is viewed primarily as an instrument of education or as an instrument of order, rather than as a goal in itself, the society no longer conceives of punishment as a last resort, to be used only reluctantly. Lipson describes Soviet law as the instrument of state morality as follows:

Coercion to virtue is esteemed not only for virtue's sake but also as a means of reducing the incidence of lawbreaking. The number of violations of public order is swollen by the difficulties of the society and by the broadly inclusive notion of what *amounts* to a violation. The more precarious the equilibrium of the state, the greater the perceived danger of subversion; the narrower the line, the harder it is not to deviate from it. Even short of disorder, subversion, and deviation, the failure to do one's part in raising the wealth of the state is an offence against the presuppositions of the leaders and thus against the laws of the realm. If *homo oeconomicus* is not yet respectable enough to be allowed on the stage, let his lines be given to *homo juridicus*: Soviet morality permits the government to threaten pain in order to push the citizen to many acts to which it cannot yet pull him by hope of reward. (Lipson, 1965)

It is not only that the law of a total state has as its essential condition that the society conceive of itself as a single great family. Single great families in which the question of values is open to discussion are imaginable. There needs to be also a conception of the inevitability of events, a sense of place in the interpretation of the grand sweep of history, a logical connection, and, ultimately, a belief in the righteousness of killing for the sake of logic. This sort of certainty as to what is right, and the willingness to adopt the most extreme punitive measures in defense of it, is the essence of the conception of law in a total state. Father knows all in such a family, and he may, if he thinks it necessary, rule by the rod. This conception of law necessarily contemplates minimal restraint on authority.

By contrast, a democratic society envisions constraint on those who are granted the right to invoke the processes of punishment in the name of the law. They must draw their rules clearly, state them prospectively. The rules themselves must be rational, not whimsically constructed, and carried out with procedural regularity and fairness. Most important of all, rule is from below, not above. Authorities are servants of the people, not a "vanguard" of elites instructing the masses. The overriding value is consent of the governed. From it derives the principle of the accountability of authority, accountability primarily to courts of law and ultimately to a democratically constituted legislature based on universal suffrage.

References

Barnes, H.E. and N.K. Teeters. (1951). *New Horizons in Criminology*. New York: Prentice-Hall.

Barth, A. (1963). *Law Enforcement Versus the Law*. New York: Collier Books.

Bendix, R. (1963). *Work and Authority in Industry*. New York: Harper and Row.

Berman, H.J. (1963). *Justice in the U.S.S.R.* New York: Random House.

Blau, P. (1955). *The Dynamics of Bureaucracy*. Chicago: University of Chicago Press.

Clark, B.R. (1960). *The Open Door College*. New York: McGraw-Hill.

Crozier, M. (1964). *The Bureaucratic Phenomenon*. Chicago: University of Chicago Press.

Fairman, C. (1943). *The Law of Martial Rule*. Chicago: Callaghan and Company.

Fosdick, R. (1920). *American Police Systems*. New York: The Century Company.

Fuller, L. (1964). *The Morality of Law*. New Haven: Yale University Press.

Glueck, S. (1952). *Crime and Correction: Selected Papers*. Cambridge: Addison-Wesley Press.

Goldstein, A.S. (1960). The State and the Accused: Balance of Advantage in Criminal Procedure. *Yale Law Journal 69*, June:1149–1199.

Gouldner, A. (1954). *Patterns of Industrial Bureaucracy*. Glencoe, IL: The Free Press.

Hopkins, E.J. (1931). *Our Lawless Police*. New York: The Viking Press.

Inbau, F.E. and J.E. Reid. (1962). *Criminal Interrogation and Confessions*. Baltimore: Williams and Wilkins.

Kadish, S.H. (1962). Legal Norm and Discretion in the Police and Sentencing Processes. *Harvard Law Review 75*:904–905.

Kidd, W.R. (1940). *Police Interrogation*. New York: R.V. Basuino.

Korn, R.R. and L.W. McCorkle. (1959). *Criminology and Penology*. New York: Holt.

Lenin, V.I. Sochineniya [Works] (Moscow–Leningrad, 1926–1932, 2nd ed.), 23, pp. 273–274. (1957). In Wolin, S. and R.M. Slusser (Eds.), *The Soviet Secret Police*. New York: Frederick A. Praeger. P. 6.

Leonard, V.A. (1951). *Police Organization and Management*. Brooklyn, NY: The Foundation Press.

Lipson, L. (1965). Hosts and Pests: The Fight Against Parasites. *Problems of Communism 14*, No. 2, March–April:72–73.

Maitland, F.W. (1885). *Justice and Police*. London: Macmillan.

Mather, F.C. (1959). *Public Order in the Age of the Chartists*. Manchester: The University Press.

Morris, N. (1951). *The Habitual Criminal*. Cambridge, MA: Harvard University Press.

National Commission on Law Observance and Enforcement. (1930–1931). *Publications, Nos. 1–14*. Washington, DC: U.S. Government Printing Office.

Newman, D.J. (1962a). Pleading Guilty for Considerations: A Study of Bargain Justice. In Johnston, N., L. Savitz, and M.E. Wolfgang (Eds.), *The Sociology of Punishment and Correction*. New York: John Wiley and Sons. Pp. 24–32.

Newman, D.J. (1962b). *The Decision as to Guilt or Innocence*. Chicago: American Bar Foundation.

O'Hara, C.E. (1956). *Fundamentals of Criminal Investigation*. Springfield, IL: C.C Thomas.

Orfield, L.B. (1947). *Criminal Procedure From Arrest to Appeal*. New York: New York University Press.

Parker, W.H. (1957). *Parker on Police* (Wilson, O.W. Ed.). Springfield, IL: C.C Thomas.

Paulsen, M.G. and S.H. Kadish. (1962). *Criminal Law and Its Processes*. Boston: Little, Brown.

Ramsay, A.A.W. (1938). *Sir Robert Peel*. New York: Dodd, Mead.

Reckless, W.C. (1961). *The Crime Problem*. New York: Appleton-Century-Crofts.

Reith, C. (1938). *The Police Idea: Its History and Evolution in England in the Eighteenth Century and After*. London: Oxford University Press.

Report and Recommendations of the Commissioners' Committee on Police Arrests for Investigation. (July 1962). District of Columbia:42 Commissioners' Committee on Police Arrests for Investigation. P. 42.

Roucek, J.S. (1961). *Sociology of Crime*. New York: Philosophical Library.

Royal Commission on the Police Cmnd. (1962). *Royal Commission on the Police Cmnd. 1728*. London: Her Majesty's Stationary Office.

Rubin, S., H. Wiehofen, G. Edwards, and S. Rosenzweig. (1963). *The Law of Criminal Correction*. St. Paul, MN: West.

Selznick, P. (1949). *TVA and the Grass Roots*. Berkeley, CA: University of California Press.

Selznick, P. (1961). Sociology and Natural Law. *Natural Law Forum* 6:95.

Skolnick, J. (1966). *Justice Without Trial: Law Enforcement in a Democratic Society*. New York: John Wiley and Sons.

Sutherland, E.H. and D.R. Cressey. (1960). *Principles of Criminology*. 6th ed. Philadelphia: Lippincott.

Tappan, P.W. (1960). *Crime, Justice and Correction*. New York: McGraw-Hill.

Trebach, A.S. (1964). *The Rationing of Justice: Constitutional Rights and the Criminal Process*. New Brunswick, NJ: Rutgers University Press.

U.S. Administrative Office of the Courts. (1963). *Administrative Office of the United States Courts, Annual Report of the Director*.

Vetri, D.R. (1964). Guilty Plea Bargaining: Compromises by Prosecutors to Secure Guilty Pleas. *University of Pennsylvania Law Review 112*, April:865–895.

Wilson, O.W. (1962). *Police Planning*. Springfield, IL: C.C Thomas.

Wolin, S. and R.M. Slusser. (1957). *The Soviet Secret Police*. New York: Frederick A. Praeger.

3
Historical Roots of the Legal Control of Police Behavior*

SAMUEL WALKER

In the spring of 1956 a member of the American Bar Foundation research team asked a Wisconsin police chief what he thought about the exclusionary rule. "Oh, we never exclude anyone from the court room," the chief assured him.[1]

At that time, the exclusionary rule was in effect in Wisconsin, as it was in a number of states prior to the Supreme Court's landmark 1961 decision in *Mapp v. Ohio* (367 U.S. 643 (1961)). The incident dramatizes a number of important issues in the history of the legal control of police behavior.

The first is the growth of formal legal controls over police behavior during the past several decades. The exclusionary rule is but one of the most controversial and most intensively studied of a wide range of such controls (see Davies, 1983). The central argument of this essay is that the growth of these controls is, arguably, the most important development in recent police history (Walker, 1992). For the purpose of this discussion, *legal controls* are defined as including any and all written rules regulating police conduct. This includes statutes, court decisions, and administrative policies.

The growth of legal controls in policing, meanwhile, is but one part of a larger development in the entire criminal justice system. Commentators have generally labeled this development the "due process revolution" and associated it primarily with the Warren Court era of the Supreme Court. A more appropriate label would be the "rule revolution." One problem with focusing on the Supreme Court is that it fails to adequately account for either the origins of the growth of legal controls, its continued devel-

---

* Research for this paper was supported in part by a fellowship from the Ford Foundation.
[1] Interview, Herman Goldstein. Goldstein was a member of the field research team of the American Bar Foundation Survey of the Administration of Criminal Justice.

opment in the last two decades, or the many issues related to the practical consequences of these controls.

A second set of issues concerns the nature and consequences of legal controls. How and why have the existing rules developed? Why has the effort to control the behavior of American police officers taken the particular form it has? Do the existing rules work? Are some more effective than others? What are the conditions of successful legal control? The 1956 Wisconsin incident reminds us that the mere existence of the exclusionary rule guaranteed nothing. Do rules have any unintended consequences? If so, are they positive or negative?

One of the problems with the existing literature on the legal control of the police is that far too much attention has been given to the exclusionary rule and to certain aspects of it (particularly the "loss" of criminal cases) (Davies, 1983).[2] Too little attention has been given to other rules, to the general phenomenon of rule development, and to various indirect and unanticipated consequences of rules.[3]

It is appropriate to acknowledge at the outset one possible objection to the argument presented in this paper. It paints a picture of a linear development of legal controls in policing, moving from no controls to an elaborate network of controls. In part, this represents an exercise in overcompensation. It attempts to correct for the general neglect of what is a very important historical development. At the same time, however, some powerful countertrends are also at work that tend to weaken the new legal controls.[4]

The trend toward weaker controls is driven by two social forces. First, public fear of crime, drugs, and gangs has put tremendous political pressure on the police to "get tough," even through extreme measures.[5] The Supreme Court, meanwhile, is now dominated by a majority that is very responsive to the expressed needs of law enforcement. In the 1990–1991 term alone, the Court continued to erode Fourth and Fifth Amendment protections for suspects, even accepting a coerced confession in one notable case. These decisions not only loosen the legal controls over the police but, in a more general sense, send a message that extreme measures may be excused.

---

[2] The preoccupation with that particular aspect of the rule is a consequence of (1) the politically volatile aspect of crime control in recent American politics, and (2) the fact that dismissal of cases is readily quantifiable through the techniques preferred by contemporary social scientists.

[3] For one of the most important attempts to explore this generally neglected issue, see Punch (1983).

[4] I am indebted to David Weisburd for suggesting this point, which did not appear in the initial draft of this paper.

[5] A good example would be the occasional "sweep" arrests conducted by the Los Angeles police department, in which more than 1000 suspected gang members have been arrested on a single weekend.

We do not have a very good sense at this point about the relative strength of either the trend toward greater legal controls or the counter-trend. Careful readers of the pages that follow will note that they describe formal legal controls. Only in the case of deadly force do we have any persuasive empirical evidence that these controls directly affect on-the-street behavior. More research is needed regarding the quality of routine police work. Today, this question arises in the context of the controversy surrounding the beating of Rodney King by Los Angeles police officers on March 3, 1991. Recorded on videotape by a bystander, and subsequently broadcast repeatedly by the national news media, the King tape dominates the public image of contemporary policing. Many people have concluded that policing has made no progress since the worst days of the 1960s riots. The author of this paper is not prepared to accept that view. The paper that follows argues just the contrary. Nonetheless, the King videotape is a sobering reminder that the development of formal controls may or may not affect on-the-street police behavior.

The Prehistory of Legal Control: American Policing to 1960

The prehistory of legal control of the police begins roughly about 1960. The precise date is a bit arbitrary, but the mid-1950s and mid-1960s certainly represent two different eras in American policing (Walker, 1980).

Prior to the mid-1950s there were no meaningful legal controls over routine police behavior. By all accounts, American policing in the nineteenth century was utterly lawless. Physical brutality was rampant and essentially unpunished (Fogelson, 1977; Walker, 1977). In one of the most provocative explorations of police history, Wilbur Miller argues that because of the very different contexts of political and administrative control, the London police developed a tradition of civility while their New York counterparts (and by extension all American police) were completely uncontrolled. Challenges to police authority in this country were regarded as challenges to an officer's personal authority. Officers responded to such challenges in the most direct, personal fashion (Miller, 1977).

The lawlessness of the police was a consequence of a political, legal, and administrative vacuum in which all the potential sources of control failed to operate. Elected officials with formal responsibility for local police departments were interested primarily in the opportunities for graft and patronage.[6] The courts took a "hands off" posture with respect to the

---

[6] See the police as "adjuncts of the machine" (Fogelson, 1977).

constitutional aspects of criminal justice administration.[7] Nor did the police administrators exercise any meaningful control over police officer behavior. This latter point, which is extremely crucial, requires some elaboration.

Nineteenth-century police departments did maintain official manuals or rule books, but they appear to have been completely worthless. Investigations found that they were regarded as jokes by the officers and often not readily available. Even more important, for our purposes, the early rule books did not contain any specific rules pertaining to on-the-street officer behavior. This includes the subjects that have been of great concern in recent years: arrest, search, interrogation, and physical and deadly force.

The principal documents of police "reform" in the first 100 years of policing are also silent on this issue. Fuld's *Police Administration* (1909), Raymond Fosdick's *American Police Systems* (1920), the Wickersham Commission's *Report on Police* (U.S. National Commission on Law Observance and Enforcement, 1931a), and other key documents give no attention to the problem of controlling on-the-street police officer behavior. The principal concerns of reformers included political influence over policing, nonenforcement of the law (especially relating to drinking), the formal structure of political control of police departments, and personnel standards. One searches the many nineteenth-century reports and investigations for any discussion of what we understand as the critical issue of police discretion.[8] The various crime commission investigations of the early twentieth century are equally silent. And we should remember that these commissions involved the foremost scholars of the period. The 1922 Cleveland Survey, which established the model for those that followed, was codirected by Roscoe Pound and Felix Frankfurter (The Cleveland Foundation, 1922).

The notable exception to this generalization was the rising concern about the "third degree," or the coercion of testimony by suspects, often by the most brutal methods.[9] Public concern about the third degree reached its apex with the 1931 Wickersham Commission *Report on*

---

[7] The demise of the "hands off" doctrine with respect to police, prisons, and virtually all other aspects of criminal justice was the essential feature of the "due process revolution" of the Warren Court.

[8] In fairness, it should be noted that virtually all of these early investigatory reports are biased sources: produced by self-styled reformers who began with the assumption that policing was seriously flawed. The published accounts by police officials themselves, however, are not encouraging either. Most are celebrations of the heroic work done by the police, with no attention given to the issues under discussion here.

[9] See the attention given the subject by the chiefs of police in the proceedings of the International Association of Chiefs of Police. Selections from 1905 to 1910 are reprinted in Dilworth (1976:63–81).

Lawlessness in Law Enforcement (U.S. National Commission on Law Observance and Enforcement, 1931b). The report alerted a wider public audience to the problem of police lawlessness. Yet, from our perspective, it is significant that the coercion of testimony was seen as a special and limited problem. The authors did not see a general problem of police misconduct, involving a number of different actions.

The absence of legal controls over the police was primarily a matter of intellectual framework. The best minds of several generations did not understand the problem as we do today and did not see legal control as a possible solution. Police reform in the first half of the twentieth century was dominated by the ideology of Progressivism. Policing would be improved by hiring qualified people, freeing them from political influence, and giving them sufficient resources (Walker, 1980:125–160, 169–170). It never occurred—and could not have occurred—to these reformers that "good" people could do "bad" things: that a person who met their standards of being qualified for policing could physically beat up a citizen or conduct a blatantly illegal search. Today, we understand that such things can—and do—happen. That is because we are informed by a sociological perspective on police work. That understanding did not appear until the late 1950s and, together with several other forces, shaped the development of legal controls over the police (Newman, 1966:177–187; Walker, 1992).

The Watershed: From the Mid-1950s to the Mid-1960s

The decade from the mid-1950s to the mid-1960s constitutes the watershed in American policing. The years 1956 and 1966 might as well have been a century apart. The process of change involved the complex interplay of several powerful legal, political, and intellectual forces.

The Supreme Court and the Police

The Supreme Court was perhaps the most important force for change in this critical period. The history of the Court's rulings on the police can be divided into two periods, separated by the 1961 *Mapp* decision.

With *Powell v. Alabama* in 1932, the Court began its scrutiny of the criminal process. It proceeded through *Brown v. Mississippi* (1936), *McNabb* (1943), *Rochin* (1952), and *Mallory* (1957). Extremely tentative at first, it picked up increasing momentum in the 1950s, and then entered a new and vigorous phase with *Mapp* in 1961. *Mallory* is particularly notable because it provoked the first serious (although unsuccessful) congressional effort to overturn a Supreme Court decision on police procedure, foreshadowing the reaction to *Mapp* and *Miranda* in the 1960s (Pritchett, 1961).

This essay is not the occasion for a full history of the Supreme Court's growing scrutiny of police procedures (see, for example, Abraham, 1982; White, 1988:317–368).[10] From our perspective, the important point is that the line of cases reflected a significant change in judicial thinking. This represented not only new constitutional doctrine, but also a growing awareness of the depth of police misconduct and the need for a judicial remedy. This new judicial thinking, which found its parallel in some state supreme courts, pointed in the direction of the legal control of routine police behavior.

What prompted this new judicial thinking? Several factors appear to have been at work. The emerging civil rights movement heightened the consciousness of innumerable Americans, including the legal community. Although the civil rights movement's litigation efforts concentrated on *de jure* segregation, they inevitably provoked concern about the fate of racial minorities in other areas of American life, including the police (Cox, 1968; White, 1988).

As the 1960s proceeded, the Supreme Court intervened in a steadily growing number of areas of criminal justice administration—the right to counsel, juvenile court proceedings, prison conditions, the death penalty, and so on. As one commentator observed, the Court fashioned a code of criminal procedure out of the Bill of Rights (Friendly, 1965). The high water mark of Court scrutiny of police practices was, of course, *Miranda v. Arizona* in 1966. Moreso than in any other case, the Court's opinion contained a detailed set of rules for how the police should handle a specific situation. This is, of course, the famous "*Miranda* warning." It seems appropriate to view the entire body of case law on on-the-street police behavior as a detailed set of rules governing a broad range of situations.

The role of the Court was extremely important in pointing toward the legal control of the police. But it was hardly the only force at work and, by itself, may not have been sufficient. It is necessary to put the Court and its decisions in a broader intellectual, political, and administrative context.

Intellectual Breakthrough: The American Bar Foundation Survey of the Administration of Criminal Justice, 1956–1960

In terms of the intellectual framework underpinning the legal control of the police, the historic intellectual breakthrough was the American Bar

---

[10] For an illuminating discussion of how the Warren Court gained confidence about its interventionist role after a few tentative forays, see White (1988:317–368).

Foundation (ABF) Survey of the Administration of Criminal Justice. Although largely forgotten today, the ABF Survey created what became the dominant paradigm in the study of criminal justice (Walker, 1992).[11]

In brief, the Survey marked the beginnings of a sociology of the administration of justice. Most important, it was the first to conceptualize the administration of criminal justice as a "system"[12] pervaded by the exercise of discretion (Walker, 1992). The latter contribution is extremely relevant for the discussion here. The idea that legal control of the police was necessary required an awareness that there was a serious problem demanding some innovation remedy.

The intellectual contributions of the ABF Survey were a product of its methodology. The Survey undertook the first systematic direct observation of criminal justice officials at work.[13] The earlier crime commission investigations had all relied on official statistics and made no attempts to observe the law in action.[14] Within a matter of weeks of beginning field research in February 1956, the entire research team was stunned by their observations. Research Director Frank Remington quickly reformulated the project's objectives, focusing on discretion at various critical decision points.[15] Team members were struck by the rampant lawlessness of official behavior, the disregard for legal norms in decision making, and the extent to which decisions such as arrest were routinely made for reasons unrelated to arrest.[16] The Survey's findings circulated on a very restricted basis, because of an earlier promise of confidentiality, but had a profound effect on everyone who saw them. Criminologist Donald Cressy commented that "criminology will never be the same again."[17] Sanford Kadish later called the data an "eyeopener."[18]

For a variety of reasons, publication of the Survey's findings was delayed several years. When they did reach a broader audience through

---

[11] The best summary of the Survey's work is Newman (1966). A fuller treatment appears in Walker (1993).

[12] The President's Crime Commission is generally regarded as having founded the concept of a criminal justice "system." See, especially, President's Commission on Law Enforcement and Administration of Justice (1967a:58–59). But in fact it systematized and popularized the basic concept that originated with the ABF Survey.

[13] There were a few notable exceptions to this rule: with respect to policing, Warner (1940); bail, Foote (1954).

[14] See the critique in Sherry (1955).

[15] The original field reports and internal memos are housed in the Criminal Justice Library at the University of Wisconsin Law School. For the intellectual reorientation of the Survey, see, especially, Lloyd Ohlin, Memo to O.W. Wilson, March 15, 1956; Frank Remington, Memo to Goldstein and Warner, May 11, 1956; Frank Remington, Memo to All Field Research Personnel, June 8, 1956.

[16] The classic treatment, based on the ABF field research, is LaFave (1965).

[17] Anecdote related by Herman Goldstein.

[18] Interview, Sanford Kadish.

the normal channels of publication, the impact was profound. The first significant publication based on the Survey's field reports, Joseph Goldstein's 1960 *Yale Law Journal* article on police discretion marked the first serious discussion of the subject (Goldstein, 1960:543–588). In a similar fashion, Sanford Kadish's article on the absence of legal norms in the correctional area helped stimulate new thinking and, eventually, new law and policy in that arena (Kadish, 1961).

Goldstein's article on police discretion is of particular relevance to our discussion here. It launched serious discussion of the subject, but did not control the subsequent debate. He reacted in horror and argued that police discretion was illegal and should be abolished. The ensuing debate on police discretion rejected his approach in favor of an alternative promulgated in large measure by Herman Goldstein, one of the original members of the ABF team. Over the next decade and a half a broad consensus was reached around the idea that discretion was an inescapable part of police work, that it had some beneficial aspects, that the proper approach was to control rather than attempt to abolish it. Furthermore, such control was best achieved through written administrative policies (Walker, 1993). Herman Goldstein disseminated his views in a series of articles (Goldstein, 1963, 1967a, 1967b), in important sections of the U.S. President's Commission's *Task Force Report: The Police* (1967),[19] and in the American Bar Association's "Standards Relating to the Urban Police Function" (1980). Both of the latter two documents were important for their discussion of the complexity of the police role, the pervasiveness of discretion in the face of multiple tasks and often conflicting pressures, and the need for administrative controls to guide that discretion.

The Politics of Crime and Justice

The decade of the 1960s is unique in American history in that never before had issues pertaining to the administration of criminal justice played such a major role in national politics. It has properly been called the "law and order decade" (Walker, 1980).

The phrase "law and order" embraces two very distinct political movements. The one that appeared first chronologically and is most relevant to our concerns is the civil rights movement. In brief, civil rights forces across the country challenged routine police practices, leveling charges of brutality, verbal abuse, and discriminatory arrests and shootings of blacks. The conjunction of the civil rights movement and the Supreme Court's

---

[19] In particular, Goldstein and Frank Remington were responsible for the then pioneering discussion of the complexity of the police role and the recommendation for administrative controls over police behavior in Chapter 2 of the Task Force Report.

rulings on the police created a powerful dynamic, with each one reinforcing the other in the direction of greater legal control of police behavior.[20]

One important consequence of the politics of law and order was an unprecedented examination of the administration of justice. A burst of research provided a new body of knowledge on the workings of the justice system. In addition, several national-level commissions undertook the task of making recommendations for improvement in the system. The American Bar Association initiated its standards for the administration of justice in 1963 (American Bar Association, 1980; Jameson, 1972). That same year the American Law Institute set out to draft a Model Code of Pre-arraignment Procedure (American Law Institute, 1975; Vorenberg, 1975). The President's Commission on Law Enforcement and the Administration of Justice was established in 1965 and finished its work in 1967 (Walker, 1980:232–235). The National Advisory Commission on Civil Disorders (1968) delivered its report, with three chapters on police–community relations, in 1968. The National Advisory Commission on Criminal Justice Standards and Goals (1973) published its reports in 1973.

As we have already indicated, these commissions and reports became the vehicle for dissemination of the emerging consensus regarding police behavior: that much if it was lawless, that control was necessary, and that administrative rulemaking was the best form of control.

The politics of law and order shifted dramatically in the late 1960s, with public concern for crime control taking precedence over concern for racial and economic justice.[21] Nonetheless, the network of controls continued to grow through the 1970s and 1980s. Because of the preoccupation with the Supreme Court by most commentators, this development is generally overlooked. Yet, the continued development of controls over the police in an allegedly conservative era is an extremely important phenomenon.

Consensus: The Control of Police Behavior Through Administrative Rulemaking

By the mid-1970s a consensus was reached on the control of police behavior through administrative rule making. The change in both the academic/intellectual sphere and the realm of police administration over the previous decade was remarkable. In the intellectual realm, the new consensus was summed up by Davis' little book *Police Discretion*, which made a persuasive case for administrative rule making by one of the

---

[20] One perspective on the period is found in Walker (1990:Chap. 11).

[21] The shift in public attitudes is most clearly evident in public attitudes toward the death penalty. Support was declining steadily until about 1966–1967, when it began to rise to its current high level.

leading authorities on administrative law (1974:703–725). His argument met little dissent[22] and, in effect, closed the debate that Joseph Goldstein had begun in 1960.

In the operational realm of police administration, the changes were no less dramatic. The traditional refusal of police officials to acknowledge the subject of police discretion had vanished.[23] The existence of discretion was now part of the "conventional wisdom," an accepted and uncontroversial idea. Moreover, police officials began to initiate controls over police discretion without any initiative from the Supreme Court. The most important elements in this chapter of recent police history are examined next.

Deadly Force

Perhaps the most important development was the growth of restrictive controls over police use of deadly force. In 1972 Police Commissioner Patrick V. Murphy issued a new and restrictive deadly force policy for the New York City police department. The policy also included an accountability mechanism, by which officers were required to file written reports after each firearms discharge, with those reports then being automatically reviewed by a departmental committee (Fyfe, 1979). Murphy established an important and influential precedent. Within just a few years many other big-city police departments also revised their deadly force policies, adopting the New York policy with minor variations (Sherman, 1978). The direction of change was a steady movement away from the common law "fleeing felon" standard and toward the "defense-of-life" standard.

By the time the Supreme Court ruled on police use of deadly force in 1985 (*Tennessee v. Garner* 471 U.S. 1 (1985)), the defense-of-life standard, with accompanying administrative review of shooting incidents, had become the norm. Perhaps the most notable aspects of the *Garner* case were that briefs for the plaintiffs cited current police policies limiting the use of deadly force and the lack of sustained criticism from the police following the decision. At that point, officers in most big-city departments had been working under policies even more restrictive than that required by *Garner*[24] and had apparently not found such policies burdensome or threatening.

---

[22] The notable exception was Allen (1976:61).

[23] On the traditional denial, see Davis (1975:Chap. 3). For the best evidence of the new acknowledgment of discretion, see the discussion of the law enforcement accreditation standards.

[24] *Garner* required neither the defense-of-life standard nor most of the other restrictions that had become prevalent, such as the prohibition on warning shots.

Accreditation

A second important indicator of the new consensus was the accreditation movement. The Commission on Accreditation for Law Enforcement Agencies was created in 1979, with representatives from the International Association of Chiefs of Police (IACP), the National Sheriffs' Association (NSA), the National Organization of Black Law Enforcement Executives (NOBLE), and the Police Executive Research Forum (PERF) (Commission on Accreditation, 1988). A set of accreditation standards was approved in 1983 and the first police department accredited a year later. By mid-1989, one hundred agencies had been accredited (Commission on Accreditation, 1989).

Two aspects of accreditation are relevant here. First, it seems clear that the accreditation movements in both corrections and law enforcement were prompted by the increase in litigation and represented an effort to avert intervention by external authorities through self-regulation (Jacobs, 1983:57). Although leaders in the law enforcement profession had long talked in terms of their being a "profession," it required the shock of intervention by external authorities to stimulate a serious attempt at self-regulation, one of the hallmarks of a true profession.

Second, the standards themselves embrace the general principle of legal control, in the form of controlling police discretion through administrative rule making. Standard 12.2 requires that "The agency has a written directives system that includes, at a minimum, the following: statements of agency policy; procedures for carrying out agency activities; rules and regulations" (Commission on Accreditation, 1988). Meanwhile, Standard 1.3 requires a written policy on use of deadly force that embodies the defense-of-life standard (Commission on Accreditation, 1988). Given the composition of the Commission on Accreditation for Law Enforcement Agencies, it is fair to say that the standards represent the consensus of the profession.

The IACP Policy Development Center

In 1987 the International Association of Chiefs of Police, with financial support from the Justice Department, established a National Law Enforcement Policy Center. The Center developed model policies on selected subjects and provided technical assistance to local agencies on related problems. Creation of the Center was further evidence of the consensus surrounding administrative rule making and a somewhat belated recognition on the part of the IACP that it had a responsibility to provide leadership in this area. By mid-1990, the Center had published seven model policies with accompanying concepts and issues policies, with fourteen other policies nearly completed.[25]

---

[25] IACP/BJA National Law Enforcement Policy Center publishes model policies and a newsletter, *Policy Review*.

Domestic Violence

The problem of domestic violence emerged as a matter of great national concern in the 1970s. The result was substantial changes in both statutes and administrative policies (Buzawa and Buzawa, 1990). With respect to the police, the basic trend was in the direction of a preference for arrest in cases of domestic assault. To this end, many departments adopted written policies (some as a result of court decrees) instructing police officers to make arrests where there was evidence of a felonious assault (Loving, 1980). The Minneapolis Domestic Violence Experiment gave powerful support to this trend with its finding that arrest deterred future violence more effectively than mediating the dispute or separating the two parties (replications of the study, however, found no such deterrent effect, see Dunford et al., 1990; Sherman and Berk, 1984; Sherman, 1992). A national survey of big-city police departments found that the percentage of departments with "arrest preferred" policies increased from 10 percent in 1984 to 46 percent in 1986 (Cohn and Sherman, 1987).

The changes in domestic violence policy paralleled those in the area of deadly force policy. The process may be summarized as follows: (1) a new issue emerged, championed by a well-organized political constituency; (2) through protest, litigation, and public education this constituency had a noticeable effect on public policy; (3) litigation produced specific changes, incorporating new administrative controls over police discretion; (4) social science research, stimulated by the intense public interest, confirmed the existence of the problem (as defined by the advocacy groups) and lent powerful support to the developing controls over discretion. In the case of domestic violence, the prior example of deadly force provided a readily imitated model.

Pursuits

The process appears to be repeating itself with respect to high-speed pursuits, another police activity where officer discretion had traditionally been left ungoverned. Rising concern about danger to citizens and police officers, increasing civil damage suits by injured parties, and new questions about the law enforcement value of pursuits have led to controls in the form of written directives (Alpert and Dunham, 1990). The Omaha police department policy, for example, embodies two forms of control. First, sergeants are given explicit authority to terminate pursuits if circumstances warrant; second, a report is required after every pursuit (Omaha Police Division, 1982).[26] Restrictive pursuit policies appear to be spreading

---

[26] The policy was revised in a radically more restrictive direction in August 14, 1990. Pursuits are now permitted only where the officer believes that the suspect has committed a violent felony and that there is substantial risk that death or serious injury will result if the suspect is not apprehended. In effect, the new policy closely parallels the defense-of-life standard for the use of deadly force.

nationally, but we do not yet have an evaluation of the extent of this movement or the impact of restrictive policies.

Roads Taken and Not Taken

Why did policing evolve in the direction of written rules, as opposed to some other form of control? We gain additional perspective on the development of legal controls over the police by considering alternative approaches that were not adopted.

As Supreme Court scrutiny of police activity increased from the mid-1950s onward, the police and their advocates strenuously objected. The most articulate advocates of police autonomy offered what might be called a "professional" model of control. The police, this argument held, were entitled to the same prerogatives as other recognized professions. Within their area of professional expertise, they should be granted broad discretion to make judgments based on their professional training and experience. At the same time, they should have exclusive right to determine standards of unprofessional conduct and to discipline their own members for breaching those standards (Moore, 1970). The full professional model included the development of specialties, the accreditation of skill within those areas (Bittner, 1970), and an organizational framework that permitted specialization.[27] The imposition of external controls was seen as leading to the "bureaucratization" of the police, rather than in the direction of "true" professional status.

If the claim of professional status represented the "high road," the "low road" involved the specter of rampant crime. Shackle the police, the argument went, and society would be overrun with crime. This argument was quickly adopted by national political figures and used with great effectiveness from George Wallace in 1964, through Richard Nixon in 1968, to George Bush in 1988.

Needless to say, the American police did not develop in the direction of an autonomous, self-governing profession. The trend has clearly been in the direction of increased bureaucratization, particularly in the form of complex written rules designed to standardize behavior. The relevant question is why events proceeded in this direction. Why was the other road to the control of police behavior not taken? After all, it had its vigorous advocates and seemingly enormous political support.

The professional model failed for several reasons. First, the police had no status as a profession. Given the long and notorious history of police corruption and inefficiency, together with the personnel standards that prevailed at this critical juncture (roughly the late 1950s to mid-1960s), the idea that the police were or could ever hope to be the equals of the

---

[27] See the recommendation of the President's Crime Commission (1968:274–277).

"true" professions such as law and medicine was absurd. Even low-status professions such as social work and public school teaching had difficulty making such a claim. In this respect, then, the police as an occupation were highly vulnerable to intervention by outsiders.

Second, and perhaps more important in a larger sense, the control of police behavior through formal written rules was consistent with broader trends in American society. This includes two separate phenomena. One is the general bureaucratization of society (including, it might be noted, of the so-called "true" professions of law and medicine). The other is the growth of a "rights consciousness" in American society. The rules that have developed emerged to control police behavior for the larger purpose of protecting individual rights, defined legally in terms of due process and equal protection. The growth of a vast body of law protecting individual rights was one of the most important and lasting developments of the 1960s. The full dimensions of this "rights revolution" are still not clear, but it is impossible to doubt that it has had and continues to have a profound effect on American life.[28] Friedman (1985) views this development in terms of a "law explosion" which reflects "a general expectation of justice" that pervades American society.

The "professional model" of police control, in short, attempted to swim against the tide of history. The "bureaucratic model," with its growing network of written rules and regulations, swam with the tide. This explains why one road was not taken and why the legal control of the police has taken the form it has.

That tide was far broader and deeper than the Warren Court. The development of controls over policing described earlier is almost entirely a post-Warren Court phenomenon. Furthermore, these controls have emerged without benefit of direct rulings by the Supreme Court. The *Garner* decision on deadly force was a belated event and the Court's holding was less restrictive on police behavior than the prevailing norm among big-city police departments. This point has enormous implications for the future of legal controls, a subject to which we now turn.

The Future of Legal Control: Alternative Scenarios

The argument developed here raises a number of questions about the present status of the legal control of the police and its future.

---

[28] This is the argument in Walker (1990). For an illuminating discussion of a parallel development in medical ethics since 1966, which involves the substantial loss of professional autonomy on the part of the doctors and the advent of formal external controls, see Rothman (1991).

With respect to the future, one interpretation is implicit in the argument as already developed. The evidence suggests that the movement toward greater legal control is likely to continue in the near future. Controls over the police continued to develop through the 1970s and 1980s; the movement in this direction appears to have intensified in recent years; and, finally, the movement appears to have substantial support from a number of sources and, consequently, does not depend on the leadership of the Supreme Court.

This interpretation has important political ramifications. It greatly diminishes the importance of the Supreme Court as overseer of the criminal process. This is certainly good news for civil rights and civil liberties activists. The present conservative trend in the Court may not be as alarming as those activists fear.

There is, of course, an alternative scenario, one that is far less promising for the future of legal control of the police. This scenario attaches more weight to the purely *symbolic* role of the Supreme Court. Court decisions are often as important for their symbolic value, for the implicit message, as for their precise holding. Thus, the great contribution of the Warren Court was its symbolic role as defender of individual rights. The primary message, which went far beyond the holding of any single decision, was that there were limits to police authority and that the police were accountable to the law. (Of course, some consistuencies saw a different symbol and heard a very different message: that abstract rights took precedence over the need for effective crime control and protection of law-abiding citizens).

In recent years, the Court has been sending a different message: that crime control takes precedence over individual rights; that "good faith" and "public safety" exceptions to previously established restraints are legitimate (*United States v. Leon* 468 U.S. 897 (1984)). Libertarians and some police observers fear that the message implicit in these decisions encourages deception, incompetence, or both on the part of the police. If this is indeed the message that is "heard," the possibility arises that the entire existing structure of legal control may erode. For every problematic situation there is an exception that justifies whatever the police officer does. If this scenario is correct, then the future of the legal control of the police looks very grim indeed. In fact, as we suggested at the outset, the police today hardly need the Supreme Court to tell them to take extreme and possibly questionable measures. The general public and elected officials have been telling them the same thing in very loud voices for many years.

This issue turns on the question of what exactly working police officers "hear" about Supreme Court decisions. There is some reason to believe that they do not hear much or that what they do hear is impressionistic inaccurate, or both. Wasby's (1976) study of small-town police in Illinois is the only serious inquiry into this crucial issue. Further studies examining more recent court decisions and focusing on the extent to which important new decisions are incorporated into training materials or policy and procedure manuals would help to resolve this question.

The Conditions of Successful Legal Control

Consideration of these alternative scenarios brings us to a number of questions about the conditions of successful legal control (Walker, 1993). The basic question is, What makes a rule work? It is a truism that rules are not self-enforcing. The mere existence of a rule on a piece of paper somewhere means nothing. The anecdote we began with illustrates the point: the exclusionary rule had no apparent impact on Wisconsin in 1956. Anyone knowledgeable about policing can think of examples of the systematic evasion of a rule or rules.

The history of legal control suggests two points about the conditions of successful rules. One directs our attention to the inner world of police departments, to the administrative implementation of rules. The other directs our attention to more elusive phenomena, involving both the social psychology of policing and the broader political environment.

The Administration of Rules

The available evidence on the successful implementation of rules confirms what common sense suggests: rules are more likely to be successful when they are developed and enforced by people closest to the decision in question[29] and rules are more likely to work when there is a specific enforcement mechanism.

The best evidence involves the police use of deadly force. Fyfe (1979) found that the restrictive shooting policy adopted by the New York City police department in 1972 reduced firearms discharges by about 30 percent. Sherman's national trend data for the fifty largest cities found both a significant reduction in the number of persons shot and killed between 1971 and 1985 and a reduction in the ratio of blacks to whites shot and killed (form roughly 6:1 to 3:1) (Sherman and Cohn, 1986). There is good reason to assume that these national trends are the result of the steady adoption of restrictive policies by big-city departments.

There is also good reason to assume that the new restrictive shooting policies are successful because of the reporting and review mechanisms

---

[29] A change in Pennsylvania state law on police use of deadly force, for example, has little effect on shootings by Philadelphia police (Waegel, 1984). Rules developed and enforced by police departments themselves, on the other hand, do appear to have had some impact.

that are now generally standard procedure. In almost all departments, officers are required to file a report after any firearms discharge (regardless of the circumstances), and these reports are automatically reviewed by supervisors. These report and review mechanisms puts officers on notice that they will be held accountable for their discretionary decisions. Thus, enforcement seems to produce successful rule implementation (Fyfe, 1979).[30]

Although we have no systematic data on the subject, there appears to be a trend toward similar report and review procedures for other critical decisions by police officers. In the Omaha Police Department, for example, six different actions by police officers involving a citizen trigger an automatic report (firearms discharge, use of mace or baton, choke hold, high-speed pursuit, resisting arrest charge) (Omaha Police Division, 1989). The "chief's report" nominally goes directly to the chief of police but is in fact investigated by the internal affairs unit.

The policies on domestic violence represent a very different picture. None of the existing policies have a mandatory report and review mechanism. Thus, the officer is instructed to make arrests in the case of felonious assault, but there is no mechanism for monitoring compliance. The domestic violence policies are notable, as they represent the first attempt to control police discretion in the basic arrest decision. But given the fact that, by definition, domestic assaults occur in private places, there is no observation by noninvolved parties, a factor that might serve as a check on officer behavior.[31] It should be noted that in the experiments on the deterrent effect of arrest in domestic assaults, officer discretion was controlled by the design of the experiment (Sherman and Berk, 1984).

A unique compliance mechanism was created by a Seattle, Washington, ordinance regulating police intelligence gathering. Designed to curb police spying, the law imposed administrative controls over police intelligence gathering on political, religious, and private sexual activity. To ensure compliance, the law also created the position of auditor, a person hired independently by the city council with authority to randomly examine police investigatory files. This approach represents a wholly unprecedented monitoring of police activity by an outsider. There is as yet, however, no systematic evaluation of the impact of this mechanism (Walker, 1985a: 144–157).

In conclusion we should emphasize the dangers of overestimating the effectiveness of the existing compliance mechanisms. Even though a report may be required after each firearms discharge, and officers dutifully

---

[30] See the discussion of policy change in New York, Atlanta, and Kansas City in Sherman (1983:98–125).

[31] For a discussion of why the apparent success of the deadly force rules might not transfer to domestic violence or other areas of policing, see Walker (1986).

file them, we have no way of knowing whether officers are in fact disciplined for violating policy. Some anecdotal evidence suggests that, in some departments at least, the apparatus of control is undermined by a systematic failure to enforce existing guidelines.[32] One of the major items on the agenda of police research involves systematic inquiry into the administration of existing legal controls.

The Impact of "Consumer Demand" on Legal Control

A neglected aspect of legal control of the police is the impact of "consumer demand." Our hypothesis here is that rules work when people demand that they work. This process involves several different elements. First, consumer demand—often in the form of political pressure—is frequently responsible for the creation of rules. Second, consumer demand may affect the social psychology of police–citizen encounters in ways that constrain police behavior. Third, consumer demand is effective insofar as citizens with claims of injustice at the hands of the police have access to the resources necessary to pursue those claims.

With respect to the creation of rules, we can view the Warren Court initiatives as the product of a sustained legal challenge to existing police practices. The briefs and oral arguments in these cases were, in effect, an expression of consumer demand for controls over police behavior. By the same token, the development of the new restrictive rules on police use of deadly force was the product of a broad and sustained attack on police shootings. Public concern about domestic violence, and the growth of police rules, has been largely a product of the demands of the women's movement.

Consumer demand is also expressed situationally. In a specific police–citizen encounter, the citizen may claim that his or her rights have been violated. This may serve as a constraint on police officer behavior. A person cannot raise a claim of this sort, however, unless he or she is aware that such a right exists. Another anecdote from the ABF Survey illuminates the enormous change in public consciousness that has occurred in the past thirty-five years. Milwaukee police officers reported that in the predominantly Italian-American ward, they had to be attentive to the laws of criminal procedure. Suspects were knowledgeable about their rights and, apparently, had access to vigorous legal assistance. But in the predominantly black ward, they had a free hand because, the officers reported, blacks did not know their rights or at least did not assert them.[33]

---

[32] Comments by James J. Fyfe on the Boston police department, ACJS annual meeting, April 1990.

[33] Field Reports, ABF Survey Papers, University of Wisconsin Law School. The full history of the ABF Survey will appear as a chapter in Walker (in press).

The world has changed enormously since this anecdote was told. Consciousness of rights is now very widespread, and the change has probably been greatest within the black community. The impact of this changed consciousness has enormous implications for the effectiveness of rules governing police behavior. To the extent that the citizen's claim has some legitimacy, or is at least arguable, it may constrain the officer's behavior. Although officers may develop subtle strategies for bending or breaking rules, they also know that there are some outer limits to rule breaking.

A similar process is at work in the prison setting. An elaborate body of prisoners' rights law has developed in the past fifteen years. In the Nebraska prisons, for example, incoming inmates are presented with a copy of the institutional rules. The rulebook specifies certain rights they have, including the right to appeal disciplinary action.[34] Although we have no systematic evidence on the impact of these rules, a presumptive case can be made that the mutual recognition of limits on official behavior and the right of appeal constrain the conduct of prison guards, at least in terms of reducing the grosser forms of abuse.[35]

One of the most important unexplored issues in the administration of justice is the extent to which the institutional working environment of policing, the courtroom, and prisons has been fundamentally altered over the past twenty to thirty years. With respect to the police, our benchmark is the classic statement of the problem by Skolnick in *Justice Without Trial* (1966). Skolnick posited a tension between the norms of police work, especially the pressure to get results, and the rule of law. At the time he did his research, there were relatively few formal written rules governing police behavior. The relevant question is, To what extent has this environment changed? To what extent has the principle of accountability become established to the point where it is one of the facts of life into which a new police officer is socialized?

In this regard, it is important to remember that virtually all sworn officers today are members of a post-*Mapp* and post-*Miranda* generation. Most of the officers on routine patrol duty joined the force after the present restrictive rules on deadly force were promulgated. The history of the legal control of the police must come to terms with the implications of the long-term effect of personnel turnover and the changed environments into which frequent generations of officers are socialized.[36]

We have no systematic data on this phenomenon. There is some fragmentary evidence, however. A study of Chicago narcotics officers

---

[34] Interview with officials at the Omaha Correctional Training Center.

[35] On the impact of the prisoners' rights movement on prison administration, particularly the sense of a loss of power by prison guards, see Jacobs (1983:33–60).

[36] On the changing police subculture, see Walker (1985b).

found a surprising degree of support for the exclusionary rule.[37] A number of officers saw it as a valuable safeguard against misconduct. This study also documented, better than any other inquiry, the subtle but important changes that occurred in the supervision of narcotics cases as a result of the *Mapp* decision. Prosecutors scrutinized cases more closely before accepting them, and working relationships between police and prosecutors became closer. Sergeants exercised more oversight of detectives under their command. Some officers reported that loss of cases was a criterion for continued assignment to the detective bureau. They also reported that courtroom testimony, particularly the experience of losing a case or being embarrassed by a defense attorney or judge, was a powerful learning experience—the best training they ever got, according to some officers.

Changes along the same lines were identified by Reuss-Ianni in her study of *The Two Cultures of Policing* (1983). Studying the New York City Police Department during a period of intense change, she identified an internal clash between the old "street cops" and the new ethos of what she termed "management cops." Her study does not provide specific information directly related to our concerns here, but her general framework is consistent with the argument that the working environment of policing has become pervaded by bureaucratic rules and regulations.

The impact of a control over police behavior is also a matter of resources. To what extent does a person who feels that his or her rights have been violated, that is, that a formal control has breached, have access to some person or group who will press that claim. In other areas of the law, it is recognized that inadequate or even nonexistent "access to justice" renders the law meaningless.

In this regard, the rise of the so-called "rights industry" in recent American history has significant implications for the police. The "rights industry" is defined as the network of public interest advocacy groups.[38] This includes national and local groups devoted to civil rights, women's rights, environmental rights, the rights of the poor, the mentally ill, and so on. For our purposes, civil rights and civil liberties groups are the relevant actors (the NAACP, NAACP Legal Defense Fund, the ACLU, the National Lawyers Guild, and so on). In addition to groups, there is in most cities today a local civil rights bar, which includes private attorneys whose practice includes police misconduct cases. This "rights industry" barely existed thirty years ago, especially outside a few major metropolitan

---

[37] "The Exclusionary Rule and Deterrence: An Empirical Study of Chicago Narcotics Officers" (1987) *University of Chicago Law Review 54* Summer:1016–1055.

[38] For a critical view of the "industry," see Morgan (1984). For a favorable view, see Walker (1990).

areas. We should also consider the spread of public defender systems following the 1963 *Gideon* decision as another component of the rights industry.

We have no systematic evidence of the impact of the "rights industry," but we can make some reasonable hypotheses. Presumptively, it means that someone who has a claim of injustice has access to a potential advocate. To what extent does this serve as a "check" on police behavior? To what extent does the mere existence of such advocates affect the consciousness and subsequent behavior of police officers? There are, for example, many questions raised about the quality of legal defense provided by public defenders (if only because of heavy case loads). But it may well be that the mere existence of a public defender curbs the grossest forms of prosecutorial misconduct.

Conclusions

This review of the history of the legal control of the police raises more questions than it answers. The one thing we know for certain is that an elaborate network of formal controls over police behavior has developed over the past thirty years. It also seems evident that this is a wholly new phenomenon in policing, without precedent in previous police history. On the factors responsible for this development, there is ample room for debate among historians. The greatest uncertainty concerns the important questions about the impact of these rules. Do they achieve their intended aims? Why or why not? If so, what are the necessary conditions of effectiveness? Do the rules have unintended consequences, either desirable or undesirable?

In the end, a historical perspective tells us that a network of nominal legal controls over police behavior has developed in the past thirty years; it remains to be determined whether those controls work.

References

Abraham, H.J. (1982). *Freedom and the Court.* 4th ed. New York: Oxford University Press.

Allen, R. (1976). The Police and Substantive Rulemaking: Reconciling Principle and Expediency. *University of Pennsylvania Law Review 165*:61.

Alpert, G.P. and R.G. Dunham. (1990). *Police Pursuit Driving: Controlling Responses to Emergency Situations.* Westport, CT: Greenwood Press.

American Bar Association. (1980). Standards Relating to the Urban Police Function. *Standards for Criminal Justice.* 2nd ed. Boston: Little, Brown.

American Law Institute. (1975). *Model Code of Pre-arraignment Procedure.* Washington, DC.

Bittner, E. (1970). Accreditation of Police Skill. In Bittner, E. (Ed.), *The Functions of Police in Modern Society.* Rockville, MD: National Institute of Mental Health.

Buzawa, E.S. and C.G. Buzawa. (1990). *Domestic Violence: The Criminal Justice Response*. Beverly Hills, CA: Sage.

The Cleveland Foundation. (1922). *Criminal Justice in Cleveland*. Cleveland, OH.

Cohn, E.G. and L.W. Sherman. (1987). *Police Policy on Domestic Violence, 1986: A National Survey*. Washington, DC: Crime Control Institute.

Commission on Accreditation for Law Enforcement Agencies. (September 1988). *Standards For Law Enforcement Agencies*. Fairfax, VA.

Commission on Accreditation for Law Enforcement Agencies. (Fall 1989). *Commission Update*. XLII.

Cox, A. (1968). *The Warren Court*. Cambridge, MA: Harvard University Press.

Davies, T.Y. (1983). A Hard Look at What We Know (and Still Need to Learn) About the "Costs" of the Exclusionary Rule: The NIJ Study and Other Studies of "Lost" Arrests. *American Bar Foundation Research Journal*, Summer:611–690.

Davis, K.C. (1974). An Approach to Legal Control of the Police. *Texas Law Review 52*, April:703–725.

Davis, K.C. (1975). *Police Discretion*. St. Paul, MN: West.

Dilworth, D.C. (Ed.) (1976). *The Blue and the Brass: American Policing, 1980–1910*. Gaithersburg, MD: International Association of Chiefs of Police.

Dunford, F.W., D. Huizinga, and E.S. Delbert. (1990). The Role of Arrest in Domestic Assault: The Omaha Police Experiment. *Criminology 28*, May:183–205.

Fogelson, R. (1977). *Big City Police*. Cambridge, MA: Harvard University Press.

Foote, C. (1954). Compelling Appearance in Court: The Administration of Bail in Philadelphia. *University of Pennsylvania Law Review 102*:1031.

Fosdick, R. (1920). *American Police Systems*. New York: The Century Company.

Friedman, L.M. (1985). *Total Justice*. New York: Russell Sage Foundation.

Friendly, H. (1965). The Bill of Rights as a Code of Criminal Procedure. *California Law Review 53*:929.

Fuld, L. (1909). *Police Administration*. Montclair, NJ: Patterson Smith.

Fyfe, J.J. (1979). Administrative Interventions on Police Shooting Discretion: An Empirical Examination. *Journal of Criminal Justice 7*, Winter:309–323.

Goldstein, H. (1963). Police Discretion: The Ideal Versus the Real. *Public Administration Review 23*, September:148–156.

Goldstein, H. (1967a). Police Policy Formulation: A Proposal for Improving Police Performance. *Michigan Law Review 65*:1123–1146.

Goldstein, H. (1967b). Administrative Problems in Controlling the Exercise of Police Authority. *Journal of Criminal Law, Criminology, and Police Science 58*:160–172.

Goldstein, J. (1960). Police Discretion Not to Invoke the Criminal Process: Low-Visibility Decisions in the Administration of Justice. *Yale Law Journal 69*:543–594.

Jacobs, J.B. (1983). *New Perspectives on Prisons and Imprisonment*. Ithaca, NY: Cornell University Press.

Jameson, W.J. (1972). The Background and Development of the Criminal Justice Standards. *Judicature 55*, May:366–368.

Kadish, S.H. (1961). The Advocate and the Expert—Counsel in the Peno-correctional Process. *Minnesota Law Review 45*, April:803–841.

LaFave, W.R. (1965). *Arrest: The Decision to Take the Suspect into Custody*. Boston: Little, Brown.

Loving, N. (1980). *Responding to Spouse Abuse and Wifebeating: A Guide for Police*. Washington, DC: Police Executive Research Forum.

Miller, W. (1977). *Cops and Bobbies: Police Authority in New York and London, 1830–1870*. Chicago: University of Chicago Press.

Moore, W.E. (1970). *The Professions: Rules and Roles*. New York: Russell Sage Foundation.

Morgan, R.E. (1984). *Disabling America: The "Rights Industry" in Our Time*. New York: Basic Books.

National Advisory Commission on Civil Disorders. (1968). *Report of the National Advisory Commission on Civil Disorders*. Washington, DC: U.S. Government Printing Office.

National Advisory Commission on Criminal Justice Standards and Goals. (1973). *Police*. Washington, DC: U.S. Government Printing Office.

Newman, D.J. (1966). Sociologists and the Administration of Criminal Justice. In Shostack, A.B. (Ed.), *Sociology in Action*. Homewood, IL: Dorsey Press.

Omaha Police Division. (1982). *Standard Operation Procedures*, OPS 2–3–6.

Omaha Police Division. (1989). *Standard Operation Procedures*, OPS 50.

President's Commission on Law Enforcement and Administration of Justice. (1967a). *Task Force Report: Sciences and Technology*. Washington, DC: U.S. Government Printing Office.

President's Commission on Law Enforcement and Administration of Justice. (1967b). *The Challenge of Crime in a Free Society*. Washington, DC: U.S. Government Printing Office.

President's Crime Commission. (1968). *The Challenge of a Crime in a Free Society*. New York: Avon Books.

Pritchett, H.C. (1961). *Congress Versus the Supreme Court, 1957–1960*. Minneapolis, MN: University of Minnesota.

Punch, M. (Ed.) (1983). *Control in the Police Organization*. Cambridge, MA: MIT Press.

Report on the National Advisory Commission on Civil Disorders. (1968). New York: Bantam Books.

Reuss-Ianni, E. (1983). *The Two Cultures of Policing: Street Cops and Management Cops*. New Brunswick, NJ: Transaction Books.

Rothman, D.J. (1991). *The Strangers at the Bedside*. New York: Basic Books.

Sherman, L.W. (1978). Restricting the License to Kill—Recent Developments in Police Use of Deadly Force. *Criminal Law Bulletin 14*, November–December: 577–583.

Sherman, L.W. (1983). Reducing Police Gun Use: Critical Events, Administrative Policy, and Organizational Changes. In Punch, M. (Ed.), *Control in the Police Organization*. Cambridge, MA: MIT Press.

Sherman, L.W. (1992). *Policing Domestic Violence*. New York: The Free Press.

Sherman, L.W. and R. Berk. (1984). The Specific Deterrent Effects of Arrest for Domestic Violence. *American Sociological Review 49*:261–272.

Sherman, L.W. and E.G. Cohn. (1986). *Citizens Killed by Big City Police, 1970–1984*. Washington, DC: Crime Control Institute.

Sherry, A.H. (1955). *The Administration of Criminal Justice: A Plan for a Survey*. Chicago: American Bar Foundation.

Skolnick, J. (1966). *Justice Without Trial*. New York: John Wiley and Sons.

U.S. National Commission on Law Observance and Enforcement. (1931a). *Report on Police*. Washington, DC: U.S. Government Printing Office.

U.S. National Commission on Law Observance and Enforcement. (1931b). *Report on Lawlessness in Law Enforcement*. Washington, DC: U.S. Government Printing Office.

U.S. President's Commission on Law Enforcement and Administration of Justice. (1967). *Task Force Report: The Police*. Washington, DC: U.S. Government Printing Office.

Vorenberg, J. (1975). The A.L.I. Approves Model Code of Pre-arraignment Procedure. *ABA Journal 61*, October:1212–1217.

Waegel, W.B. (1984). The Use of Lethal Force by Police: The Effect of Statutory Change. *Crime and Delinquency 30*, January:121–140.

Walker, S. (1977). *A Critical History of Police Reform: The Emergence of Professionalism*. Lexington, MA: D.C. Heath.

Walker, S. (1980). *Popular Justice: A History of American Criminal Justice*. New York: Oxford University Press.

Walker, S. (1985a). The Politics of Police Accountability: The Seattle Police Spying Ordinance as a Case Study. In Webb, V. and E. Fairchild (Eds.), *The Politics of Crime and Criminal Justice*. Beverly Hills, CA: Sage.

Walker, S. (1985b). Racial Minority and Female Employment in Policing: The Implications of "Glacial" Change. *Crime and Delinquency 31*, October:555–572.

Walker, S. (1986). Controlling the Cops: A Legislative Approach to Police Rulemaking. *University of Detroit Law Review 63*, Spring:361–391.

Walker, S. (1988). *The Rule Revolution: Reflections on the Transformation of American Criminal Justice, 1950–1988*. Madison, WI: Institute for Legal Studies.

Walker, S. (1990). *In Defense of American Liberties: A History of the ACLU*. New York: Oxford University Press.

Walker, S. (1992). Origins of The Contemporary Criminal Justice Paradigm: The American Bar Foundation Survey, 1953–1969, *Justice Quarterly 9*:47–76.

Walker, S. (1993). *Taming the System: The Control of Discretion in Criminal Justice, 1950–1990*. New York: Oxford University Press.

Warner, S.B. (1940). Investigating the Law of Arrest. *ABA Journal 26*:151–155.

Wasby, S. (1976). *Small Town Police and the Supreme Court: Hearing the Word*. Lexington, MA: Lexington Books.

White, E.G. (1988). *The American Judicial Tradition*. Expanded ed. New York: Oxford University Press.

Part III
Changing Trends in Police Innovation: Toward Community-Based Policies of Crime Control

4
Alternative Futures for Policing*

JOHN E. ECK

In *Justice Without Trial*, Jerome Skolnick (1975) described a basic tension in policing—the inherent conflict between the rule of law and bureaucratic efficiency (see Chapter 2). Today, policing is undergoing a fundamental reexamination of its functions and strategy that could have profound implications for this tension. Current reexaminations could lead to deep meaningful changes in how officers perform their duties and relate to the publics they serve. Proposed changes in the operational strategy of policing emphasizing order maintenance give greater discretionary authority to line officers to address community concerns. By increasing officers' discretionary authority to address community problems these changes strengthen order, efficiency, and initiative at the possible expense of the rule of law. Alternatively, new approaches to policing may redefine the operational environment of officers and thus eliminate or greatly reduce the tension described by Skolnick. Or, the proposed changes may have no impact on Skolnick's dilemma. The changes may be cosmetic—altering only the terminology used to describe policing and adding a few boxes to departments' organization charts—and have little impact on the way police officers act.

This chapter explores how policing may evolve and how changes underway may affect tensions inherent in current innovations in policing. Specifically, I describe five proposed departures from current police practice—two forms of problem-oriented policing and three forms of community policing—and show how full implementation of each may affect Skolnick's dilemma. Each of the five departures from current

*I am indebted to Herman Goldstein, who has sparked some of the ideas expressed in this paper. While writing this draft I was especially aware of remarks he made before police officials attending the first annual Conference on Problem-Oriented Policing in San Diego. Craig Uchida, David Weisburd, and Herman Goldstein reviewed an earlier draft and gave me valuable comments. The views expressed in this paper are mine alone and do not necessarily reflect the views of the members or the staff of the Police Executive Research Forum.

policing methods suggests a resolution of this tension, but their prospects for resolving the tension vary.

There are several questions we must ask with respect to proposed changes and their impact on the rule of law in police work. Will the proposed changes take place? What forms of proposed operational strategies will police organizations adopt in the future? Will the conflict between the rule of law and everyday realities of police work continue under new operational strategies? And if the conflict remains, will it be fundamentally different from the dilemma posed by Skolnick? These are the questions addressed in this chapter. In short, this chapter asks whether the tension between legality and the "ideas of order, efficiency, and initiative" will continue to "constitute the principle problem of policing as a democratic legal organization" (Skolnick, 1975:6).

Changes in Policing

Widespread dissatisfaction with existing practices and interest in new strategies may result in fundamental changes in the police function, delivery of services, and public perceptions of the police. These changes might, if their proponents are correct, result in substantial benefits to the communities whose police adopt new approaches. Alternatively, current discussions and experimentation with new strategies may dissipate, and the police may continue to be a reactive force.

The most likely of these two alternative futures cannot be accurately judged at this time. The volume of written pages on community and problem-oriented policing, the attendance of police officials at seminars on these strategies, the glowing accounts in the news media, and the large number of agencies claiming to be implementing these approaches all point in the direction of substantial changes in policing.

Still, all of this may be a passing fancy. Changes on the scale required to implement fully community or problem-oriented policing may be so massive that once police officials get below the surface of the proposed reforms, institutional barriers—inside and outside police bureaucracies—will constrain further changes. Certainly there is more precedent for this scenario than the first. Recall, for example, the embrace of neighborhood team policing, followed by experimentation and rejection. Adoption of neighborhood team policing was superficial (Sherman, Milton, and Kelly, 1973), and despite some apparent success at controlling crime (Bloch and Bell, 1976; Schwartz and Clarren, 1977), it could not overcome major bureaucratic barriers (Schwartz and Clarren, 1977). Interest and effectiveness are not guarantors of acceptance.

There is reason to believe that this possible future is too conservative. Change in any institution is more common than stability, and histories of police point to successive waves of change (Fogelson, 1977; Walker, 1977;

Monkonnen, 1981). So the question is not whether change will occur, but whether these particular changes will occur. There are four reasons for believing that recent proposals for policing have a better chance of succeeding than team policing. First, public expectations of all service delivery has changed. In response, market-driven businesses have tried to become more responsive to customers' needs. Government agencies, though not facing market pressures, are still under some pressure to follow suit, and community and problem-oriented strategies claim to be more responsive than simply reacting to calls for service.

Second, public tolerance for deviant behavior and unsatisfactory environmental conditions seems to be declining. The environmental and consumers' movements are examples of this larger trend. The criminalization of previously tolerated behaviors such as drunk driving and casual drug use also are examples of this trend. In short, the public is and will continue to demand more police interventions in the control of lesser crimes, nuisances, and quality-of-life problems. Further, previously acceptable levels of crime are likely to become less acceptable. These trends will require a broader police role, beyond law enforcement, that community and problem-oriented policing seem to satisfy.

Third, changes in mainstream management theory and practice will support schemes to flatten police hierarchy and decentralize authority. Highly centralized organizations are no longer in vogue. Instead, the popular management literature calls for the same changes in corporate management (see, for example, Ouchi, 1981; Peters and Waterman, 1982; Kanter, 1983) that are only now being discussed in police circles (Couper and Lobitz, 1991; Moore and Stephens, 1991). Team policing enthusiasts did not have this advantage.

Fourth, trends in work force demographics show that the labor force from which police agencies will draw their recruits is shrinking. Police forces will have to keep older officers longer and pay all officers more to compete with other organizations in the job market. This will raise costs. As the costs of policing rise there will be increasing pressure to do more with fewer officers per capita. But, as suggested earlier, the public will also be demanding more of the police, so workloads will increase. The needs of efficiency will reinforce management changes and require departments to control workloads. Some load shedding may occur, but preventive measures will also become increasingly attractive alternatives as they control workloads without sacrificing public service.

The strength of these four trends varies from region to region and from jurisdiction to jurisdiction, so changes in policing will not progress uniformly. Further, local police cultures, political histories, economic conditions, scandals, and crises will have impacts on the progress of change in particular cities and counties. Some police agencies may make what appear to be fundamental changes, only to have them thrown out by the next police chief or city administration. Other jurisdictions may appear to lag behind only to undergo substantial changes in a flurry of reform efforts. A few police agencies will break new ground and continue to innovate. Some others may continue to police in a reactive, incident-driven style for many years. All this is to say that changes in policing will appear to be haphazard and confusing, with spurts of changes followed by periods of inaction or regression.

Nevertheless, for the four reasons enumerated earlier, community policing and problem-oriented policing will continue to take root and develop. It is not, however, clear that these two strategies will have the same effect on policing. Nor is it clear that community policing is a single strategy that will have a unitary impact on policing. To see why these new policing strategies may have different effects on policing's future, first we must examine the origins of these strategies.

The Rise of Problem-Oriented Policing and Community Policing

If community policing or problem-oriented policing are likely future police strategies, what are the implications for the rule of law in policing? To answer this question we must begin by acknowledging that both strategies make law enforcement subservient to other ends. Both strategies reject law enforcement as a defining characteristic of policing, but for different reasons. As a consequence, the tension between the rule of law and police practice may decline, but not necessarily.

By focusing the police on crime control, late nineteenth- and early twentieth-century police reformers began the process of defining the police role in terms of the application of the criminal law (Walker, 1977; Monkonnen, 1981). It is not surprising, therefore, that the first comprehensive study of policing, conducted by the American Bar Foundation, addressed the questions of how the police exercised discretion despite the lack of legal authority to do so (Goldstein, 1960), the instrumental uses of the law (LaFave, 1965), and how discretion could be controlled (Goldstein, 1963). If the application of the law is the defining role of policing, then understanding the conflicts between this role and the daily exigencies of police work, as detailed by Skolnick (1975), is of fundamental importance for developing sound police policy.

Throughout the 1960s and 1970s, administrative control of discretion continued to be an important theme of police reform proposals. One significant proposal was for structuring discretion through policy-making (Goldstein, 1967; Krantz et al., 1979). If discretion was to be guided by policy, however, then policies had to be based on the realities of police work. Problem-oriented policing arose from Goldstein's (1979) realization that, to develop sound policies that will guide the exercise of discretion, police policy-makers need detailed knowledge of the problems that police are called on to address. Discretion-bounding policies must be based on careful analysis of these problems. Further, by focusing on problems, police agencies can become more effective. Problem-oriented policing is, therefore, a direct response to the findings of the earliest police research.

Under a problem-oriented approach, the problem, not the criminal law, becomes the defining characteristic of policing. Goldstein (1979) asserted that police have focused too much on the means of doing their job and have generally ignored the ends to which these means are to be put. The criminal law is only one of many means to address problems. Instead of deciding if the criminal law is appropriate for a problem, police are likely to decide whether the problem fits their mandate by determining whether the criminal law can be applied to it. Or, having decided that the problem should be handled by them, the police determine how the criminal law should be applied to it. This imbalance of means and ends leads to the use of the criminal law where it is inappropriate and to the ignoring of problems that clearly cannot be handled by the criminal law. If police considered problems first, they could use problem analysis to learn the best means to use in various circumstances. Following this line of reasoning, Goldstein may have resolved the conflict posed by Skolnick by making the criminal law one of many instruments that the police can use to address problems. The choice faced by police is no longer whether to address a problem by legal or extralegal means, or whether to apply the criminal law or to ignore the problem, but whether the criminal law or a host of other legal options is the most effective means for addressing the problem.

Though discretion remained a major theme of writings on the police, from the mid-1970s its dominance was supplanted by a wave of effectiveness research. Studies of patrol (Kelling et al., 1974), response time (Kansas City Police Department, 1980; Spelman and Brown, 1984), and investigations (Greenwood, Chaiken, and Petersilia, 1977; Eck, 1982) questioned the universal application of these tactics. These studies influenced the development of problem-oriented policing by demonstrating how ineffective police were when they relied on the criminal law (Goldstein, 1990).

These studies also spurred interest in developing universal alternatives to random patrol, rapid response, and follow-up investigations. Studies of foot patrol's ability to reduce fear (Police Foundation, 1981; Pate et al., 1986) and evidence that perceptions of crime are linked to environmental conditions and social cohesion as well as the risks of victimization (Skogan, 1987) suggested that the police should address fear of crime as well as crime itself. Aggressive order maintenance, organizing neighborhoods, and building good police–community relations were suggested as means to control fear (Wilson and Kelling, 1982). Community policing, therefore, would be defined by these tactics, rather than law enforcement.

Community policing is a collection of tactics with a common theme; the tactics are to bring the police and members of the public closer together. So it is the tactics—foot patrols, ministations, community organizing, citizen contact patrols, and others—that define community policing and not necessarily the ends to which these tactics are to be put. As I describe later, there are at least three versions of community policing, each one based on a different conception of the major deficiencies of the police. But common to all three versions, and contrary to problem-oriented policing, is the universal application of a standard set of tactics.

In their emphasis on the universal application of a standard set of tactics, community policing and traditional incident-driven policing are similar. Community policing substitutes another set of tactics for random car patrols, rapid response, and detective follow-up. Though tactics are different, in traditional and community policing the tactics are to be used in most circumstances and to cover almost all police work. Although, community and traditional forms of policing differ in their emphasis on community relations versus law enforcement, and the choice of tactics is reflective of this difference, community policing and traditional policing apply their tactics in the same way.

The emphasis on problems rather than tactics marks the difference between problem-oriented policing and community policing (and traditional policing). Problem-oriented policing defines the police role in terms of the ends it tries to achieve—solving problems. Community policing defines the police role in terms of the means used by the police. Consequently, problem-oriented policing tactics are situation specific, whereas community policing tactics are universal. That is, for a given problem, a problem-oriented agency will engage in a search for tactics that appear to be most effective at addressing it. A community policing department will apply the same set of tactics to all problems that come to its attention.

Does the situational/universal difference between problem-oriented policing and community policing have important consequences for police performance? Both strategies require decentralization of police authority to patrol officers and first-line supervisors. Both strategies also place great emphasis on collaboration between police and community members (Kelling and Moore, 1988; Eck and Spelman, 1987). So it is unclear whether this distinction is one of emphasis, having no meaningful differences, or whether the distinction affects the service police provide the public, officers' behavior, and control of the police. In the next section I describe how features of community and problem-oriented policing may affect the conflict between the rule of law and bureaucratic efficiency.

Consequences of Community Policing

Community policing describes a loose collection of ideas linked by the premise that police and members of the public should join together to pursue common objectives. We need to distinguish among at least three forms of community policing if we are to make reasonable guesses about the future of policing. For ease of reference, I label these three forms of community policing "legitimization," "control," and "deployment."

In its simplest form, community policing means gaining the support of the public for police actions. Insofar as this has been a theme throughout modern police history (see, for example, Vollmer, 1971; Wilson, 1968; Reith, 1975) this form of community policing is an extension of the realization that without legitimacy, police cannot be effective. Indeed, even if no changes in operational strategies were to be undertaken, police officials would still want to develop more extensive public support, especially within poor and minority communities where antagonism toward the police is the greatest. That is, even if police respond only to incidents and rely almost exclusively on their powers under the criminal law, we would still demand that they act in a manner that is consistent with democratic principles and engenders respect and cooperation from citizens.

Klockars (1988) claims that much of what is called community policing is merely an attempt by the police to gain legitimacy without making any fundamental changes. This may be so. Nevertheless, we should not discount these efforts to improve police–community relations if they have the result of reducing conflicts between police and minority communities. Recent evidence of police misuse of force and racist behavior in Long Beach and Los Angeles (Independent Commission, 1991), disregard of complaints from minority group members in Milwaukee (Criminal Justice Newsletter, 1991), and not-too-distant events in Philadelphia (Philadelphia Police Study Task Force, 1987) are vivid reminders that police should be very concerned about how they treat citizens. Community policing efforts that have as their sole objective improving the legitimacy of the police in the eyes of majority and minority communities cannot be dismissed lightly.

Still, legitimization of policing efforts is only an extension of current police practices and is not a major shift in police strategy. If this is as far as community policing reforms go, then the tensions described by Skolnick will not be affected. Officers would still have to resolve conflicts between strict adherence to legal procedure and the demands of a bureaucracy sensitive to concerns about legitimacy.

Another form of community policing emphasizes local control over policing—shifting the locus of power from city hall and police head-quarters to community meeting rooms and precinct stations. Control community policing is often linked to legitimization insofar as accusations of police misuse of force are often accompanied by recommendations for greater citizen oversight of the police. But shifting control to neighborhoods goes further by recognizing that people working and residing in different areas of the city have different problems that they want to see addressed.

To the extent that this form of community policing stems from the unresponsiveness of elected officials to neighborhood demands, this approach is doomed to failure. Such changes require the support of elected officials who control the appointment of police chiefs, approve budgets, and enter into agreements with police unions. If elected officials are unresponsive to neighborhood interests then they are unlikely to be supportive of a decentralized police bureaucracy that is responsive. If elected officials are responsive to the concerns of diverse interests then the need for this form of community policing diminishes.

As much police action is not under the direct observation of supervisors or community members, it is unlikely that decentralized control of the police will have an impact on police behavior. As Brown (1988:298) points out, simply decentralizing authority is insufficient to make the police responsive; political reforms must accompany these administrative changes. As a practical matter, police are unlikely to permit outside control. Community meetings and surveys may be used to keep police officials abreast of community sentiments, but the daily decisions on how communities will be policed will be left to the line officers, their supervisors, and commanders.[1] Skogan (1990) claims that disorganized communities lack the ability to control the police so police pursue their own objectives which are irrelevant to community needs. It is therefore difficult to imagine that this form of community policing will reduce the tension described by Skolnick (1975).

A third form of community policing emphasizes deployment modes and tactics for engaging the public and police in the coproduction of safety. Foot beats, ministations, community organizing, and other procedures have been suggested as useful means for this purpose (Trojanowicz and Bucqueroux, 1989). If these procedures actually reduce crime and the fear of crime they hold out some promise. Unfortunately, research on the effectiveness of deployment community policing suggests that it will not have the desired impact. Greene and Taylor (1988) reviewed the major community policing studies and found that the theories, research designs, and measurements employed in community policing studies provide no support for the hypothesis that these tactics are effective at reducing

---

[1] This is a testable hypothesis, of course. Given the claims by the police officials that their community policing initiatives are making officers more responsive to the direction of community members, research is clearly needed to determine how responsive officers and supervisors are and in which ways they are responsive.

crime and fear of crime in neighborhoods. Skogan (1990), while providing support for the hypothesis that fear of crime leads to neighborhood deterioration, finds that community policing is unlikely to make much difference in the communities that need it the most. Community organizing is least likely to help the most disorganized neighborhoods (Skogan, 1990), and intensive community organizing can lead to heightened levels of fear and withdrawal from collective crime prevention actions (Rosenbaum and Heath, 1990). The evaluation of the New York Police Department's Community Police Officer Program (CPOP) provides further support for these pessimistic conclusions. According to the evaluators, CPOP officers were reasonably good at identifying and addressing problems[2] but found it difficult to organize communities and build sustained collaborative efforts (McElroy, Cosgrove, and Sadd, 1989; Weisburd and McElroy, 1988).

Adopting and pursuing deployment community policing could have major negative consequences for the police. As with more standard policing strategies, this form of community policing places its strongest emphasis on the means of policing. So instead of counting arrests, tickets, and other law enforcement actions, deployment community policing administrators will count other activities. When the District of Columbia Police Department, for example, initiated what they called "community empowerment policing," their plan required "officers to fill out monthly reports stating not only how many arrests they made, but also how many households they contacted, how many community meetings they attended, the number of street lights replaced, and abandoned cars towed and crack houses boarded" (Horwitz, 1989). Administrative pressures when combined with grass roots support will provide greater impetus for officers to circumvent the rule of law.

The separation of the patrol force into community policing officers and incident-handling officers can create additional problems. Officers assigned to neighborhoods may treat neighborhood residents differently than do nonneighborhood officers who pass through the area or have to handle incidents in the neighborhood. Anderson (1991) provides a good illustration of such problems as seen from the perspective of the citizens of two Philadelphia neighborhoods: traffic officers were seen as being much harsher and objectionable than precinct officers assigned to the area. Disparities in treatment will create conflicts within the police agency as well as conflicts between the police and the public.

There is another possible set of consequences from the adoption of deployment community policing: neighborhood triage. Highly organized

---

[2] At the same time, CPOP officers engaged in little analysis of problem circumstances and tended to employ standard law enforcement tactics (McElroy, Cosgrove, and Sadd, 1989).

communities that have little crime or disorder may get little policing because they do not need it. Communities that are afflicted with problems may be evaluated by the police on the basis of their abilities to provide sustained organized efforts to curb crime and disorder. Arguing that public safety is affected more by the actions of the public than the police, public officials and police may withdraw support from neighborhoods that cannot be organized. As the police cannot withdraw completely from a neighborhood, these areas will be receive reactive incident-based policing. If community triage is used it will accentuate class disparities in the delivery of police services (Bayley, 1988).[3]

This review of three forms of community policing suggests that none of the three forms is likely to reduce the conflict between the rule of law and the demands of the police operational environment. Under one form of community policing (deployment), this conflict could increase. The relationship forms and effects of community policing are summarized in the Appendix.

Consequences of Problem-Oriented Policing

There are two ways the implementation of problem-oriented policing could evolve. Problem-oriented policing could develop along the lines elaborated by Goldstein (1990) in which members of police agencies undertake thorough analyses of problems, engage community members and other agencies in a broad search for appropriate solutions, and critically evaluate outcomes of problem-solving efforts. I call this "situational" problem-oriented policing. Alternatively, problem solving could become a synonym for proactive enforcement efforts with only superficial analysis, symbolic engagement of the public and other agencies, consideration of a limited range of alternatives, and minimal efforts to determine effectiveness. I call this "enforcement" problem-oriented policing. In short, problem-oriented policing could become the new name for directed patrolling and tactical enforcement. There are ample examples of both sorts of problem solving in agencies beginning to implement this approach and it is unclear in which direction departments will go if a problem-oriented approach begins to dominate policing. Given the diversity in policing throughout the United States, it seems likely that over time police agencies embracing a problem-oriented approach will vary from

---

[3] Though I have not seen evidence of such a strategy being pursued, a few police officials have suggested policies that would logically lead to such outcomes. Further, the extolling, by national leaders, of local activists who took on drug dealers and revitalized their communities suggests that other drug-plagued communities that cannot achieve the same results will receive little additional support.

those using a situational form to those applying an enforcement form.[4]

Agencies using enforcement problem-oriented policing may exacerbate the conflict between the rule of law and the operational environment of police practice. This form of problem-oriented policing would have the result of focusing police attention on the application of familiar law enforcement tactics, a return to means-over-ends policing. Administrative efficiency would require the use of crackdowns and other enforcement efforts without first determining whether these tactics are appropriate. Absent a concerted attempt to develop objective, problem-specific performance measures that can reveal the impact on the problem, success will be judged on the basis of arrests made, drugs seized, and other activity measures. If coupled with legitimization community policing, it may be possible, in the short run, to allay community concerns about these tactics (Bayley, 1988). Weisburd, McElroy, and Hardyman (1988) give an example of how a mix of enforcement problem-oriented policing and legitimization community policing was used by the New York Police Department's Community Police Officer Program.

(T)he strategy adopted by the CPOP unit consisted of three parts. First, they provided a great deal of intelligence information to the Narcotics Unit which had jurisdiction and responsibility for narcotics enforcement throughout the patrol borough. Second, the officers and supervisor went to community meetings to explain that they could not use aggressive enforcement tactics against the street narcotic trade without the understanding and support of the community.... Finally, the unit applied aggressive patrol tactics on the streets in which the drug sales were concentrated. These tactics include stopping and questioning people who were "hanging out," questioning people in automobiles with out-of-town plates, ticketing doubleparkers and arresting or issuing summonses to those who were known dealers. In some cases, the arrest charges were actually a pretext for arresting and searching a suspected dealer. Frequently, several CPOP officers would work together, along with the sergeant, in carrying out these tactics. (1988:41)

Regardless of the effectiveness of this approach (Weisburd, McElroy, and Hardyman, 1988 do not describe the results of these police actions) the tension between the rule of law and bureaucratic efficiency remains. In this case, to clear an area of drug dealing, officers were willing to violate the rights of some people using the streets. The major difference between this form of police work and more traditional forms is that the police explained their actions in advance to some community members.

Though described as problem solving, the method of handling a problem in the preceding example falls short of what was originally meant by a problem-oriented approach. Goldstein (1979, 1990) has been quite explicit

---

[4]Further, we are likely to see blends of problem-oriented policing forms and community policing forms.

about the need to undertake a broad search for solutions. Part of this search involves determining the limits of police authority and the authority of other agencies called on to help resolve a problem. If the powers of the police and the other agencies are insufficient to deal with problems of the type under consideration, then the problem-solving process should include a request for the additional authority needed to address these problems.

Close adherence to Goldstein's (1990) description of problem-oriented policing could reduce the conflict between the rule of law and the police operational environment. If the police culture begins to value careful tailoring of responses to the particular needs of problems and success is judged by the impact on problems, then officers will look for tactical options that are less likely to conflict with the rule of law.

For example, instead of using a tactical enforcement squad to stake out an area with a high volume of robberies, physical environmental changes may be used to make the area less attractive to offenders. A sergeant and her squad of officers (all assigned to routine patrol) used this approach to handle a robbery problem at a trolley station in San Diego.

Their problem description states that the station has been an ideal location for criminal activity. They described the station as being elevated and surrounded by a four-foot wall. The passengers or criminal activity cannot be seen from the parking lot or street. The stairs leading up to the station are enclosed by a brick wall. Numerous gang fights, stabbings, felony assaults, narcotics, and vice crimes have occurred at the station. The officers' analysis included:

- The number of crime reports to both the city and trolley security.
- Photographs of the 47th Street trolley station including comparisons of the other stations.
- Interviews of trolley patrons at adjacent stations. What are the riders' fears? Are they aware of any problems?
- Information from Councilman Pratt's office and support for the effort.
- Who designed the trolley station and why?
- Is the City liable?
- Is it cost effective to change the design of the wall? (Welter, 1990:14)

Analysis revealed that on an average day, only three riders used the station and that some trolley riders went to stations further from their homes to avoid this station. The sergeant and members of her squad discussed the problem with officials from other city agencies and the general manager of the trolley system. Because of the documentation provided by the officers, the trolley board decided to redesign the station by replacing the wall with a guard rail at a cost of $200,000. Data from the department's Crime Analysis unit suggest that violent crimes decreased around the trolley stop (Welter, 1990).

As this case illustrates, it is sometimes possible to address a crime problem without using the criminal law. In situations like this, conflicts between the rule of law and "ideas of order, efficiency, and initiative" are less likely.

Tactics based on civil law may provide more powerful tools to solve problems than tactics based on criminal law. Many local government agencies specialize in the regulation of behavior through the application of civil law. Health inspectors, building inspectors, alcohol control officials, child protective service workers, fire marshals, housing officials, city attorneys, and others have special powers or legal expertise that can be brought to bear on problems. Though legal requirements vary, civil proceedings are likely to receive more scrutiny by outside officials than arrests.

Even when enforcement of the criminal law is required, officers have greater opportunity to plan their approach, identify the specific targets of their crackdown, and adhere to legal norms if they have undertaken a systematic problem analysis. In this way, the application of the criminal law can be narrowly focused.

Focusing on solving problems rather than the application of a pre-determined set of tactics will provide an incentive to officers to find tactics that address a problem without violating legal norms. Relatively few problems, however, can be solved by eliminating them. More common will be a reduction in the number of incidents stemming from a problem or a reduction in the harm per incident. The solution to some problems may require making improvements in the treatment of special groups—for example, child abuse victims, elderly offenders, the mentally ill, or the homeless—or finding and empowering other agencies to handle the problem (Eck and Spelman, 1987). Emphasis on eliminating problems can be dysfunctional, however. If police administrators set uniform and unrealistic objectives then officers will be under pressure to show that these objectives have been achieved, even when they have not been. This will shift officers' attention from responses to problems that work to responses that fill administrative expectations. How this may affect the tension between the rule of law and police operational environment is unclear. To the extent that administrative expectations can be more easily filled using criminal enforcement tactics, a return to means-over-ends policing will perpetuate the conflict. But if administrative expectations are more easily met by using tactics that do not involve the criminal law, this tension may be reduced.

Problem-oriented policing can make police practice more visible to supervisors and members of the public. Unlike incidents that officers can handle alone and without scrutiny from supervisors and members of the public, addressing problems usually requires a great deal of participation by others. Police agencies currently engaged in problem-oriented policing have procedures to inform supervisors of the status of problem-solving efforts, resource needs, and difficulties encountered. The involvement of other local government agencies, members of the public, and other police resources increases the number of people who are familiar with police behavior. This reduces officers' discretionary authority and can increase compliance with the norms of society outside police agencies. With repeated interactions over time it is possible that officers may be able to co-opt others and create a closed network of collaborators who can address problems without much oversight.

Such collusion is illustrated by the following example described to me by a police supervisor involved in the events. A group of officers assigned to a specialist problem-solving squad tried to address a neighborhood traffic problem. The citizens and the officers felt that the addition of a few stop signs at strategic intersections in the neighborhood would resolve the problem. The officers approached the traffic engineering department but were turned down because the intersections did not meet the traffic engineering department's specifications required to site stop signs. The officers discussed the matter with lower-level workers in the traffic engineering department and found a way to circumvent the department's rules. The workers gave the officers blank forms for use when a sign is stolen, damaged, or needs replacing. The officers filled out and submitted these forms as if the signs had been installed and were now missing. A road crew was dispatched to install the signs at the intersections.

This relatively minor rule violation was carried out by a specialist unit. Collusion seems less likely to occur with generalist patrol officers who will confront a variety of problems needing different individuals for each problem. But problem solvers in special units, confronting similar problems repeatedly, may develop closed networks. A work group could develop norms that are counter to the norms of the agencies and communities the collaborators represent. Such a development could lead to violations of due process or corruption. Nevertheless, it will be harder for groups of individuals from diverse backgrounds to circumvent the rule of law than it is for groups of officers sharing a common organizational culture and work environment.

Problem-oriented policing has the potential of reducing the conflict between the rule of law and the police operational environment. It has this potential for several reasons: The criminal law becomes one of many means that can be used to address problems; careful analysis can ensure that when the criminal law is required to address a problem, it is applied narrowly to specific individuals for specific legal purposes; and police decision making is open to more people, inside and outside the police agency, than it is under current police practice. These benefits can be achieved only if police agencies require officers to conduct careful analyses of problems, encourage collaboration with others, and measure success by observing the impact problem-solving efforts have on problems.

Conclusions

In this chapter I outlined five new forms of policing—three forms of community policing and two forms of problem-oriented policing—that purport to forge a partnership between members of the community and the police. None of the forms of community policing and one form of problem-oriented policing are likely to reduce the tension described by Skolnick (see the Appendix for a summary). At best they will make police actions more acceptable to the public, even if due process is violated. One form of problem-oriented policing does hold some potential for reducing, if not resolving, this tension.

The potential success of Goldstein's concept of "situational" problem-oriented policing for addressing Skolnick's dilemma is in large part attributable to its origins. Goldstein developed a problem-oriented approach in response to a concern about how to control officer discretion. As the exercise of discretion is a critical element in the tension between the rule of law and bureaucratic efficiency, it should not be terribly surprising that a policing strategy that explicitly addresses discretion may also reduce the tension.

There are five related features of Goldstein's formulation of problem-oriented policing that make it more likely to resolve Skolnick's dilemma.

1. It demands careful analysis of problems to determine the causes of the problem, the options available to address these causes, and the resources and legal authority needed to apply one or more of the options.
2. It involves situational selection of tactics rather than universal application of a standard set of tactics.
3. It requires measuring performance by evaluating the impact on problems and eschews documenting activities for performance measurement purposes.
4. It calls for searching for a broad range of alternatives for resolving problems instead of relying predominately on law enforcement responses.
5. It calls for the police to work in partnership with members of the public, other government agencies, and anyone else who has a stake in the problem.

Collectively, though not separately, these elements of problem-oriented policing can focus police attention on the ends they are to achieve without placing disproportionate emphasis on the means used to achieve these objectives. But if problem-oriented policing focused exclusively on the ends of policing, without some concern for the means used, then police officers would be encouraged to find ways to circumvent restrictions on their legal authority and ignore due process. The requirements of problem analysis, broad search for solutions, examination of nonenforcement options, and collaboration with others direct officers toward methods for addressing problems that do not require extralegal means. As officers are not constrained to criminal law enforcement options they can look for methods that work but do not violate legal norms.

The forms of problem-oriented policing and community policing that do not address Skolnick's dilemma have at least one of three characteristics:

1. They prescribe generic universal tactical responses to problems, for example, foot patrols, citizen surveys, community organizing, ministations, and decentralization.
2. They establish policing objectives that are unobtainable, for example, revitalizing neighborhoods.
3. They focus on achieving an objective with little regard for the methods selected.

Singly or in combination, these characteristics of a policing strategy will perpetuate the dilemma Skolnick described. Focusing on the means of policing places emphasis on fulfilling bureaucratic standards but ignores the legal context within which policing takes place. If officers only wander around talking to people, attend meetings of citizens, or sit in storefront stations the worst one could say of these activities is that they improve community relations but do little to address substantive community concerns. But these officers also will be engaged in invoking the criminal law while on the beat, and because they are given no other alternatives to handle community problems, they will continue to use questionable methods.

If policing objectives are extremely broad and unobtainable, like reducing crime or revitalizing declining communities, officers will become cynical and frustrated in their inability to achieve these objectives. This will also lead to abuses of authority. The Christopher Commission's report on policing in Los Angeles draws a direct link between the Los Angeles Police Department's image as crime controllers and the organizational culture that permitted a few officers to act brutally (Independent Commission, 1991). Replacing the crime control mission with a community revitalization mission will recreate this behavior in another context because the forces that impact neighborhood decline are largely beyond police and community control (Bursik and Webb, 1982; Bursik, 1988; Sampson, 1987; Shaw and McKay, 1942; Skogan, 1990).

Policing strategies that focus on problem solving but do not broaden the options used by officers will also create a culture of the ends justifying the means. If officers are told only to address problems, but are not told to look beyond enforcement, they will use enforcement to solve all problems. Some temporary relief may be forthcoming from such efforts (Sherman, 1990), but in many circumstances the results are likely to be less than hoped. This is likely to lead to frustration on the part of officers, who, faced with continued pressure from the community and supervisors, will go beyond their legal authority.

Having achievable goals and a wide range of means for accomplishing them can substantially reduce the tension between bureaucratic efficiency and due process. Controlling crime is not an achievable goal for the police and the criminal law provides very few options for the police or the community. Though problem-oriented policing holds the promise of reducing the tension between bureaucratic efficiency and due process, it is dependent on the police and the public establishing and maintaining a balance between goals and means. Striking this balance is not easy. In the future, observers of the police will be kept busy studying whether this balance can be struck or whether we recreate, in the guise of community policing, the tensions inherent in the policing strategy being abandoned.

Appendix: Policing Forms, Characteristics, and Predicted Effects

Form	Characteristics	Predicted effects on tension
Current policing		
	Patrol officers react to calls. Crime control and use of legal authority are principal means used. Performance is measured by enforcement activities.	As described by Skolnick (1975)
Community policing		
Legitimization	Patrol officers continue as in current policing strategy. Police chief and higher-ranking officials meet with community leaders. Use of general community surveys. Strict control on use of force. Extensive use of neighborhood watch and meetings with the public.	Little difference, but fewer complaints from citizens not involved in incidents.
Control	Neighborhood advisory boards meet with commanders of police subdivisions. Officers are tasked to handle concerns. Enforcement is the principal method applied. Most officers' time is engaged in responding to calls as above. Officers' performance is judged by minimum complaints from advisory boards.	Little difference, but possible increase in differences in levels of police services across neighborhoods

Appendix: *Continued*

Form	Characteristics	Predicted effects on tension
Deployment	Special groups of officers are deployed to use a standard set of methods—foot patrols, community organizing, etc. Officers' performance is judged by numbers of activities conducted or by improvement in neighborhood conditions.	Same as control, or increased tension. Possibility of disparate treatment by officers assigned to different units
Problem-oriented policing		
Situational	Officers' time is divided between handling calls and addressing problems. Careful analysis of problems is used to identify tactics to apply in specific circumstances. A wide array of responses are applied to problems. Officer's performance is judged by effectiveness of solutions and minimum use of legal sanctions.	Reduced tension Decrease in violations of due process and civil liberties Increased use of noncriminal law options Search, by police, for greater legal authority to address problems for themselves or other agencies
Enforcement	Officers' time is divided between handling calls and addressing problems. Most problems are addressed by enforcement tactics. Officers' performance is judged by quick handling of problems and immediate results of enforcement.	Increased tension Similar to traditional unless combined with a form of community policing

References

Anderson, E. (1991). *Street Wise*. Chicago: University of Chicago Press.

Bayley, D.H. (1988). Community Policing: A Report From the Devil's Advocate. In Greene, J.R. and S.D. Mastrofski (Eds.), *Community Policing. Rhetoric or Reality*. New York: Praeger.

Bloch, P. and J. Bell. (1976). *Managing Criminal Investigations: The Rochester System*. Washington, DC: Police Foundation.

Brown, M.K. (1988). *Working the Street: Police Discretion and the Dilemmas of Reform*. New York: Russell Sage Foundation.

Bursik, R.J., Jr. (1988). Social Disorganization and Theories of Crime and Delinquency: Problems and Prospects. *Criminology 26*:519–551.

Bursik, R.J., Jr. and J. Webb. (1982). Community Change and Patterns of Delinquency. *American Journal of Sociology 88*:24–42.

Couper, D.C. and S.H. Lobitz. (1991). *Quality Policing: The Madison Experience*. Washington, DC: Police Executive Research Forum.

Criminal Justice Newsletter. (1991). Reputation of Milwaukee Police Damaged by Dahmer Case. *Criminal Justice Newsletter 22*:2–3, August 15.

Eck, J.E. (1982). *Solving Crimes: The Investigation of Burglary and Robbery*. Washington, DC: Police Executive Research Forum.

Eck, J.E. and W. Spelman. (1987). *Problem Solving: Problem-Oriented Policing in Newport News*. Washington, DC: Police Executive Research Forum.

Fogelson, R.M. (1977). *Big City Police*. Cambridge, MA: Harvard University Press.

Goldstein, H. (1963). Police Discretion: The Ideal Versus the Real. *Public Administration Review 23*:140–148.

Goldstein, H. (1967). Police Policy Formulation: A Proposal for Improving Police Performance. *Michigan Law Review 65*:1123–1146.

Goldstein, H. (1979). Improving Policing: A Problem-Oriented Approach. *Crime and Delinquency 25*:236–258.

Goldstein, H. (1990). *Problem-Oriented Policing*. New York: McGraw-Hill.

Goldstein, J. (1960). Police Discretion Not to Invoke the Criminal Process: Low-Visibility Decisions in the Administration of Justice. *Yale Law Journal 69*:543–594.

Greene, J.R. and R.B. Taylor. (1988). Community-Based Policing and Foot Patrol: Issues of Theory and Evaluation. In Greene, J.R. and S.D. Mastrofski (Eds.), *Community Policing: Rhetoric or Reality*. New York: Praeger.

Greenwood, P.W., J.M. Chaiken, and J. Petersilia. (1977). *The Criminal Investigation Process*. Lexington, MA: D.C. Heath.

Horwitz, S. (1989). Fulwood Seeks to Immerse D.C. Officers in Community. *Washington Post*, December 4, p. A1.

Independent Commission. (1991). *Report of the Independent Commission on the Los Angeles Police Department*.

Kansas City Police Department. (1980). *Response Time Analysis:* Vol. II. *Part I Crime Analysis*. Washington, DC: U.S. Government Printing Office.

Kanter, R.M. (1983). *The Change Masters: Innovation and Entrepreneurship in the American Corporation*. New York: Simon and Schuster.

Kelling, G.L. and M.H. Moore. (1988). *The Evolving Strategy of Policing. Perspectives in Policing No. 4*. Washington, DC: National Institute of Justice.

Kelling, G.L., T. Pate, D. Dieckman, and C.E. Brown. (1974). *The Kansas City Preventive Patrol Experiment: A Technical Report*. Washington, DC: Police Foundation.

Klockars, C.B. (1988). The Rhetoric of Community Policing. In Greene, J.R. and S.D. Mastrofski (Eds.), *Community Policing: Rhetoric or Reality*. New York: Praeger.

Krantz, S., B. Gilman, C.G. Benda, C.R. Hallstrom, C., and E.J. Nadworny. (1979). *Police Policymaking: The Boston Experience*. Lexington, MA: D.C. Heath.

LaFave, W. (1965). *Arrest: The Decision to Take a Suspect Into Custody*. Boston: Little, Brown.

McElroy, J.E., C.A. Cosgrove, and S. Sadd. (1989). An Examination of the Community Patrol Officer Program (CPOP) in New York City (unpublished report). New York: Vera Institute of Justice.

Monkonnen, E. (1981). *Police in Urban America, 1860–1920*. New York: Cambridge University Press.

Moore, M.H. and D.W. Stephens. (1991). *Beyond Command and Control: The Strategic Management of Police Departments*. Washington, DC: Police Executive Research Forum.

Ouchi, W.G. (1981). *Theory Z: How American Business Can Meet the Japanese Challenge*. Reading, MA: Addison-Wesley.

Pate, A.M., M.A. Wycoff, W.G. Skogan, and L.W. Sherman. (1986). *Reducing Fear of Crime in Houston and Newark: A Summary Report*. Washington, DC: Police Foundation.

Peters, T.J. and R.H. Waterman. (1982). *In Search of Excellence: Lessons from America's Best-Run Companies*. New York: Harper and Row.

Philadelphia Police Study Task Force. (1987). *Philadelphia and Its Police: Toward a New Partnership*. Philadelphia, PA.

Police Foundation. (1981). *The Newark Foot Patrol Experiment*. Washington, DC.

Reith, C. (1975). *The Blind Eye of History: A Study of the Origins of the Present Police Era*. Montclair, NJ: Patterson Smith.

Rosenbaum, D.P. and L. Heath. (1990). The "Psycho-Logic" of Fear-Reduction and Crime Prevention Programs. In Edwards, J., S.R. Tindale, L. Heath, and E.J. Posavac (Eds.), *Social Psychological Applications to Social Issues*. Vol. I. *Social Influence Processes and Prevention*. New York: Plenum Press.

Sampson, R.J. (1987). Communities and Crime. In Gottfredson, M.R. and T. Hirschi (Eds.), *Positive Criminology*. Newbury Park, CA: Sage.

Schwartz, A.I. and S.N. Clarren. (1977). *The Cincinnati Team Policing Experiment: A Summary Report*. Washington, DC: The Urban Institute and Police Foundation.

Shaw, C.R. and H.D. McKay. (1942). *Juvenile Delinquency and Urban Areas*. Chicago: University of Chicago Press.

Sherman, L.W. (1989). Repeat Calls for Service: Policing the "Hot Spots." In Kenney, D.J. (Ed.), *Police and Policing: Contemporary Issues*. New York: Praeger.

Sherman, L.W. (1990). Police Crackdowns: Initial and Residual Deterrence. In Tonry, M. and N. Morris (Eds.), *Crime and Justice: A Review of Research*. Vol. 12. Chicago: University of Chicago Press.

Sherman, L.W., P.R. Gartin, and M.E. Buerger. (1989). Hot Spots of Predatory Crime: Routine Activities and the Criminology of Place. *Criminology 27*:27–55.

Sherman, L., C. Milton, and T. Kelly. (1973). *Team Policing: Seven Case Studies*. Washington, DC: Police Foundation.

Skogan, W.G. (1987). The Impact of Victimization on Fear. *Crime and Delinquency 31*:135–154.

Skogan, W.G. (1990). *Disorder and Decline: Crime and Decline: Crime and the Spiral of Decay in American Neighborhoods*. New York: Free Press.

Skolnick, J.H. (1973). The Police and the Urban Ghetto. In Niederhoffer, A. and A.S. Blumberg (Eds.), *The Ambivalent Force: Perspectives on the Police*. San Francisco: Rinehart Press.

Skolnick, J.H. (1975). *Justice Without Trial: Law Enforcement in a Democratic Society*. 2nd ed. New York: John Wiley and Sons.

Spelman, W. and D.K. Brown. (1984). *Calling the Police: Citizen Reporting of Serious Crime*. Washington, DC: U.S. Government Printing Office.

Trojanowicz, R.C. and B. Bucqueroux. (1989). *Community Policing. A Contemporary Perspective*. Cincinnati, OH: Anderson.

Vollmer, A. (1971). *The Police in Modern Society*. Montclair, NJ: Patterson Smith.

Walker, S. (1977). *A Critical History of Police Reform: The Emergence of Professionalism*. Lexington, MA: D.C. Heath.

Weisburd, D. and J.E. McElroy. (1988). Enacting the CPO Role: Findings From the New York City Pilot Program in Community Policing. In Greene, J.R. and S.D. Mastrofski (Eds.), *Community Policing: Rhetoric or Reality*. New York: Praeger.

Weisburd, D., J.E. McElroy, and P. Hardyman. (1988). Challenges to Supervision in Community Policing: Observations on a Pilot Project. *American Journal of Police 7*:29–59.

Welter, J. (1990). Squad Popping. *Upfront 11*:14–15.

Wilson, J.Q. (1968). *Varieties of Police Behavior*. Cambridge, MA: Harvard University Press.

Wilson, J.Q. and G.L. Kelling. (1982). The Police and Neighborhood Safety: Broken Windows. *Atlantic Monthly 127*, March:29–38.

5
Community Policing and the Rule of Law

STEPHEN D. MASTROFSKI and JACK R. GREENE

> *A government of laws, and not of men.* (John Adams)
> *[T]he law is such an ass.* (George Chapman)

Over the course of American history, much has been made of the distinction between "government by laws" and "government by men." Different times and circumstances have evoked calls for more of one and less of the other, to rectify what reformers perceived as the faults of the current imbalance between the two. When government seems too corrupt, inefficient, or unequal in its treatment of the governed, stronger laws and more rules and regulations are called for. When government seems too unresponsive, inflexible, and ineffective, the call is to lighten the burden of rigid laws and allow citizens to govern themselves as exigencies dictate.

The last decade has witnessed the emergence of a diverse set of reform proposals that have come to be characterized as "community policing." One of the themes of this movement is the readjustment of the balance between "laws and men" in the governance of police. In brief, advocates of community policing propose that greater weight be given to the "men" part of the equation—couched in terms of "community." Correspondingly, the bonds of formal law and bureaucratic rules must be loosened to allow police policies and practices to be guided by community norms and sentiments. If the 1960s came to be characterized as a decade of the "due process revolution," when legal restraints were ascendant in efforts to reform police, then the 1980s may come to be known as the decade of the "quiet revolution," when reformers began to find merit once again in a policing not so heavily mediated by legal institutions, such as courts, litigation, statutes, and administrative rules and regulations, and infused more with decentralized and direct democratic processes that link police and policed more intimately (Kelling, 1988).

This chapter responds to the government-of-laws-versus-men issue at two levels. At one level we are concerned with the possibility of community policing, what it might be. Although we recognize the reality of the tension between a government of laws and a government of men, we hold that the relationship is not strictly zero sum, that it is possible to increase the role of community without degrading the rule of law, and that police accountability is thus enhanced.

At a second, practical level, we argue that achieving such a community police requires major changes in the organization and practice of policing in urban America. We maintain that such changes are far more profound and difficult to achieve than recent reform rhetoric and "community policing" programs acknowledge. We conclude by suggesting that such a community police arrangement, though having many virtues, would not be an unmitigated good; rather, it would create a new set of thorny problems for future police and their communities to address.

Community Policing, Accountability, and Compliance

The liberal philosophy holds that enduring governments must be accountable to someone beside themselves; that a government responsible only to its own conscience is not for long tolerable.   (Walter Lippmon)

Among its many objectives, community policing aims to alter the structure of accountability and control of the police. There are at least four subsystems of accountability that would be affected by community policing. First is the system of criminal, civil, and administrative law and the institutions with authority to make policy and oversee police operations (e.g., legislative bodies, mayors, city managers, courts, civil service boards, regulatory bodies). Second is the department's formal internal system of command and control—the rules, regulations, and policies promulgated by its administrators. Third are groups both within and outside the organization that provide (formally or informally) standards of work performance for police. These standards can arise from work group norms within the rank and file that have evolved informally over time, or they can arise from external groups attempting to establish "professional" standards of performance based on rigorous testing. A fourth accountability subsystem draws on the "community"—the expectations of those who live in or use the area policed. "Community" is the most amorphous of all the systems, often lacking routine mechanisms to convey its expectations. The press, various business, civic, and interest groups, political leaders, public opinion surveys, local traditions, and displays of "culture" are the usual means of communicating community expectations.

These four systems are, of course, not independent, but are, both by design and otherwise, intertwined. The police department's internal system of accountability is expected to be consistent with the dictates of external legal authority, enlarging on them and specifying how police should carry them out (Davis, 1975; Goldstein, 1977). Perhaps to a lesser degree, we expect the organization's policies and practices to follow the received occupational wisdom on how best to do police work (Bayley and Bittner, 1989) and to do so within the broad boundaries formed by the local community's preferences (Wilson, 1968). That these systems of police accountability are sometimes at odds with each other is well documented, but the general expectation is that police resolve these conflicts by finding a compromise among their diverse expectations that pays at least some attention to the demands of each. That styles of policing vary so much among departments in the same state, or even the same metropolitan area, is testimony to the considerable latitude of organizations and their individual decision makers to respond to situational exigencies and circumstances.

What makes community policing a particularly interesting reform is the effort to bring all four of these accountability systems into closer harmony, that is, to make compliance with their separate expectations converge within a smaller domain of police practice and thus increase accountability.[1] Perhaps the most dramatic shift envisioned is the attempt to find some middle ground between the first and fourth compliance systems (legal institutions and community). But also involved are efforts to break down the barriers between the informal police subculture and departmental hierarchy and the community by appealing to a common interest in the goal of more effective policing. This is accomplished by acknowledging the importance of discretion exercised at the rank-and-file level, giving those in the lower ranks more say over what they do and how they do it, and providing more opportunities for those officers to learn the community's perspective (see Goldstein, 1990:Chap. 9).

Etzioni (1975) has outlined a theoretical framework for compliance systems that helps us understand the hoped-for process of community policing. According to Etzioni, compliance systems for organizations are formed through the interaction of two forces: (1) the kind of power that is exercised over lower-level organizational members and (2) the kind of involvement that lower-level members have in the organization. The most effective organizations are those that rely on the type of power that is congruent with the involvement of the members. Two of Etzioni's congruent compliance types help to inform this discussion (1975:12–13). They are "coercive-alienative" and "normative-moral" compliance systems.

Historically the "coercive-alienative" compliance system is characterized by contemporary reformers as "traditional" management styles (Schein-gold, 1984:Chap. 5) in attempting to control officer behavior almost exclusively through law, rules, and regulations. Punishment is the central

---

[1] See Goldstein (1990:47–49) for the most explicit statement of this perspective.

element of this system, and over time it has alienated many officers, thereby diminishing its impact in controlling their behavior, which is therefore directed mostly toward giving only the appearance of compliance while actually subverting the objectives of formal law and authority and avoiding punishment. The exercise of coercion as the dominant method of gaining compliance, Etzioni tells us, is advisable only when lower-level participants are clearly alienated from their work.

The current level of officer alienation therefore seems ample justification for the coercive management style, but contemporary reformers suggest that the alienation is the product of a vicious cycle and is quite contrary to the effective development of an element of police reform honored mostly in the rhetorical sense by police agencies: professionalism (Klockars, 1988). Hoping to break this cycle and harmonize the impact of compliance systems now working (too often) at cross-purposes, community policing proponents advocate changing police organizations to conform to Etzioni's "normative-moral" form of compliance. Under this vision, the law and formal rules of the organization retain coercive potential, but the need to apply coercion is vastly reduced because the involvement of lower-level organizational participants and the community encourages their moral commitment to mutual aims and interests. This strategy is ambitious, for it seeks both to change the principal source of power exercised over lower organizational members (even including members of the community as peripheral participants) and to change the nature of those currently excluded from policy making (i.e., preparing them for the responsibilities of decentralization and community input).

By seeking common ground among the demands of these four subsystems of accountability, community policing thus attempts to negotiate an accommodation that reduces the centrifugal and fragmenting effects of systems that are often at odds or at best only loosely connected. This chapter focuses primarily on the opportunities, challenges, and consequences of bringing the legal and community subsystems in greater harmony, although necessarily this will involve some discussion of the other two subsystems as well.

A Community Policing Compatible With the Rule of Law

Community policing advocates have argued that the "law" as popularly understood (ordinances, statutes, case law, and administrative regulations) offers police insufficient guidance in deciding how best to serve the public (Goldstein, 1990; Kelling, 1987; Sparrow, Moore, and Kennedy, 1990:Chap. 4; Sykes, 1986; Trojanowicz and Bucqueroux, 1990; Wilson and Kelling, 1982). Sometimes it even contravenes community preferences or the widely held views among street-level officers of what constitutes adept police work.

What binds diverse conceptions of community policing is the need to increase the role of the "community" in deciding what police should do, to whom, and how. Advocates diverge on the amount of scope the law should give the police in making these decisions (e.g., the extent to which due process should apply to minor order maintenance situations), but all acknowledge that community policing must be bounded to some extent by legal authority that issues from sources beyond the "community" (see Mastrofski, 1988). There is then in the literature on community policing a certain acknowledged tension between "the community" and "the law." Within this framework the principal issues to resolve are (1) how much influence should the community be given and (2) what are the best ways to structure that influence.

How Much Community Influence?

> A certain quantum of power must always exist in the community, in some
> hands, and under some appellation.   (Edmund Burke)

Where are the proper boundaries between what the law tells police to do and what the community tells them? Answering this question first requires acknowledging the limits of the law in structuring police discretion. The police make two kinds of decisions that require guidance and accountability in a democratic society: what kinds of problems to get involved in and what to do once involved. Few would argue that the law is irrelevant to these decisions. It is clear that the law empowers police, giving them the authority to intervene and take certain actions (e.g., arrest) in specific circumstances (where evidence suggests the probability of a violation). Without a legal basis for intervention and action, it is undoubtedly true that the police would show less inclination to get involved in many problems and take certain legal actions. Recent laws giving police broader arrest powers in certain domestic violence situations are an example. But we know that police use the law instrumentally, as a means to accomplish a variety of ends, and they therefore draw on it selectively, applying it in ways that appear (legally) inconsistent. Most traffic law violators caught by police receive no citation; many alleged offenders in domestic disputes avoid arrest; minor thieves and disorderly persons often receive warnings instead of arrests; and these decisions are often based on factors other than the legal evidence (Black, 1980; Brown, 1981:Chap. 7; Smith and Visher, 1981).

The law not only empowers police; it also constrains them. Indeed, the law's greatest potential to influence police would seem to lie in its capacity to define forbidden actions (e.g., excessive force, illegal search and seizure) rather than to specify desired ones (Bittner, 1983). That has been the thrust of the "due process revolution" that expanded the scope of constitutional protections to defendants by demarking the boundaries of unacceptable police practice. But research has shown that the police can be quite adept at subverting legal proscriptions (Chevigny, 1969; Manning, 1974; Medalie, Zeitz, and Alexander, 1968; Milner, 1971; Rubinstein, 1973; Skolnick, 1975, 1985; Sutton, 1986; Wald et al., 1967), and more importantly, the system for monitoring police compliance is limited to those relatively few instances where police actions are made visible in cases that receive review in court (National Institute of Justice, 1982).

Thus, after more than two decades of intense research and scholarly rumination, it is now widely accepted among students of the police that the law exerts only limited influence on what police do. This is because (1) police objectives extend well beyond simply enforcing the law, (2) enforcing the law is not always the best way to accomplish these objectives, and (3) limited police resources make total enforcement of the law an impossibility and selective enforcement inevitable (Klockars, 1985:Chap. 5). So, as a practical necessity, police decisions about when to intervene and what to do once involved are guided by a variety of "extralegal" factors, which may include the officer's own biases and predilections, certain features of the police department and courts, and the locally popular views held by the public.

Given this limited scope of the law as a mechanism of accountability, it seems entirely possible and desirable that a department seeking to become a "community police" force would not necessarily *replace* the law with the community as the source of legitimate governance, but rather would seek to *supplement* it. That is, the most appropriate objective for a community police would be to find ways to enlarge or extend police accountability to the public without diminishing their accountability to the law.[2]

Community contributions to police governance can be made in three ways: identifying problems (agenda setting), establishing priorities, and selecting methods to handle those problems. Under the good government model ascendant in police reform since the 1920s, the "political" arena is an appropriate place to undertake the first two tasks (with, of course, expert input from the police). Elected officials have traditionally carried out these functions by participating in the electoral process and by debating and passing public policies that frame what problems the police can and should address. Passing local budgets has been a (cumbersome) way of establishing priorities. Selecting the methods for accomplishing police objectives falls within the realm of "administration" under the

---

[2] Compare this objective with that of administrative rule making, which seeks to enlarge police accountability to the *law* by refining, extending, and elaborating the department's rules about what the laws mean and when and how they are to be executed. But the source of this legal supplementation is in this case the police executive, not the public.

good government model, and there the "expert" police administrator dominates—to ensure effectiveness, efficiency, and fairness in service delivery.

Critics have suggested that good-government reforms have been carried to such an extreme that local elected and appointed officials have abandoned their responsibility to govern police (Goldstein, 1977:Chaps. 6 and 7; Hudnut, 1986; Fraser, 1986), and there is some evidence to suggest that elected officials are now only peripherally involved in police oversight and policy development (Wilson, 1968; Gardiner, 1969; Brown, 1981; Scheingold, 1984; Heinz, Jacob, and Lineberry, 1983).[3] Into this vacuum community policing advocates wish to introduce "community" as a means of police governance.

Unlike community control advocates of the late 1960s and early 1970s, community police exponents do not propose to strengthen ties of accountability through bodies with formal governing powers (e.g., mayors, local legislators, civilian review boards), but rather hope to develop informal linkages between the police organization and the public that bypass existing formal governing structures. And although the community control doctrine perceived a sharp distinction between the community and the police, one that presumed a strong oversight function for the community in an adversarial environment between police and policed, the community police perspective offers instead a vision of shared values, a "coproductive" relationship, most often characterized as a "partnership" in which communities offer input, advice, and guidance to police while working hand-in-hand to carry out strategies to fulfill their mutual objectives. Whereas community control advocates wanted to decentralize the governing authority or "control" of the police, community policing advocates want the community to serve in an advisory capacity only (Trojanowicz and Bucqueroux, 1990; Skolnick and Bayley, 1986; Sparrow, Moore, and Kennedy, 1990).

The scope of this "advisory process" is still rather nebulous in community policing programs throughout the country. Some programs provide a certain amount of voice to community residents on an agenda framed entirely by the police. Others afford the opportunity for the community to frame the agenda to a limited degree. Part of the problem in broadening participation is in defining communities and determining how to integrate community and police agency priorities.

Most of the community policing literature, both conceptual and programmatic, construes "communities" as being geographically bounded, most often into "neighborhoods." Although sociologists have imbued "community" with a rich variety of meanings, in the terms of the police reform literature, the "community" in each neighborhood is the group or

---

[3] For some contrary evidence, see Mastrofski (1988).

groups of people who reside, work, recreate, or are otherwise legitimately involved in the area on a regular basis.[4] In jurisdictions that have many neighborhoods, the idea of a community police thus connotes a police force that engages and responds to the public in a decentralized fashion, being sensitive to variations in the features of neighborhood and their denizens (Greene and Taylor, 1988). Implicitly, local government and its elected representatives are insufficiently able to hear and represent the complexity of such numerous and diverse "neighborhoods," thus necessitating new forums for police–community dialogue.

What then is the appropriate domain of neighborhood influence regarding police policy and practice? One can begin by saying that police need not do the bidding of the neighborhood when it requests things that the law clearly forbids (e.g., violations of constitutional rights). Here the police are obliged only to obtain an authoritative interpretation of the law and explain it to the neighborhood.

Where the law offers broad police discretion—and this is often the case on the kinds of problems the public asks the police to handle—the nature of police policy and practice may be open to neighborhood input. There is no broader range in police discretion than that of selective involvement in the community's affairs. When legal violations are at issue, we call the exercise of this discretion "selective enforcement," a specific case of the broader selective involvement (which can include circumstances that do not necessarily involve legal violations). Thus, identifying problems and establishing priorities for dealing with those problems are prime functions for each neighborhood to consider and solicit police responsiveness.

If one neighborhood signals that speeding cars are its top priority, then the department should see to it that the officers serving that neighborhood give speeding cars top priority. If another neighborhood identifies open-air drug markets as its major problem, then that should be the assigned officers' major concern. If another wants abandoned cars cleared, then that becomes the priority of officers on that beat. And even if one asks for its officers to spend more time developing positive relations with the youth of the area, that is what their police should do.

This requires an open acknowledgment by both police and the public of the limitations of police resources, the necessity of selective enforcement (or, more generally, "problem solving"), and acceptance of differing priorities and styles of policing from neighborhood to neighborhood—albeit, all within the limits of the law. The presumption is that within the bounds of law and resources available, the police will be guided by the preferences of the "community." These preferences do not have the force of law, as a local ordinance or an order from the mayor might, but they do create an obligation for the police to justify to the community any

---

[4] See Goldstein (1990:25) for a different conceptualization of community.

significant divergence of their practices from the community's priorities. Moreover, such police sensitivity to community needs establishes an effective bond between the police and the neighborhood community, such that the normative force of community expectations shapes police responses. This, of course, reflects the model of compliance emphasizing normative power and moral involvement.

A more difficult arena in which to establish the scope of appropriate community input is that of deciding strategies and tactics. Even if the police are the experts on how best to get things done, may not the community have some say in the choice of methods? Suppose, for example, that drug dealing in the schools is the problem, and the police must decide whether to use undercover agents, more visible enforcement methods, or preventive educational programs. Is it appropriate for the community to forbid undercover operations if it finds them offensive? Or suppose that a department decided to deal with a juvenile gang problem by conducting "sweeps" through neighborhoods. If a neighborhood objects because the residents perceive the police to be too rough and undiscriminating between the troublemakers and the innocent, what should the police be expected to do? Or suppose that a neighborhood prefers foot patrol to motorized units. Should the department accede to its wishes, even if that degrades the capacity of officers to serve efficiently the *entire* neighborhood and those adjacent to it?

Most police, and perhaps even most citizens, would defer to police "professional" judgment on matters of strategy and tactics, even in the face of strong objection. Here the appropriate type of police accountability to the community might be an explicit expectation that the police would in advance clearly explain and justify the methods they intend to use, and they would hear and respond to questions and criticisms from the community. Community input on police methods would be advisory only, and in this case there would be no presumption of police acquiescence.

Although advisory in nature, community input in the selection of police tactics and strategies has the potential of actually improving police legality as well as community relations. First, the a priori discussion of tactics and strategies provides time for a reasoned consideration of potentially negative impacts. For example, if a neighborhood sweep is to be implemented, some consideration of who might be caught in such a sweep, and at what cost to the law-abiding community, is more likely to occur in a beforehand discussion with the community. Second, public discussion of police methods forces the police to rethink them. Are they legal? Can they be defended in court? A variety of legal actors and interest groups outside the neighborhood will have the opportunity to comment as well, the public discussion serving as a sort of legal trial balloon. Such visibility enables diverse elements of the jurisdiction to mobilize the legal system at an early stage if the course of action entertained by the neighborhood and their police is believed to transgress the boundaries of the law. Finally, a neighborhood engaged in a dialogue with its police may come to hold a better appreciation for the constraints that law places on officers. Carefully conducted, this process can thus work to ease popular pressure on the police to engage in legally questionable strategies and tactics.

Structuring Community Influence

If police are to increase a neighborhood's involvement in determining how it is policed, then three issues must be addressed: (1) To what extent should the community be organized? (2) Who should be represented? (3) What should the community do?

The Extent of Community Organization

The people are to be taken in very small doses.   (Ralph Waldo Emerson)

Community policing proposals and programs are wide ranging in the nature and degree to which neighborhoods are organized. At one extreme are those programs that presume no level of organization beyond perhaps the family or household. Officers are expected to deal with citizens or household representatives on an individual basis, either when citizens decide to raise matters of concern or when officers solicit their input, as they might in door-to-door surveys. At the other extreme are permanent citizen organizations with the sole function of providing input to police, such as the police consultative committees that arose in London as an aftermath of the Brixton riots.[5] Another structural dimension is the extent to which such organizations are independent of the police. Some organizations, such as Neighborhood Watch, are typically promoted by the police and are designed at the outset to fit neatly into the *police* conception of community–police interaction. Other organizations are created entirely separately from police—and even sometimes with an adversarial or watchdog posture to local government—such as some civilian review boards of the 1960s.

The more organized the neighborhood's means of giving voice to its preferences, the easier it is for police to obtain input, deal with diversity of viewpoints within the neighborhood, and mobilize the community to support and assist police efforts. On the other hand, to the extent that a neighborhood is organized regarding police issues, the police may find that their range of policy-making discretion is narrowed or, at least, that they are more accountable for their actions. To the extent that the

---

[5] The Police and Criminal Evidence Act of 1984 required that police commanders attend these groups' meetings.

community organization depends on police for resources, issue identification, and legitimacy, these restrictions on the police are meliorated, but organizations not dependent on police for their existence are capable of creating significant challenges to police policy, thus complicating police administration, if not restricting departmental discretion.

Urban areas vary in their capacity to nurture and sustain grass roots citizen organizations (Rosenbaum, 1988; Yin, 1986), something that community policing advocates are beginning to appreciate. The police role in facilitating neighborhood organization will vary accordingly. Some neighborhoods are already well organized, and the police problem is simply one of developing channels of communication with existing organizations. Other neighborhoods may have untapped potential that merely requires encouragement and stimulation from the police. And some neighborhoods are so fraught with conflict or anomie that the first order of police business is to establish sufficient order and public safety for the civic virtue of citizen participation to take root. Assessing neighborhoods in terms of their needs for police support is thus an important part of the community policing effort (Greene and Taylor, 1988). But, ultimately, a citizen organization that remains dependent on police support to sustain membership interest and activity ends up being merely a civilian extension of the police department, not an effective device for community input.

The Representation of Diverse Interests

> *Unanimity is almost always an indication of servitude.*
>
> (Charles de Remusat)

Some community policing advocates have argued that urban neighborhoods demonstrate a high degree of consensus about policing priorities and practices for a given area, as if they speak with one voice (Kelling, 1987). This may be true for a variety of crimes police have traditionally regarded as serious (murder, robbery, burglary, rape), but for the host of lesser disorders, neighborhood consensus is the exception, not the rule (Mastrofski, 1988). It is therefore imperative that police obtain input from the widest possible array of neighborhood interests.

How should community policing widen citizen access to the police, ensuring the broadest possible expression of views? Door-to-door surveys and polls (Trojanowicz et al., 1987) may be an efficient way to accomplish this, but they tend to focus on narrow, personal problems; they are a passive form of input; their results are easily manipulated by those who collect the data; and they lack the sort of give-and-take public discussion and debate that would help citizens and police work through complex issues relevant to the entire neighborhood.

Neighborhood organizations and other public forums do provide the opportunity for citizens and police to engage in such a dialogue, but the extent to which such organizations offer representative viewpoints is often problematic. It is well established that participation in such groups is heavily skewed toward those who have higher socioeconomic status and are long-term residents. Neighborhoods that have predominantly low-income and transient residents have proven the most difficult for developing and sustaining such organizations. Indeed, a study focusing directly on the representativeness issue found that the perceptions of neighborhood organization activists do not correlate with the perceptions of the neighborhood at large regarding the identification of problems in the neighborhood (Rich, 1986).

Of course, this skewedness in participation is found in other forms intended to give voice to a broad range of political interests: voting, party participation, protests, political action committees, and so on. Although this may be a political fact of life, it is possible for the police to endeavor to facilitate the broadest possible range of community input, and they should do so. Certain organizations (businesses, schools, and churches) seldom need much encouragement to participate, but other groups, often alienated from local government, may need to be convinced that they will be given a chance to have their voices heard.

The problem of representation is further complicated in that not all parties with legitimate interest in a given neighborhood reside there or have property interests there. Commuters, workers, shoppers, people seeking entertainment, residents of proximate areas, and others from the "outside" all have legitimate interests in how the neighborhood is policed. How can the police ensure that they too are given ample opportunity to provide "community" input? And how will their interests be weighted with respect to those who reside, rent, or own property in the neighborhood?

So, one major task of a "community-oriented" police department is to identify as many sources of community interest as possible and to attempt to ensure their representation in discussions of priorities and policy making. Ultimately, of course, the police department must make a decision and take a stand, but in the early stages of discussion and debate, it often makes more sense to allow disputing groups to air their views and for the police to listen and serve as mediators.

If police aggressively solicit such participation from diverse, alienated, even hostile segments of the community, they will undoubtedly find it more difficult to elicit and perceive *a single* expression of the community will. Discussions and debates will sometimes be chaotic, seemingly trivial, and endless. Intergroup conflicts may well be illuminated and perhaps even heightened, because the local press finds they make attractive stories. It may encourage posturing by those with political ambition and the playing out of petty rivalries among groups of citizens. Initially, at least, such an approach will seem not to build consensus, but to undermine it. But the illumination of conflicting interests within a community is not necessarily bad. It may provide the basis from which consensus or compromise is reached. Or, at a minimum, it may highlight the important issues that fragment the neighborhood, thus helping external authorities, such as the police, decide what to do.

The Duties and Activities of Community Organizations

Let the people think they govern, and they will be governed.

(William Penn)

Most police administrators are understandably uncomfortable with reforms that complicate the policy-making process, as it is quite challenging even without new (and often unpredictable) groups being added. Entering into this "blooming, buzzing confusion" of neighborhood politics, the administrator's first impulse is, like that of the street officer, to establish order, cool things down, and make sense of the situation in terms of the department's categories for "slotting" problems (Prottas, 1978). The more cynical among the police will view such encounters as "gripe sessions," during which the adept administrator will allow citizens to vent grievances without really addressing problems.

Another approach is for police to use the neighborhood leadership to manipulate neighborhood opinion and overwhelm objections to police practice. A police administrator in a large city boasted to one of us that he considered his personally selected citizen council his "civilian staff." Their principal function, as he saw it, was to mobilize support for his policies and quiet criticism. He noted several instances when their intercession on his behalf had been crucial.

Another alternative, and one that has dominated most of the community policing programs fielded in the last decade, is to emphasize the "coproductive" aspect of community policing while downplaying the policy input and oversight aspects of community participation. Community crime prevention programs are, by and large, prepackaged formula programs that seem to show remarkably little sensitivity to the diversity of neighborhoods' makeup, problems, and conditions. Neighborhoods are "sold" the package, and their involvement focuses on such things as property marking, crime reporting, childrens' safe houses, neighborhood cleanup campaigns, and newsletters. Without a clear organizational commitment from top to bottom to make the community important in police policy making, the neighborhood organizations become mere tools for police to *manage* the public, setting the agenda and convincing the community that its priorities are the department's. Co-optation of the community seems a real likelihood.

The extent to which these programs work to increase citizen *voice* is not at all clear at this point, but it may be that citizen participation in such organizations is hard to sustain precisely because citizens catch on to the real nature of the role in which police have cast them. For example, community relations programs of the 1960s and 1970s have been criticized for their one-sided approach to police and community discourse (Greene, 1989). Many of these programs were established in the wake of social disorder as a means for placating minorities. When residents believe that they are being "used" by the police for the department's ends, they not only withdraw from participation but become more vocal in their criticism as well. Absent a voice and declining in loyalty, residents exit these programs and become sometimes formidable opponents to the department (see Hirschman, 1970). Future evaluations of community policing should therefore pay careful attention to the challenge of stimulating actual community voice rather than achieving cooptation.

Ultimately, the more progressive and committed departments may use the neighborhood organization forum to develop a consensus or compromise that is compatible with the department's perspective on the issue. But a true *community* police effort will accept such conflict as an essential part of the process of governance. In any event it is little more than a rhetorical sleight of hand for a community policing program to focus only on getting the citizens to work *with* the police on a variety of coproductive strategies. To adjust an election campaign slogan of the 1960s, what communities need is "a voice, not an echo."

The Risks of an Expanded Community Role

The Risks of Failure

What if they formed a community police and nobody came? This is undoubtedly the greatest risk attached to the sort of police–community relationship we envision. Community policing attempts to revive some aspects of ward politics, albeit in a nonpartisan, sanitized form, that some, perhaps romantically, believe to have existed when urban political machines were in their heyday. The extent to which "the good old days" really produced a police responsive to neighborhood preferences is a matter for historians to explore and debate, but it is clear that a very different political environment exists in urban America today.

Local political parties no longer mobilize neighborhoods, and it is not at all clear that police can effectively serve that function (Rosenbaum, 1987, 1988). Traditional forms of political participation (voting and party activity) at the local level are at an all time low (Abramson and Aldrich, 1982; Almond and Verba, 1973; Burnham, 1982; Cavanagh, 1981; Crotty and Jacobson, 1980). In addition, many of the forces that determine the quality of life in urban neighborhoods operate in arenas well beyond the neighborhood level, in the halls of state and federal governments, metropolitan authorities, and the board rooms of banks and corporations far removed from the neighborhood's vicinity and scope of influence (Gottdiener, 1987). And those "disadvantaged" neighborhoods most needful of political voice are the very areas least capable of generating and sustaining the organizations that are a necessary instrument of their "empowerment." That neighborhood organizations emerge and endure at all on the contemporary scene should perhaps strike us as a remarkable phenomenon (Gitel, 1980; Boyte, 1980; Henig, 1982; Crenson, 1983; Castells, 1983; Sharp, 1978). But under current conditions there must surely be great skepticism regarding their capacity to offer a new structure for the form of grass roots democracy, which is undoubtedly the strongest basis for its public appeal (Manning, 1984, 1988).

Structuring the reform about the proposition that communities must become more directly and actively engaged in directing police policies and practices is, then, risky. That is perhaps why some advocates have proposed a more passive role for the community under the "community policing" banner (Goldstein, 1990:25; Trojanowicz and Bucqueroux, 1990:Chap. 3). Nonetheless, community policing may be an important element in any effort to revive local civic culture. It is therefore all the more appropriate to anticipate some of the problems that might develop if community policing were successfully implemented as true grass roots participation.

The Risks of Success

Every reform, however necessary, will . . . be carried to an excess, that itself will need reforming.   (Samuel Taylor Coleridge)

We have argued that it is possible in theory for the community to increase police accountability without infringing on the "rule of law," because the law leaves so much discretion to the police anyway. If a police department and the citizens of its jurisdiction were able to implement such an approach, there are a number of risks that attend the benefits of reform, and these deserve careful consideration.

The first risk, and the greatest one to those who place highest value on limited government, is the risk that the once-discredited role of police-man as neighborhood politico will now be relegitimated, even if cloaked in terms more palatable for contemporary politics. Rather than hand-in-hand with the ward heeler, tomorrow's community police will work with neighborhood, civic, and special interest groups. We think that this can serve to enhance police accountability, but we wonder whether it is a good idea to require of the police that they serve to amplify the neighborhood's voice on the broad range of problems for which many advocates now urge the police to accept responsibility: broken windows, public health, trash, transportation, schools, and all manner of social dysfunction (Goldstein, 1990; Wilson and Kelling, 1982). Should the police seek to fulfill the role traditionally reserved for the legislative branch of our government: seeing that government bureaucracies correct errors, inefficiencies, and inequities? And even more important, do we really want our police to serve as the political lightning rod for all or most of the ills and political issues that beset the neighborhoods they police?

Given the depth and complexity of problems faced by many urban neighborhoods today, it is apparent that some considerable political mobilization will be necessary to make local government more responsive. But the history of police involvement in electoral politics is not a happy one, and great risks attach to any effort to invite the police to shoulder this burden.[6] Police coercive and investigative powers, used improperly, can have a chilling effect on democratic processes. Police have been and always will be political, but asking them to take the lead role on a political stage that moves from the street corner to city hall heightens citizen vulnerability to police abuse of power.

The red tape, turf protectiveness, lack of coordination, and general inefficiency of local service provision are real in many urban areas and require attention. But it would be better, perhaps, to revitalize the parts of local government that are already responsible for representation of constituents' interests and for making local government work. In asking police to do what elected representatives should do, the greatest risk is not that they may do it badly, but that they may do it too well.

Even if police limit their efforts to develop closer community linkages to the traditional realms of police concern (crime and disorder), several risks attach to the need to decentralize the department. First among these is the fragmentation of police policy and practice. Debates over "community control" or political decentralization of police in the late 1960s and early 1970s addressed the merits and demerits of issues that now resurface, albeit from proposals in more tempered form (cf. Altshuler, 1970; Wilson, 1968:290). Community policing proposes that departments maintain central control over a variety of key decisions (e.g., personnel matters, organizational structure, resource allocation, general rule and policy making, review, oversight, and evaluation of operations), but decentralize decision-making about strategies and tactics, allowing "community" to have some say in those decisions through mechanisms falling generally outside the established processes of local governmental authorities. This would move police organizations more toward what Wilson (1968:286) characterized as the "communal" model of order maintenance, but in a manner more palatable to police executives. The police retain decision-making authority but decision-making within the department is decentralized so that lower-level commanders and supervisors are given

---

[6] For a review of some of these risks and arguments for greater police involvement in local politics, see Muir (1983).

the flexibility to respond to local conditions. Community policing creates an organizational commitment to solicit community input on how to police. There is then a legitimate expectation in the community that the police will carefully consider that input and be responsive to it inasmuch as the law, professional judgment, and overarching jurisdictionwide constraints allow.

If implemented successfully, community policing will yield distinctive styles of policing in different neighborhoods, and those styles will in large part reflect the concerns, preferences, and conflicts of those who live in and otherwise routinely use those neighborhoods. People, groups, and organizations whose enterprises and interests transcend neighborhood boundaries will sometimes find this diversity frustrating and press for greater interneighborhood uniformity in policing. Traffic and parking enforcement, the regulation of disorderly conduct, the enforcement of drug and vice laws, the control of juveniles, minor theft and mischief—all mundane police work—will become targets of even more intensive debate and public scrutiny than they currently are. And police will not be able to resort to the convenient fiction of uniform standards of enforcement in responding to these pressures. They will be obliged to articulate defenses for unequal enforcement of laws and different problem-solving priorities.

It is possible that seemingly diverse neighborhoods will, through this more visible process of decentralized neighborhood advocacy, come to appreciate their shared concerns. Even in Gotham, many things that aggravate uptown residents aggravate downtown residents too. But when uptowners and downtowners come to realize that they want the same things from their police, this may heighten competition for those services among areas where neighborhood consciousness has been raised.

Unfortunately, the community policing literature tends to ignore broad distributional issues about how police resources are to be allocated among neighborhoods, focusing, as this chapter has, on the process of how police relate to each neighborhood. But the *capacity* of the police to fulfill a given neighborhood's wishes will be substantially determined by the level of police resources committed to that neighborhood, and this calls for a consideration of community politics that transcends neighborhood boundaries. It will be interesting to see whether community policing becomes a means to "empower" some neighborhoods to have greater control over an ever-declining police resource base while others enjoy a net gain. Will there be a shift in the distribution of police services? Who will benefit and who will suffer?

The nature and extent of any distributional shifts in service delivery among neighborhoods are difficult to predict at this point; however, it seems likely that most cities experiencing community policing as we have envisioned it will also experience a greater awareness of differences in levels of police service distribution. Heightened *neighborhood* consciousness, endorsed and encouraged by police, will stimulate competition among neighborhoods for scarce police resources. Greater access to police administrators and open discussion of neighborhood problems will undoubtedly lead to more neighborhood-level attention to who is getting what.[7]

Police should be prepared to defend their allocation of resources among the community's various geographic areas. Currently, most departments allocate patrol resources according to workload (e.g., calls for service) levels. It is not entirely clear that this will be the most appropriate method under a community policing arrangement (Goldstein, 1990). And if it is used, savvy neighborhood organizers will recognize that the obvious way to increase the department's allocation of resources to a given neighborhood is to organize to generate more demand from that neighborhood. Indeed, police assigned to that neighborhood and committed to its welfare may well be in the business of encouraging neighborhood denizens to report more problems to the department to justify a reallocation of resources.

Where distributional politics becomes highly charged, the police may find it expedient to refer the issue to elected officials. This has three advantages: (1) It takes the political heat off the police. (2) It places responsibility for policy making squarely on the shoulders of those who were elected to office to make such obviously political decisions. (3) It increases the visibility of these choices to the public. This strategy has the distinct disadvantage (from the chief's perspective) of reducing the department hierarchy's autonomy in resource allocation. The department need not be relegated to the sidelines, however, as it can still serve as an active commentator on the "professional" implications of any given proposal, thus influencing the decision.

In addition to the external pressures described earlier, the organizational decentralization necessary for community policing will create certain challenges for police administrators within the department itself. Although decentralization increases decision flexibility at lower organizational levels, it restricts headquarters' freedom in some respects. Decentralization places a premium on keeping officers assigned to the same area for long periods, which conflicts with the need of administrators to transfer officers for a variety of personnel and work demand reasons. To the extent that the department is successful in stabilizing the geographic

---

[7] On the other hand, police management of citywide distribution issues may actually be enhanced through a continuing analysis of community demand. Current methods of allocating police resources often ignore the minor problems that so concern neighborhood residents. Presumably these models would be revised under community policing. Continuous monitoring of demand for these services would enable police administrators to make better-informed distributional decisions.

assignments of its officers, it must come to grips with the possibility of "too much of a good thing." Officers invested with a sense of belonging, ownership, or "turf" in a given neighborhood can "go native," or at least shift their allegiance sufficiently that their priorities become parochial (Muir, 1977:80).

Another potential problem is the possibility that community policing would contribute to greater police favoritism and corruption. A number of advocates and critics of community policing have raised this possibility. Advocates hope that the level of officer professionalism, improved supervision techniques, enhanced organizational capacity to monitor officer activities, and strengthened internal affairs units will minimize this risk. And it is also true that the old partisan political machines that so thoroughly integrated the police in the seamier aspects of the nineteenth- and early twentieth-century urban political economy are now defunct. It would be dangerous, however, to assume that the police of today are somehow more immune to corruption than their predecessors. The opportunities for corruption remain, even if organized differently today. The illicit drug industry, in particular, can make huge sums available for police protection. Whether developing a more intimate relationship with a neighborhood increases the opportunities and benefits for corruption depends largely on how drug trafficking is organized in a given neighbor- hood. The decentralization of policing would seem to give smaller, decentralized drug operations greater opportunities to pursue corrupt arrangements with police. The extent to which these arrangements can be controlled by means compatible with community policing remains to be demonstrated empirically.

Whether departments can indeed achieve a "community" police and deal effectively with its attendant risks remains largely untested empirically, primarily because there have been few such programs that have tried or been able to implement successfully the nature and extent of community involvement that make the community a *true* partner in policy making. And where such programs may have been implemented, there have been no comprehensive, even-handed evaluations of their success in enhancing police accountability to the community or the law. What empirical research *has* demonstrated, however, are the difficulties of getting and sustaining community involvement at levels sufficiently high to consider that this aspect of the *theory* of community policing has really been tested (Rosenbaum, 1987, 1988; Weisburd and McElory, 1988).

Conclusions

In this chapter we have, in a sense, tried to have our cake and eat it too. That is, we have set forth arguments for a police reform that rhetorically at least seeks substantial grass roots participation in the governance of local police, one that supplements the rule of law rather than detracts from it. This, we believe, can be done by making explicit and more visible the "community" processes that already operate *sub rosa* to shape styles of policing in American cities. We have also suggested that what are generally passed off today as "community policing" programs are shallow, faint, diluted, and unsatisfying renderings of what community policing might be. Better to have no community policing at all than the limp, watered down versions that serve up only a thin gruel of citizen participation. But finally, we have noted that "doing the right thing" with community policing carries with it a number of risks: that the community will fail to respond to the challenges of its new role; that police will become too powerful in political arenas from which they have been largely excluded; that police policy and practice will become too geographically fragmented; that enforcement of the laws will be come more unequal; that interneighborhood rivalries will be heightened; that police exposure to the politics of who-gets-what will be intensified; and that officer parochialism and corruption will increase.

One cannot make light of these challenges. Indeed, they are of such magnitude that we should hold suspect any claim that a department has "achieved" community policing in one, two, or even five years. This is unfortunate for most police departments, because their top administrators, whose tenure is typically quite short, are under tremendous pressure to institute change and declare success. This encourages resort to quick fixes and the management of appearances, and mitigates against attempting long-term organizational and community development programs. This suggests to us that if community policing is to endure in more than the rhetorical sense, communities will probably not be able to rely on the police to implement it. That is to say, the impetus for community participation must be sustained more by the community's continuing commitment to achieve it than by police willingness to try it. Ironically, such "customer" input may do more to improve police management than the reforms that come from the "management experts" (see Peters and Waterman, 1982). It is this irony that makes community policing both an interesting phenomenon to study and, at least potentially, a compelling one to experience.

References

Abramson, P. and J. Aldrich. (1982). The Decline of Electoral Participation in America. *American Political Science Review 76*, No. 3:502–521.

Almond, G. and S. Verba. (1973). *The Civic Culture*. Princeton, NJ: Princeton University Press.

Altshuler, A. (1970). *Community Control*. New York: Bobbs-Merrill.

Bayley, D.H. and E. Bittner. (1989). Learning the Skills of Policing. In Dunham, R.G. and G.P. Alpert (Eds.), *Critical Issues in Policing: Contemporary Readings*. Prospect Heights, IL: Waveland Press.

Bittner, E. (1983). Legality and Workmanship: Introduction to Control in the Police Organization. In Punch, M. (Ed.), *Control in the Police Organization*. Cambridge, MA: MIT Press. Pp. 1–11.

Black, D.J. (1980). *Manners and Customs of the Police*. New York: Academic Press.

Boyte, H. (1980). *The Backyard Revolution*. Philadelphia, PA: Temple University Press.

Brown, M.K. (1981). *Working the Street: Police Discretion and the Dilemmas of Reform*. New York: Russell Sage Foundation.

Burnham, W.D. (1982). *The Current Crisis in American Politics*. New York: Oxford University Press.

Castells, M. (1983). *The City and the Grass Roots*. Berkeley, CA: University of California Press.

Cavanagh, T. (1981). Changes in voter turnout, 1964–1976. *Political Science Quarterly 96* (Spring):53–65.

Chevigny, P. (1969). *Police Power*. New York: Pantheon Books.

Crenson, M.A. (1983). *Neighborhood Politics*. Cambridge, MA: Harvard University Press.

Crotty, W. and G. Jacobson. (1980). *American Parties in Decline*. Boston: Little, Brown.

Davis, K.C. (1975). *Police Discretion*. St. Paul, MN: West.

Etzioni, A. (1975). *A Comparative Analysis of Complex Organizations*. Rev. ed. New York: Free Press.

Fraser, D.M. (1986). Politics and Police Leadership: The View from City Hall. In Geller, W.A. (Ed.), *Police Leadership in America: Crisis and Opportunity*. New York: Praeger.

Gardiner, J.A. (1969). *Traffic and the Police: Variations in Law Enforcement Policy*. Cambridge, MA: Harvard University Press.

Gitel, M. (1980). *Limits to Citizen Participation*. Beverly Hills, CA: Sage.

Goldstein, H. (1977). *Policing a Free Society*. Cambridge, MA: Ballinger.

Goldstein, H. (1990). *Problem-Oriented Policing*. New York: McGraw-Hill.

Gottdiener, M. (1987). *The Decline of Urban Politics: Political Theory and the Crisis of the Local State*. Newbury Park, CA: Sage.

Greene, J.R. (1988). Community Policing and American Law Enforcement: Problems in Implementing Social Change. Paper presented at the 10th International Congress on Criminology, Hamburg, Germany.

Greene, J.R. (1989). Police and Community Relations: Where Have We Been and Where Are We Going? In Dunham, R.G. and G.P. Alpert (Eds.), *Critical Issues in Policing: Contemporary Readings*. Prospect Heights, IL: Waveland Press.

Greene, J.R. and R.B. Taylor. (1988). Community-Based Policing and Foot Patrol: Issues of Theory and Evaluation. In Greene, J.R. and S.D. Mastrofski (Eds.), *Community Policing: Rhetoric or Reality*. New York: Praeger.

Heinz, A., A. Jacob, and R.L. Lineberry. (1983). Crime, Politics, and the Cities. In Heinz, A., H. Jacob, and R. Lineberry (Eds.), *Crime in City Politics*. New York: Longman.

Henig, J. (1982). *Neighborhood Mobilization: Redevelopment and Response*. New Brunswick, NJ: Rutgers University Press.

Hirschman, A.O. (1970). *Exit, Voice and Loyalty: Responses to Decline in Firms, Organizations and States*. Cambridge, MA: Harvard University Press.

Hudnut, W.A. (1986). The Police and the Polis: A Mayor's Perspective. In Geller, W.A. (Ed.), *Police Leadership in America: Crisis and Opportunity*. New York: Praeger.

Kelling, G.L. (1987). Acquiring a Taste for Order: The Community and Police. *Crime and Delinquency 33*, No. 1:90–102.

Kelling, G.L. (1988). Police and Communities: The Quiet Revolution. Washington, DC: National Institute of Justice. Klockars, C.B. (1985). *The Idea of Police*. Beverly Hills, CA: Sage.

Klockars, C.B. (1985). *The Idea of Police*. Beverly Hills, CA: Sage.

Klockars, C.B. (1988). The Rhetoric of Community Policing. In Greene, J.R. and S.D. Mastrofski (Eds.), *Community policing: Rhetoric or Reality*. New York: Praeger.

Manning, P.K. (1974). Police Lying. *Urban Life 3*:283–306.

Manning, P.K. (1984). Community Policing. *American Journal of Police 3*, No. 2:205–227.

Manning, P.K. (1988). Community Policing as a Drama of Control. In Greene, J.R. and S.D. Mastrofski (Eds.), *Community Policing: Rhetoric or Reality*. New York: Praeger.

Mastrofski, S.D. (1988). Community Policing as Reform: A Cautionary Tale. In Greene, J.R. and S.D. Mastrofski (Eds.), *Community Policing: Rhetoric or Reality*. New York: Praeger.

Mastrofski, S.D. (1988). Varieties of Police Governance in Metropolitan America. *Politics and Policy 8*:12–31.

Medalie, R.J., L. Zeitz, and P. Alexander. (1968). Custodial Police Interrogation in Our Nation's Capitol: The Attempt to implement Miranda. *Michigan Law Review 66*, No. 7:1347–1422.

Milner, N.A. (1971). *The Court and Law Enforcement: The Impact of Miranda*. Beverly Hills, CA: Sage.

Muir, W.K. (1977). *Police: Streetcorner Politicians*. Chicago: University of Chicago Press.

Muir, W.K. (1983). Police and politics. *Criminal Justice Ethics 2*, No. 2:3–9.

National Institute of Justice. (1982). The Effects of the Exclusionary Rule: A Study of California. Washington, DC: U.S. Government Printing Office.

Peters, T.J. and R.H. Waterman. (1982). *In Search of Excellence*. New York: Harper and Row.

Prottas, J.M. (1978). The Power of the Street-Level Bureaucrat in Public Service Bureaucracies. *Urban Affairs Quarterly 13*, No. 3:285–312.

Rich, R.C. (1986). Neighborhood-Based Participation in the Planning Process: Promise and Reality. In Taylor, R.B. (Ed.), *Urban Neighborhoods: Research and Policy*. New York: Praeger.

Rosenbaum, D.P. (1987). The Theory and Research Behind Neighborhood Watch: Is It a Sound Fear- and Crime-Reduction Strategy? *Crime and Delinquency 33*, No. 1:103–134.

Rosenbaum, D.P. (1988). Community Crime Prevention: A Review and Synthesis of the Literature. *Justice Quarterly 5*, No. 3:323–395.

Rubinstein, J. (1973). *City Police*. New York: Farrar, Straus and Giroux.

Scheingold, S.A. (1984). *The Politics of Law and Order: Street Crime and Public Policy*. New York: Longman.

Sharp, E.B. (1978). *Citizen Organizations and Participation in Law Enforcement Advocacy and Coproduction: The Role of Incentives*. Ph.D. dissertation, University of North Carolina, Chapel Hill.

Skolnick, J.H. (1975). *Justice Without Trial: Law Enforcement in a Democratic Society*. 2nd ed. New York: John Wiley and Sons.

Skolnick, J.H. (1985). Deception by police. In Elliston, F.A. and M. Feldbery (Eds.), *Moral Issues in Police Work*. Totowa, NJ: Rowman and Allenheld.

Skolnick, J.H. and D.H. Bayley. (1986). *The New Blue Line: Police Innovation in Six American Cities*. New York: Free Press.

Smith, D.A. and C.A. Visher. (1981). Street-Level Justice: Situational Determinants of Police Arrest Decisions. *Social Problems 29*:167–177.

Sparrow, M.K., M.H. Moore, and D.M. Kennedy. (1990). *Beyond 911: A New Era for Policing*. New York: Basic Books.

Sutton, L.P. (1986). The Fourth Amendment in Action: An Empirical View of the Search Warrant Process. *Criminal Law Bulletin 22*, No. 5:405–429.

Sykes, G. (1986). Street Justice: A Moral Defense of Order Maintenance. *Justice Quarterly 3*, No. 4.

Trojanowicz, R. and B. Bucqueroux. (1990). *Community Policing: A Contemporary Perspective*. Cincinnati, OH: Anderson.

Trojanowicz, R., R. Gleason, B. Pollard, and D. Sinclair. (1987). *Community Policing: Community Input Into Police Policymaking*. East Lansing, MI: Michigan State University, National Neighborhood Foot Patrol Center.

Wald, M., R. Ayres, D. Hess, M. Schantz, and C.H. Whitebread. (1967). Interrogations in New Haven: The Impact of Miranda. *Yale Law Journal 76*:1521–1648.

Weisburd, D. and J.E. McElroy (1988). Enacting the CPO Role: Findings from the New York City Pilot Program in Community Policing. In Greene, J.R. and S.D. Mastrotski (Eds.), *Community Policing: Rhetoric or Reality*. New York: Praeger.

Wilson, J.Q. (1968). *Varieties of Police Behavior: The Management of Law and Order in Eight Communities*. Cambridge, MA: Harvard University Press.

Wilson, J.Q. and G.L. Kelling. (1982). The Police and Neighborhood Safety: Broken Windows. *Atlantic Monthly 127*, March:29–38.

Yin, R.K. (1986). Community Crime Prevention: A Synthesis of Eleven Evaluations. In Rosenbaum, D.P. (Ed.), *Community Crime Prevention: Does It Work?* Beverly Hills, CA: Sage. Pp. 294–308.

6
The Challenge of Reinventing Police and Community

MICHAEL E. BUERGER

The landscape of modern policing is littered with innovative programs that enjoyed a brief moment in the sun, generated a few self-congratulatory articles in the police practitioner magazines, then quickly and quietly disappeared in response to budgetary pressures or managerial changes.[1] The inherent problem of police innovation is that it almost always is an initiative that originates with "management cop culture" and is imposed on the "street cop culture" (Reuss-Ianni, 1983). As a result, police innovation generally suffers from special-unit ghettoization and strong resistance from rank-and-file officers, which either eviscerates the program or makes its expansion impossible. Police initiatives that purport to alter the basic police–citizen relationship encounter further difficulties in identifying "the community" and in empowering community participation in policing.

Street cops do not see a need for substantive change in what they do; they embrace only changes that remove the controls and restrictions under which they chafe. Street cops know that they can outlive any "innovation": the most innocuous form of resistance is just to put up with it until the funding money runs out. At the other end of the spectrum, the more reactionary elements of the police may actively seek to corrupt innovations as a screen for "business as usual."

The insularity of the rank-and-file from both the spirit and the substance of innovation bodes ill for the notion of what is being called the "reinvention" of the police. The degree to which "reinvention" merely means "redefinition" in symbolic terms affects both the substance of the

---

[1] In 1986, the National Neighborhood Foot Patrol Center published a 20–year overview of 96 police initiatives "gleaned from articles appearing in *The Police Chief*" magazine: 43 were identified as "community-oriented programs"; 26 were identified as "youth-oriented"; another 13 targeted particular identifiable groups (the elderly, visible minorities, victims of specific crimes); and 14 were "targeted at specific problems or employing limited or unique means." Not all of the described programs, NNFPC warned, were still in operation at the time of publication (Trojanowicz et al., 1986), a caveat emblematic of the history of police innovation overall.

programs and the outcomes that can be expected. Although proponents of police initiatives talk in terms of cooperation, critics remind us that police initiatives hold the potential to increase government interference in the lives of citizens—an iron fist wrapped in a velvet glove of seductive, "feel-good" terminology. Corruption of the language of innovation, to support crime-suppression agendas and tactics that have been the bedrock of the police subculture since the 1960s, remains a constant concern.

The Background

Police innovation during the decade of the 1980s has been promoted under two categorical labels: problem-oriented policing, first articulated by Herman Goldstein in 1979, and community-oriented policing (COP), also referred to as "community policing." Problem-oriented policing is one of the few programmatic innovations that promises to change substantially the way in which the police relate to the public.

The dominant perspective of policing is heavily influenced by the primary method of control associated with the work—the authority to enforce the criminal law. This influence is so strong that police officers are commonly referred to as law enforcement officers—a misnomer that uses only one of the methods they employ in their work to characterize all that they do. This common view has not only distorted our perception of the police role; it has disproportionately influenced the operating practices, organization, training, and staffing of police agencies. If, in a sharp departure from this traditional perspective, one begins with an analysis of each of the varied problems police handle and only then proceeds to establish the most effective response, one's perspective of policing is reversed. *Rather than cling to the simplistic notion that the criminal law defines the police role, we come to realize that policing consists of developing the most effective means for dealing with a multitude of troublesome situations.* And these means will often, but not always, include appropriate use of the criminal law. (Goldstein, 1990:2, emphasis added)

Community-oriented policing is regarded as the more nebulous of the two concepts, easily claimed but difficult to define. To many commentators, "community policing" is the latest police fad, a label in search of a definition. Everybody is doing it, it seems, but no one can really define it. David H. Bayley summarized it best:

Community policing is the new philosophy of professional law enforcement in the world's industrial democracies. . . . It represents progress and innovation. Wherever change is occurring, community policing is the watchword. . . . Although widely, almost universally, said to be important, it means different things to different people—public relations campaigns, shopfront and mini-police stations, rescaled patrol beats, liaison with ethnic groups, permission for the rank-and-file to speak to the press, Neighborhood Watch, foot patrols, patrol-detective teams, and door-to-door visits by police officers. Community policing on the ground often seems less a program than a set of aspirations wrapped in a slogan. . . .

It is probably fair to say that community policing . . . is more rhetoric than reality. It is a trendy phrase spread thinly over a customary reality. (Bayley, 1988:225, citing Skolnick and Bayley, 1986)

In its basic manifestation, "community policing" can be attained by simple declaration. As such, it is no more than a unilateral police decree, defining the police relationship to the public in symbolic form only, without any necessary change in police practice or structure. In turn, this calls into question the role of the community, as well as the truth of the assertion. This form of community policing is nothing more than business as usual with a new ad campaign.

In its most ambitious form, community policing stands for a radical redefinition of the police role and practices in the community, making the police and ordinary citizens "coproducers" of order and crime prevention. The tension between "redefinition of the police role" and Bayley's warning that COP is but "a trendy phrase spread thinly over a customary reality" is of great interest to those concerned about the control of the police.

Problem-Oriented Policing

The late 1960s and early 1970s were marked by police fads centering on equipment: new radio systems, enhanced 911 centers, pepper-foggers, body armor, electronic surveillance gear, and so on. These technological advances were embraced by the rank-and-file because they enabled line officers to "do the job" better and in better style. Although nominally controlled by the police administration, the benefits of the technological advances centered on the individual officer, who felt either safer or more capable as a result of acquiring the new equipment.

Police fads of the late 1970s and 1980s centered more on programs, things that police departments can *do* in the face of seemingly intractable social problems.[2] The published results of the Minneapolis Domestic Violence Experiment (Sherman and Berk, 1984) contributed to the adoption of mandatory- or preferred-arrest policies for domestic assault in 175 major city police departments (Sherman and Cohn, 1987), well before replication of the results was undertaken. Neighborhood Watch, Operation I.D., and other packaged programs have spread like wildfire in the name of doing "crime prevention," despite independent research indicating that the effectiveness of those programs is limited (Rosenbaum, 1986). More recently, the preliminary positive results of the Drug Abuse

---

[2] The seductiveness of hardware is still strong, however; Carl Klockars has noted, for instance, the "nine-millimeterization of the police" (personal communication, 1990) based on a perception of greater firepower available to the criminal elements.

Resistance Program (DARE) have led to its adoption nationwide, in the name of "education." It is something the police can *do* about the drug problem at a time when that problem seems to be a black hole, swallowing massive enforcement efforts without a trace.[3] The benefits of programmatic innovations accrue less to individual officers than to police *departments*, as the innovations serve to concentrate public attention on the technological solutions instead of outcomes, a product of the "loosely coupled" organizational response.[4]

Regardless of their limitations, all the programs move the police officers involved in them beyond the simple paradigm of "cops and bad guys." Each tries to go beyond the symptomatic manifestations of a problem, either to reach the root causes of the criminal behavior or to change the fundamental nature of the police response. In 1979, and throughout the 1980s, Herman Goldstein suggested that the police establishment should do that systematically.

In his seminal article, Goldstein criticized the police establishment on two counts. First, police "professionalism" traditionally meant a narrow devotion to the " 'means over ends' syndrome, placing more emphasis in their improvement efforts on organization and operating methods than on substantive outcome of their work" (Goldstein, 1979:236). Second, traditional evaluation methods lumped widely divergent types of activity under overly broad headings like "arson" and "robbery," categorical labels that often mask radically different types of problems. As an alternative, Goldstein proposed that the police "develop a more systematic process for examining and addressing the problems that the public expects them to handle" and "engag[e] in a broad exploration of alternatives to present responses, weighing the merits of these alternatives . . . choosing from among them" (1979:236).

---

[3] As Goldstein and Susmilch noted (1981:3), police innovation is marked by "a readiness to turn to any newly articulated approach, however undeveloped it may be, in the hope of reducing the magnitude of [the seemingly intractable problems confronted in policing]." This faddishness has the potential to work against true problem-oriented policing as envisioned by Goldstein: see Goldstein and Susmilch's note that "Because we learned that our efforts . . . to explain in detail how we acquired the data on which we based our recommendations *detracted from our ability to communicate with department personnel,* we decided in advance to highlight our findings *and keep to a minimum the explanations of how they were derived*" (1982b:7, emphasis added). This suggests that even in progressive departments like Madison, building a capacity for analysis and scanning will be an uphill battle. It is much easier to adopt an existing program developed elsewhere.

[4] For examples of the "loosely coupled model" in policing, see Manning's (1980) discussion of narcotics work in *The Narcs' Game;* Brown's (1981) *Working the Street;* and the general discussion by Stephen Mastrofski, R. Richard Ritti, and Debra Hoffmaster in "The Organizational Determinants of Police Discretion: The Case of Drinking-Driving" in Klockars and Mastrofski (1991).

Goldstein defined problems as "the incredibly broad range of trouble-some situations that prompt citizens to turn to the police, such as street robberies, residential burglaries, battered wives, vandalism, speeding cars, runaway children, accidents, acts of terrorism" (1979:242). Some of these categories fall within the purview of traditional police law enforcement, but Goldstein urged a broader vision and a wider range of police activities—some embracing traditional "crime prevention" schemes, others relating to the quality of interaction between the police and crime victims—beyond responding quickly to a call and taking a report. In some instances, he argued for giving greater attention to problems previously dismissed as trivial, such as noise complaints.

Operationalizing the concept of problem-oriented policing means defining, first, *what* constitutes "a problem" and, second, *who* may legitimately deem something "a problem." In the absence of citizen input, police identification of "problems" leans to police crimefighter preferences, traditionally targeting out-of-favor groups. Even when citizen participation occurs, the problem identification process is biased toward the organized, articulate segments of the community. The possibility of fostering greater community division in the name of community cohesion is one of the greatest potential dangers noted by critics of both problem- and community-oriented policing initiatives.

In the 1980s, several different approaches to this central question of problem identification were undertaken: the Madison, Wisconsin, pilot programs; the Police Executive Research Forum's (PERF's) problem-oriented initiative with the police in Newport News, Virginia; Citizen Oriented Police Enforcement (COPE) in Baltimore County, Maryland; and Repeat Call Address Policing (RECAP) in Minneapolis, Minnesota. The Madison projects conducted by Goldstein and Charles E. Susmilch were largely exploratory: police officers suggested the topics, and the researchers examined the issues and resources (Goldstein and Susmilch, 1981, 1982a, 1982b, 1982c). Although nominally an attempt to operationalize Goldstein's concept on a departmentwide basis, encouraging line officers to proactively identify problems, the Newport News experience reported a constriction of information sources. Noting the occasionally unreliable or insufficient nature of crime analysis information, the program's reviewers reported that "Most of the time, officers relied on their own experiences and the chain of command for identifying possible problems" (Eck and Spelman, 1987:45). The COPE teams in Baltimore County, Maryland, began as a fear-reduction strategy, but moved into problem-oriented policing after experimenting with departmental and citizen-survey target identification. COPE activities derived from *collective* citizen definitions of *problems* worthy of police attention, as the patrol force's activities had been subject to *individual* citizen definition of *incidents* worthy of police intervention (Cordner, 1985). RECAP defined problems in terms of the quantum of calls for police service to individual addresses (Sherman, 1987; Sherman et al., 1988, 1989).

Goldstein's definition of the problem-oriented policing process proceeds "logically from knowledge gained about a particular problem to the fashioning of an appropriate response" (1990:15). In its translation into police operational practices, especially at the lower levels of the hierarchy, problem-oriented policing runs the danger of "proceeding logically from knowledge *currently held*" to the fashioning of a response. "Currently held" represents the best case; "prejudices masquerading as knowledge" represents the worst, and is one of the control issues that weighs most heavily on supervisors of problem-oriented police endeavors. Prior to RECAP, target identification for the experiments in problem-oriented policing was done on relatively subjective bases: the collective insight of a departmental task force in Madison, the input of citizens solicited for their concerns about crime in their Baltimore County neighborhoods, and a task force (supplemented by pursuing official crime statistics) in Newport News. Though nominally more objective, RECAP's computer-generated selection procedure failed to account for proportionality of use, arguably producing false positives. False positives are essentially net-widening factors, extending police scrutiny (if not actual control) into areas where police participation is neither necessary nor prudent.

The core of problem-oriented policing is enhancing the ability of police to look beyond the present definitions of a problem, to see the forces and factors that contribute to and maintain the status quo. Cutting that exploration short may produce an operational evisceration of the philosophy (Goldstein, 1987), artificially limiting the range of available responses and restricting police operations to short-term, low-level tactical gains instead of long-range problem solving.

Community-Oriented Policing

If community policing has a standard operational dimension, it is probably that outlined by Bayley:

> [T]he redeployment of police personnel so as to encourage regular, routine, non-emergency interaction with the public . . . through footpatrols, park-and-walk patrols, and fixed police posts . . . [to] become a more noticeable, less anonymous presence. [The officers] become better acquainted with the community so that they can anticipate, and possibly prevent, crime and order problems from arising . . . the new modes of deployment encourage people to solicit assistance from the police for problems that are important but not necessarily criminal or urgent. (Bayley, 1988:228–229)

Though there are legitimate reasons to question the almost talismanic use of the phrase *community policing*, several major police departments have diverted resources into redeployment schemes of exactly that type.

Community-oriented policing currently has two faces: it is a broad philosophy of police–citizen interaction (which is difficult to operationalize), or it is a series of police-initiated programs that included nonmotorized deployment schemes and crime prevention projects. For most police departments claiming to "do" or "have" community-oriented policing, the latter definition appears to be the most appropriate description.

In 1986, the National Neighborhood Foot Patrol Center published the results of a nationwide survey on community-oriented policing initiatives. Eight categorical divisions were used to describe the programs, of which six were means of deployment of police personnel. Only two suggested actual or potential citizen participation, including citizen volunteer units. Of 233 police departments surveyed, 173 had foot patrol (75 percent of the total). Within that group;

115 (49 percent of the total group) had *only* foot patrol;
18 (8 percent) combined foot patrol with some other non-park-and-walk activity;
60 (25 percent) did not employ foot patrol, but the largest subdivision within the category was "park-and-walk" alone, without any other deployment or outreach strategies (36 departments).

Only 46 departments (20 percent of total group) reported some form of non-foot-patrol, non-park-and-walk program as the basis of their "community-oriented" strategies.

Another telling feature of commitment to programmatic community-oriented policing is the relatively small proportion of officers reported to be participating. In 96 of the departments (41 percent), fewer than 10 officers were involved in the community-oriented program; 75 of those departments (one third of the total group) committed five or fewer officers. An additional 55 departments either gave "no estimate" or reported that "manpower fluctuated."

If we can correctly assume that the "manpower fluctuated" and "no estimate" categories reflect a relatively low commitment to the deployment, either in numbers or in time, 56 percent of the total group reporting community-oriented policing elements have a low level of investment. Of those departments reporting participation levels of approximately 50 percent or higher (the usual proportion of officers assigned to patrol duty, itself a suspicious figure in this context), the model program category was a park-and-walk scheme: in effect, part-time community policing (Trojanowicz et al., 1986).

Foot patrol is not the only definition of community-oriented policing. Skolnick and Bayley (1986) previously outlined some of the major projects of the early 1980s: the combination of sector teams, substations, community mobilization, and outreach to the minority community in Santa Ana; emphasis on crime prevention and a bolstering of the ministation program in Detroit; the Directed Area Response Team (DART) and community storefronts in Houston; Oakland's partnership between the police and the downtown business community. In addition to the cities visited by Skolnick and Bayley, other communities across the United States have been experimenting with a wide variety of programs that are called "community-oriented policing."

The Neighborhood Foot Patrol Program of Flint, Michigan, began as a crime prevention strategy, a limited proactive police effort to supplement traditional rapid response motorized patrol (RMP), and rapidly grew beyond its mandate into something akin to what is called "community policing" (Trojanowicz, 1982).[5] Michigan State University's evaluation of the three-year experiment, using a variety of measures, showed an 8 percent decrease in recorded crime on the foot beat areas during a time when overall crime increased in Flint[6]; a reduction in calls for service; increased citizen perception of safety; increased citizen reporting of crime; greater awareness of community support of police activities (though that was a qualified finding); and, by inference, decreased citizen apathy about crime.

The New York City Police Department's Community Patrol Officer Project (CPOP) was an attempt to incorporate the positive aspects of previous deployment schemes into a new program of police services. Using a general foot beat mode of deployment, the program charged its community patrol officers (CPOs) with a variety of activities in their individual beat areas, including problem identification and community organizing. Planning, problem solving, community organizing, and providing an information link between the department and the community were all articulated roles for the CPOs. Like COPE and the Neighborhood Foot Patrol programs, CPOP was not designed to be primarily an enforcement-focused team. Many of the officers' (and each unit's) measured activities centered on traditional crime prevention activities: meetings, recruiting block watchers, neighborhood safety programs, drug awareness programs, and information dissemination. Enforcement activities were clearly within the mandate of CPOs, however, and the interim report noted that enforcement actions were frequently chosen by CPOs as problem-solving methods (Farrell, 1986:41–42).

As the RECAP experiment was starting, the Mayor's Office created the safety for everyone (SAFE) Unit in Minneapolis to address the findings of a survey of homeowners in the city: a perceived decline in the "livability" of the neighborhoods, particularly those conditions that constitute crime and disorder, was prompting middle-class homeowners to seriously consider moving to the suburbs within the coming five years.

---

[5] Indeed, the National Neighborhood Foot Patrol Center at Michigan State University, evaluators of the Flint project, has recently become the National Center for Community Policing.

[6] The two exceptions to this were robbery and burglary, but the evaluation report notes that those crimes are most prevalent in Flint during the nighttime hours, when foot beat officers were not on duty.

Centered in the civilian-controlled Community Crime Prevention Bureau, many of SAFE's operations paralleled those described for the COPE unit in Baltimore County, particularly in its formal liaison activities with neighborhood groups. In its early phases, SAFE promoted activities like Neighborhood Watch, Block Watch, Operation I.D., and McGruff Houses, which came with ready-made program directions, if no substantial record of success (Rosenbaum, 1986). SAFE subsequently expanded into dissemination of crime information, drug house enforcement activities, and specialized enforcement actions (occasionally in concert with RECAP; the two units supported each other with additional personnel for large scale activities like RECAP's juvenile sweeps and SAFE's party ordinance enforcement in neighborhoods around the University of Minnesota (Buerger, 1992)). The Minneapolis Police have since expanded their commitment to community-oriented policing, responding to citizen initiatives from the Whittier and Jordan neighborhoods experimenting with other special-focus teams, and establishing a community policing bureau equivalent to patrol, investigations and services.

Except for the Minneapolis initiatives, the major documented programs of "community-oriented policing" were originally conceived under other labels. Most of the initiatives began before the community-oriented label achieved its status as a buzzword, and have since been "repackaged" to fit the current marketable interest. Although such redefinition may fuel cynical comments on police faddishness, the redefinition is justifiable: the activities of those programs embody the spirit of community-oriented policing and are more readily measured than the hypothetical benefits of park-and-walk programs.

Problems of Community and Police Identity

These changes in police concern lead to two primary questions with which the police establishment must grapple. First, what substantive role can the community (howsoever defined) play in the desired partnership? Second, how must the police role change to move beyond programmatic functions to a point where community-oriented policing is a mutually recognized description of the relationship of the police to the community they serve?

Defining "Community"

How is "the community" to be defined, and by whom? As has been noted by other commentators (e.g., Mastrofski, 1987; 1988:48ff.), there is no single "community" in our cities. Even in geographically defined, ethnically homogeneous neighborhoods, consensus about goals and methods may be impossible to obtain. If the experience of community organization for the sole purpose of crime prevention is any guide, mere enlistment of participation will be nearly impossible. Yates (1973) reported a "failure to thrive" phenomenon among single-issue community organizations: in some cases, even though there is an "organization," its active membership is small, as small as a single motivated individual.[7] This is hardly "the community," particularly in the commonsense definition that police officers will employ. True community-oriented policing will be obliged to recognize multiple subcommunities within its jurisdictions, sometimes discrete, sometimes overlapping, and sometimes competing and/or antagonistic.

Some such subcommunities already exist and are easily identified; they have an existing formal structure and recognized spokespersons. There is an understandable tendency to tailor community-oriented initiatives to existing organizations, if only to have a place to start. The critical issue, in terms of abuse of the community policing mandate, is that the various existing groups who forge alliances with the police become special interest groups. Just because they exist, they become the de facto definition of the "community" in that area; their collective definition of problems and needs becomes the reality through which the police define operations and community-oriented objectives.

That special relationship creates turf and the possibility that other voices representing other segments of the community of a given area will not be heard (at the conclusion of the RECAP experiment, for instance, at least two separate groups claiming to represent the same neighborhood were jousting for recognition from the City Council). Turf is a two-way street, as well: the community groups who enjoy formal recognition from the police may in turn be vocal advocates for the police before the local political authorities.

The issue has always been subject to rank-and-file manipulation, as line officers tend to define "the community" in terms of the middle-class property owners with whom the police officers most readily identify. Rank-and-file officers promote the "thin blue line" metaphor to establish an "us versus them" dichotomy on police policy issues. "Us" is the natural alliance of the police and the property-owning taxpayer, usually the white middle-class voter who has relatively little need of direct police services. "Them" are the inner-city residents, typically black, latino, or other recognizable minorities, who are often dependent on tax-funded public assistance of one form or another and who have regular contact with the police.

---

[7] Community activist organizations are subject to the danger of a Gresham's Law for voluntary organizations: "bad (or at least highly idiosyncratic) members drive out good."

In its most reprehensible form, "us versus them" plays on white suburban fears of the nonwhite inner-city residents, the "symbolic assailants" (and burglars and rapists), in an effort to thwart efforts to control "street justice" and other reactionary practices by the rank-and-file officers. Defense tactics in the trial of the four Los Angeles police officers accused of criminally beating Rodney King successfully employed this fear-based strategy. The violence and looting that followed the acquittal of those officers in April 1992 demonstrated the catch-22 nature of the "us versus them" appeal: the issue for many commentators and presidential candidates was the reaction rather than the cause, and the police practices that triggered the riots quickly vanished from the public debate.

Even in less vivid terms, the language of community-oriented policing raises the spectre of civil rights violations. A central tenet of both Neighborhood Watch-type crime prevention and community participation in policing has been the identification of "strangers," people who "don't belong" in a neighborhood. This resort to a nostalgic definition is not only at odds with the realities of many sections of today's cities, but opens the door for abuses of constitutional rights on the order of the "California Walkman" case, *Kolender v. Lawson* (461 U.S. 352 (1983)). Civil libertarians object when the police on their own initiative investigate allegedly "suspicious" persons like Mr. Lawson. By actively promoting citizen reports of "suspicious persons" under the guise of "crime prevention" or "coproduction," the police gain the legitimacy of a citizen complaint to intrude on the privacy—the freedom from unwarranted government intrusion—we enjoy even in public spaces, an extension of a point originally made by Reiss (1971) about private spaces.

Equally dangerous, the emphasis on the criminal as a stranger, an outsider, ignores the realities of crime in the inner city. All too often, the predators live in the same neighborhood, just down the block, across the alley, down the hall in the same household. They "belong" in the neighborhood, and are familiar to their victims. They have various ways of knowing who has what worth stealing, and how to gain access to their homes. The tactics devised to thwart an outsider do not address the danger the resident criminals pose to their victims: a constant presence, an ever-present threat, but only episodic materialization of that threat.

To move the community-oriented concept into its next phase, police organizations will have to develop ways to reach out to both the unorganized and the organized-but-unpopular (Mastrofski, 1988:52). At the same time, they must somehow avoid manipulating one of the more readily identifiable subcommunities for illegitimate purposes, as the police unions apparently did with the business community during the "fear city" campaign at the end of the Newark Foot Patrol Experiment (Police Foundation, 1981).

How does a police department empower a "community" to participate in the policing missions, as an equal rather than as a client? What are the mechanisms for defining "the community's" responsibility in law enforcement and order maintenance? And even if such a role can be successfully defined, what are the mechanisms for "holding the community accountable" for fulfilling its end of the bargain? One of the most frustrating tasks for community organizers has been finding a role for citizens that goes beyond just "being the eyes and ears of the police," that is, providing information to the police about criminal activities in their neighborhood. Creating true community empowerment will certainly mean going beyond traditional anticrime activities, moving into social welfare and financing issues that are essentially *terra incognita* for the police. Moreover, such forays into new territory have the potential to pit the police against other competing political interests (Bayley, 1988; Wyckoff, 1988).

Changing the Police

If the police do manage to rouse the sleeping dragon of "the community," they will face a series of corresponding questions that force them to look inward. Traditional crime prevention activities have remained firmly within the control of the police, talking to the community in a benevolent mentor role. True community-oriented policing will require that one-way street to bear two-way traffic. How do the police share power with "the community" (alternatively, how do the police voluntarily surrender autonomy), other than through the formal mechanism of control by elected officials? The pilot projects have not attempted to grapple with this, as they have essentially been testing the waters of the basic concept. Indeed, the New York Police Department describes the CPOP program in these terms:

With these [community involvement] efforts, and *without having ceded any of its authority to the community*, the Department has implemented a strategy which permits citizens to feel that they have some control over their environment. (Farrell, 1986:25)

This is straightforward paternalism, typical of the professional movement's emphasis on the police-as-expert. Giving the citizens a *feeling* of control is not the same as giving them actual control, and some real power—a real mission—may be needed to fully enlist the community in the way envisioned by some community-oriented philosophies.

Even partial success will require dealing with other internal issues. How do police agencies move from programmatic community-oriented policing to a philosophy of community-oriented policing that imbues (and is accepted by) every aspect of departmental operations? How does a department operationalize "community orientation" into its recruitment, orientation, and training functions? These questions become even more critical when community policing moves beyond its current self-selection phase into general applications involving all of the rank-and-file.

At the moment, community-oriented policing appears to be an add-on, another boundary-spanning device similar to the old community relations units, in all but a few cities. For the vast majority of rank-and-file police officers, it is not "real police work," and the officers involved in community-oriented programs are no longer doing police work. CPOP officers reported a lack of department support below command level (Farrell, 1986:79ff.). The Detroit ministation programs quickly became a dumping ground for "expendable personnel" and "report-writing dead-heads," and ministation officers expressed feelings of isolation from the patrol force (Skolnick and Bayley, 1986). Minneapolis patrol officers contemptuously refer to units like SAFE and RECAP as "the ex-police," and express chagrin when officers recognized as "good cops" are assigned to community-oriented units (they also express bewilderment that the officers seek such assignments). So long as the programs remain "extra" or "special" programs, they will be identified as something that is not real police work; to fulfill the promise of community-oriented policing, police managers must find a way to make it real police work.

The basis for equating foot patrol with community-oriented policing lies in the near-mystical belief that taking the police out of the car will magically produce a better relationship between police officers and the citizens they police. That improved relationship will burst the dam of resentment that has held back from the police vital information about crime. Once community-oriented policing is established, citizens will become "the eyes and ears of the police," providing timely information that will permit the police to suppress criminal activity. The police will then be able to fulfill their professional mission of crime control in a way that they have been unable to do heretofore.

There is limited evidence that this transformation is automatic. To date, the Flint program has the only well-documented claim to success in terms of reduced crime and calls for service. Flint, Newark, and Boston (among others) reported an increase in citizen satisfaction with the police or increased perceptions of safety as a result of foot patrol efforts, but the Police Foundation's evaluation of the Newark Foot Patrol Experiment found no statistically significant evidence of crime reduction as an outcome of foot patrol deployment (Police Foundation, 1981:5).

Moreover, the Newark Foot Patrol Experiment's findings contain some indications that even the public's "warm fuzzies" for foot patrol deployment may decay over time. The preponderance of statistically significant differences in the foot patrol study occurred only in the "added beat" areas, but not in those beat areas where foot patrol was retained (with some notable exceptions that appear to be idiosyncratic). This suggests that beneficial effects occur initially as the result of the novelty of a program, not necessarily as a function of the program itself.

More important, however, may be the deterioration of the initial "warm fuzzies" for the officers involved. Pilot projects of community-oriented policing for the most part have thrived through the efforts and enthusiasm of the already converted. Most of the successful new programs discussed here and in other publications owe much of their success to the enthusiasm of the officers themselves. Almost all of the pilot or experimental programs were started with volunteers[8] and evaluated after a fairly short time in the field; most of them involve relatively small numbers of officers.

Officers who volunteer for community-oriented pilots are naturally those most amenable to closer, friendlier contacts with the public. In addition, they achieve a new social setting (both within the department, linking up with other self-selecting volunteers, and in the community), which we reasonably might expect would act as positive reinforcement for the officers.

Practitioners and academic observers of the police note that there is a "seven-year burnout" syndrome: after about seven years in any job, cops begin to get stale and grouchy, sliding into cynicism and bad work habits. The other side of that coin—recorded only in a series of anecdotal observations at this point—is that even the worst burnout case can be revived and "put back on the rails" by a positive change of assignment. Whether it is a product of the Hawthorne Effect of a new social arrangement (Roethlisberger and Dickson, 1939) or simply the response to the challenge of a new learning situation, officers generally respond positively to a change in assignment (both in self-reports and in supervisors' evaluations).

Two of the officers assigned to RECAP described themselves in similar terms, expressing a desire to find some different way to meet their personal goal for being a police officer. Their initial success provided positive feedback to their role change, and by midyear, both their mood and citizen reaction to the project were positive. By the end of the experimental year, however, after the initial successes had been removed from the active caseload, and the officers were working only on the intractable addresses, the initial mood had deteriorated, and frustration had set in over a lack of coercive tools to bring to bear on the slumlords and managers who refused to cooperate with this new, positive police profile (Buerger, 1992).

Additional stress is involved in taking on as ambitious and nebulous a task as "establishing community-oriented policing." The COPE teams

---

[8] CPOP involved volunteer sergeants and volunteer officers (Farrell, 1986:9–10); the RECAP and Whittier officers were hand-picked volunteers, as are many SAFE officers; the Flint and Houston projects either recruited "the best and the brightest" or gave foot patrol officers much greater latitude in picking their assignments than would be expected in routine police operations (Wycoff, 1988).

essentially floundered through their first phase (Cordner, 1985); RECAP officers experienced periodic bouts of frustration when their well of ideas ran dry; and in New York,

[b]ecause they lack knowledge and skills in the non-traditional areas of involvement, it is generally very difficult for the CPOs to conceptualize roles for the community in areas which heretofore were viewed as being the sole responsibility of the police. (Farrell, 1986:76)

These findings hint at long-term effects similar to those noted during the Cincinnati Team Policing experiment, wherein initial gains in job breadth and job satisfaction eroded by the end of eighteen months (Wyckoff, 1988:113, citing Schwartz and Clarren), although the source of the difficulties may have been different in Cincinnati.

It is perhaps as unreasonable to draw negative conclusions as it is to draw positive ones at this stage: part of the process should properly be learning how to cope with such frustrations and developing mechanisms that problem- or community-oriented officers can use to refresh their attitudes.

One final question remains. Can the essence of community-oriented policing be transferred to those officers who do *not* self-select for the special programs?

There would be no need for the police establishment to be talking about "community-oriented" policing if not for the fact that the police have lost—police critics would say "forfeited"—the respect and support of a significant segment of the community they police. In that sense, community-oriented policing to date is only a bit more than the old "police–community relations problem" come back to life. At issue is the character of everyday interactions between the police and the citizens of the community, particularly those citizens who receive the lion's share of direct police service: the poor, the chemically dependent, the socially disorganized, the visible minorities.

Basically, the dilemma is this. The street cop culture truly and firmly believes that "kick ass and take names" (e.g., Skolnick and Bayley, 1986:13) is the best way to do both crime control and "asshole control" (Van Maanen, 1978:221). To the street cops, the status quo of law enforcement is the Cadillac of police service, and the police subculture constitutes an assembly line that continues to produce that model. To the street cops, management's attempts to impose rules constraining that model are attempts to "fix something that ain't broken" (an outright denial, of course, of the signals from other sources—the community and their political representatives, the courts, juries making awards in civil suits, etc.—that if "it ain't broken," it's definitely in need of a tune-up).

Enter the consumer advocates, particularly those whose constituencies both demand the greatest amount of service from the police and receive the brunt of the reprehensible police practices that still lurk in the street cop culture: the verbal denigrations, the "beat-and-release" practices designed to "teach respect" to the disrespectful, and so on.[9] The consumer advocates scoff at the Cadillac image, claiming that the police product is actually an Edsel: "half of [the city's] residents fear the police almost as much as they do the city's hoodlums and thugs" (Skolnick and Bayley, 1986:11). "Sales" fall off; no longer is community respect automatic, and increased criticism of police operations is heard. Management cops respond to these market pressures as professional managers do, by taking a long, hard look at their product.

Finding evidence that supports an "Edsel" theory more than a "Cadillac" one, the management responds by designing and marketing a new vehicle, calling it problem- or community-oriented policing. The plans look good, the developmental models wow the heck out of the public in test marketing, and the new models are rushed into mass production as something the police can *do* about the crisis.

Unfortunately, the new models go into mass production on the same assembly line that produced the Edsel. The end result is not a Cadillac or even a new car, but the same old Edsel with a Cadillac hood ornament slapped on it. The public may be fooled for a little while, but when the glitz of the advertising campaign wears off, what is left is still basically an Edsel.

Reuss-Ianni's observations in *Two Cultures of Policing* do not include another salient feature of management cop culture: it is self-perpetuating. Management cops are constantly on the lookout for promising young cops who can be either assigned to or groomed for skill positions that require sensitivities greater than those that imbue the street cop culture: the police establishment's version of "the fast track." Because the field is still limited to its historical profile, with no lateral entry, management cops find their new blood in the ranks of the street cops. Those who qualify for the fast track generally come to the attention of the upper levels by

---

[9] "[Reiss and Black] found—based on field observation of Boston, Chicago, and Washington, D.C. police by thirty-six observers—that 72 percent of the officers expressed either 'extreme' or 'considerable prejudice.' Those views were not solicited but were recorded when voluntarily expressed" (Skolnick and Bayley, 1986:21–22, citing Reiss and Black, "Patterns of Behavior in Police and Citizen Transactions," from the report of the President's Commission on Law Enforcement and the Administration of Criminal Justice, Washington, DC: Department of Justice, 1976). What is most striking about the quote is that three-quarters of the officers *volunteered* these statements, as though orienting the observers to the "realities" of street-cop culture. Though an entire generation of police officers has come of age since those observations were made, and the proportions are perhaps balanced by more officers whose beliefs lie in other quarters, periodic headlines, anecdotal information, and videotapes keep reminding us that these attitudes remain deeply entrenched in certain elements of the police community.

their reputation as "good cops"; that is, they are street cops whose aggressiveness and street-smarts impress the formal and natural leadership of the street cop ranks. Potential management cops are marked for advancement by a combination of street cop skills and management cop attitudes, and are usually removed from their on-street apprenticeship as soon as a skill or promotional position is available. The circumstances of their departure engender resentment, which leads in turn to the trivialization of their assignments (if not of the officers themselves) in the street cop culture: not real police work.[10]

One practical effect of this is to reinforce the street–management split. The natural leaven of officers who have earned the respect of their peers, but nevertheless have the community-oriented attitudes encouraged by management, is removed from the environment where their influence is most needed. Management cops essentially abandon the field of policing's moral issues to the entrenched reactionary elements of the street-cop culture. A second practical result, as discussed earlier, is the placement of highly motivated officers onto an emotional rollercoaster of early success followed by slow or rapid deterioration of the situation when initial expectations prove too difficult to achieve, repeat, or sustain. As a worst case, the department stands to lose the commitment of the good officers; but even in the best case, it does not enlist the buy-in of the largest portion of its officers.

Community-oriented policing enjoys the luxury of voluntarism. Community-oriented police *programs* are conducted outside the normal realm of police business. Someone else—the street cop—takes the brunt of all the nasty calls, the tedium of twenty-four-hour availability, and the frustration of the endless stream of calls to reinforce the private order (Reiss, 1971) of unpleasant or dysfunctional people. The acid test for community-oriented policing will be when it leaves the sanitary and well-organized confines of Neighborhood Watch meetings; when the torch is passed from the best and the brightest to the Joe Lunchbuckets of the department; when COP has to move beyond voluntarism to become a mandatory performance criterion in the turbulent world of call-driven police work.

It is at this point, if it ever arrives, that the dangers of illegal policing and of corruption of the police–community relationship are greatest. Elements of the police establishment even now deliberately exploit class differences—"us" and "them"—in an attempt to gain community support

---

[10] A frequent lament among first-line supervisors in the Minneapolis Police Department during the author's tenure there was that management kept taking all the good young cops away from them, leaving the slugs and the attitude problems in the precincts. Sergeants and lieutenants recognize instinctively that they, too, would benefit—that is, their work life would be much easier—if they had more of the services of these good cops.

for punitive street justice. In a community- or problem-oriented context, with the additional support of some of the more conservative academic commentators (e.g., Wilson and Kelling, 1982; Wilson, 1983), that manipulation would undoubtedly continue, further eroding the equal protection supposedly afforded to all citizens.

Officers who do not share the commitment to the values of community policing manipulate citizens' fear of crime, attempting to make the community an alternate source of authority (against professional police management) that will approve street justice as a legitimate police tactic. Management will still be responsible for making its officers conform to accepted professional standards (Weisburd et al., 1988); even if the street cop half of the police establishment forsakes its commitment to equal justice, the courts will not. Management will still have a legal responsibility to maintain means-based supervision, even when it means forfeiting the ends-oriented results that it promulgated in the first place. The result is a mixed message to both the community and the cops.

The potential for exacerbating the already tense relations between management and street cop cultures is great. If the street cops do manage to muster local community support behind illegitimate police practices (so long as they are applied to jointly determined targets), management will be in a position of having to "negotiate police conduct with the community," as has been previously suggested by Bayley (1988). Street cops alone do not have great leverage to oppose proper management dictates, union interference notwithstanding. Street cops acting in concert with a fearful or vindictive community, on the other hand, have a political proxy through which bring pressure on management *against* professional controls on police behavior. It would be ironic if management's positive community-oriented initiatives were to be subverted by street cops, but it would not be entirely unprecedented.

In this context, however, the fragmentation of "the community" may weigh against attempts by street cops to subvert professionalism and its managerial controls. The very phrase *community oriented* implies that the police will be responsive to the concerns of the community, and one of the greatest complaints that "the community" has had over the years is the way that some cops treat citizens. Officers working in middle- and working-class neighborhoods may have a chance to win the majority of the residents over to their side, plumping the "thin blue line" image to defend the community from "them"; officers working in disadvantaged neighborhoods, essentially neighborhoods inhabited by "them," will not have such an opportunity. In theory, the professional control tactics employed against corruption (including frequent rotation of assignments to thwart the development of special relationships) could be used to defeat rank-and-file sabotage of police professionalism. Less certain at this point is whether the relative unity of the police rank-and-file citywide will outweigh the fragmentation of locally defined neighborhood communities.

Even were the worst-case scenario to come about, it is not certain that it would last long. Community support for illegitimate police tactics will last only as long as the tactics are exclusively applied to a jointly recognized "them." The history of police abuses suggests that once set loose, street police officers discard precise target discrimination fairly quickly. The supposed community allies of the police may find themselves on the receiving end of the illegitimate tactics, sundering the alliance and creating anew the cycle of community opposition to police excess.

All of this assumes a successful transition to a new police–citizen relationship that is recognizable as "community oriented." So long as community-oriented policing remains just a matter of deployment—riding on the assumption that the desired benefits will automatically fall from the tree of good intentions—what we are now calling community-oriented policing will likely fall on the already large dustheap of police innovation, replaced by a newer and sexier acronym or label. One-directional programs like crime prevention and horse patrols, and even some manifestations of community-oriented policing, vest all control within the police department and leave no room for community participation (except as passive consumers of what the police choose to market).

Although the special programs provide eye candy and a temporary feel-good relationship between the public and a hand-picked group of officers, they do not fundamentally alter the basic core of police–community interactions. True community-oriented policing cannot be made a reality by small programs or even large-scale foot patrol or park-and-walk deployments; police attitudes and the substantive nature of how the police treat *all* members of the community, not just those who show deference and appreciation, must be addressed. This leaves the police establishment still facing what Wilson describes as "the bureaucracy problem . . . getting the front-line worker . . . to 'do the right thing'" (Wilson, 1973:2–3) to make true community-oriented policing a reality.

Reinventing the police is all but impossible; the police rank-and-file energetically defend their prerogatives. Reinventing the community is almost as difficult; the most that can be done is to redefine it in symbolic terms. In a sense, the greater the emphasis placed on "community" in management-initiated police programs, the stronger the sense of "us," which inevitably requires a "them." The language and symbols of reform and innovation are not the exclusive property of police management. They are available to the entrenched, reactionary elements of street cop culture who have learned how to protect the cherished technology of policing by co-opting the language of change.

The great hazard of endeavors of "reinvention," especially those that are primarily philosophical and not well grounded in knowledge of police operations, is that reinvention will turn on itself. The reinvention itself becomes reinvented, subverted into a cloak that disguises business as usual. Cast in the symbolic terms of reinvention, business as usual avoids the normal scrutiny that might be given to police operations. In this sense, the "success" and "failure" of such innovations become largely a matter of who is most adept at manipulating the symbols.

True reinvention of the police's relationship to the communities they serve will require a major retooling of the conceptual framework of police work. A major task of that effort will be to bring the police subculture to view police work in the terms outlined by Goldstein, reducing the importance of the crimefighting definition, enhancing the despised social work component, and convincing serving and recruit police officers of the propriety of the changes. That will require bucking the riptide of the police subculture and socialization. It will not happen magically, through the incantation of carefully chosen phrases, nor will it continue of its own accord without strong, lasting intervention and nurturance by both police managers and community leaders.

The bureaucracy problem defined by Wilson—"getting the front-line worker . . . to do the right thing"—is still very much with us as we seek to reinvent or redefine the police. We are merely at the first stage, having reinvented our sense of what "the right thing" is.

References

Bayley, D.H. (1988). Community Policing: A Report From the Devil's Advocate. In Greene, J.R. and S.D. Mastrofski (Eds.), *Community Policing: Rhetoric or Reality*. New York: Praeger.

Brown, M. (1981). *Working the Street*. New York: Russell Sage.

Buerger, M.E. (Ed.). (1992). *The Crime Prevention Casebook: Securing High Crime Locations*. Washington, DC: Crime Control Institute.

Cordner, G.W. (November 1985). *The Baltimore County Citizen Oriented Police Enforcement (COPE) Project: Final Evaluation*. Presented at the American Society of Criminology, San Diego, CA.

Eck, J.E. and W. Spelman. (1987). *Problem Solving: Problem-Oriented Policing in Newport News*. Washington, DC: Police Executive Research Forum.

Farrell, M.J. (1986). *C.P.O.P. The Community Patrol Officer Program: Interim Progress Report Number 2*. New York: Vera Institute of Justice.

Goldstein, H. (1979). Improving Policing: A Problem-Oriented Approach. *Crime and Delinquency 25*, No. 2:236–258.

Goldstein, H. (June 1987). Comments to the Plenary Session on Problem-Oriented Policing of the Conference *on Policing: State of the Art III*, Phoenix, AZ.

Goldstein, H. (1990). *Problem-Oriented Policing*. Philadelphia, PA: Temple University Press.

Goldstein, H. and C.E. Susmilch. (1981). *The Problem-Oriented Approach to Improving Police Service: A Description of the Project and an Elaboration of the Concept*. Unpublished Manuscript, University of Wisconsin Law School Madison, WI.

Goldstein, H. and C.E. Susmilch. (1982a). *The Drinking-Driver in Madison: A Study of the Problem and the Community's Response*. Unpublished Manuscript, University of Wisconsin Law School Madison, WI.

Goldstein, H. and C.E. Susmilch. (1982b). *The Repeat Sexual Offender in Madison: A Memorandum on the Problem and the Community's Response*.

Unpublished Manuscript, University of Wisconsin Law School Madison, WI.

Goldstein, H. and C.E. Susmilch. (1982c). *The Problem-Oriented Approach to Improving Police Service: A Report and Some Reflections on Two Case Studies.* Unpublished Manuscript, University of Wisconsin Law School Madison, WI.

Greene, J.R. and S.R. Mastrofski. (1988). *Community Policing: Rhetoric or Reality.* New York: Praeger.

Klockars, C.B. and S.D. Mastrofski. (1991). *Thinking About Police: Contemporary Readings.* 2nd ed. New York: McGraw-Hill.

Manning, P.K. (1980). *The Narcs' Game.* Cambridge, MA: MIT Press.

Manning, P.K. and J. Van Maanen (Eds.). *Policing: A View From the Street.* New York: Random House.

Mastrofski, S.D. (May 1987). *Dilemmas of Reform: Some Difficult Problems for Community Policing.* Paper delivered at the International Symposium on Community Policing, Temple University, Philadelphia, PA.

Mastrofski, S.D. (1988). Community Policing as Reform: A Cautionary Tale. In Greene, J.R. and S.D. Mastrofski (Eds.), *Community Policing: Rhetoric or Reality.* New York: Praeger.

Police Foundation. (1981). *The Newark Foot Patrol Experiment.* Washington, DC: Police Foundation.

Reiss, A.J., Jr. (1971). *The Police and the Public.* New Haven, CT: Yale University Press.

Reuss-Ianni, E. (1983). *Two Cultures of Policing: Street Cops and Management Cops.* New Brunswick, NJ: Transaction Books.

Roethlisberger, F.J. and W.J. Dickson. (1939). *Management and the Worker.* Cambridge, MA: Harvard University Press.

Rosenbaum, D.P. (Ed.). (1986). *Sage Criminal Justice System Annuals.* Vol. 22: *Community Crime Prevention: Does It Work?* Beverly Hills, CA: Sage.

Sherman, L.W. (1987). *Repeat Calls to Police in Minneapolis.* Washington, DC: Crime Control Institute.

Sherman, L.W. and R.A. Berk. (1984). The Specific Deterrent Effects of Arrest for Domestic Assault. *American Sociological Review* 49:261–272.

Sherman, L.W., M.E. Buerger, P.R. Gartin, et al. (1988). *Policing Repeat Calls. The Minneapolis RECAP Experiment.* Preliminary Report to the National Institute of Justice. Washington, DC: Crime Control Institute.

Sherman, L.W., M.E. Buerger, P.R. Gartin, et al. (1989). *Repeat Call Address Policing. The Minneapolis RECAP Experiment.* Final Report to the National Institute of Justice. Washington, DC: Crime Control Institute.

Sherman, L.W. and E.G. Cohn. (1987). *Police Policy on Domestic Violence, 1986: A National Survey.* Crime Control Reports No. 5. Washington, DC: Crime Control Institute.

Skolnick, J.H. and D.H. Bayley. (1986). *The New Blue Line: Police Innovation in Six American Cities.* New York: Free Press.

Trojanowicz, R. (1982). *An Evaluation of the Neighborhood Foot Patrol Program in Flint, Michigan.* East Lansing, MI: National Neighborhood Foot Patrol Center (Michigan State University).

Trojanowicz, R., B. Pollard, F. Colgan, and H. Harden. (1986). *Community Policing Programs: A Twenty-Year Review.* Community Policing Series No. 10. East Lansing, MI: Michigan State University, National Neighborhood Foot Patrol Center.

Van Maanen, J. (1978). The Asshole. In Manning, P.K. and J. Van Maanen, (Eds.), *Policing: A View From the Street*. New York: Random House. Pp. 221–238.

Weisburd, D., J. McElroy, and P. Hardyman. (1988). Challenges to Supervision in Community Policing: Observations on a Pilot Project. *American Journal of Police 7*, No. 2:29–50.

Wilson, J.Q. (1973). *Varieties of Police Behavior*. New York: Atheneum.

Wilson, J.Q. (1975). *Thinking About Crime*. New York: Basic Books.

Wilson, J.Q. (1983). *Thinking About Crime*. Rev. ed. New York: Basic Books.

Wilson, J.Q. and G. Kelling. (1982). The Police and Neighborhood Safety: Broken Windows. *Atlantic Monthly* 127, March: 29–38.

Wyckoff, M.A. (1988). The Benefits of Community Policing: Evidence and Conjecture. In Greene, J.R. and S.D. Mastrofski (Eds.), *Community Policing: Rhetoric or Reality*. New York: Praeger. Pp. 103–120.

Yates, D. (1973). *Neighborhood Democracy: The Politics and Impacts of Decentralization*. Lexington, MA: Lexington Books.

Part IV
Problems of Law, Order, and Community in Comparative Context

7
The Soviet Police and the Rule of Law*

LOUISE SHELLEY

During Gorbachev's five years as a reformer (1985–1990), he launched *perestroika*. This effort to modernize the Soviet economy and transform the nature of Soviet society had the creation of a law-based state as one of its fundamental objectives. Gorbachev believed that economic reform was possible only if the state and its institutions learned to observe and respect the law. Central to this political and legal transformation was a change in the relationship between the citizen and the state. According to this perspective, individuals should not be compelled by the state but should voluntarily comply with legal norms. In return, the executors of state authority—the police and other law enforcement bodies—would be expected to respect individual rights.

In the late 1980s, for the first time in seventy years of Soviet history, the regular police (*militsiia*) were expected to abide by the rule of law. A dramatic effort was made to change Soviet policing to correspond to this new legalistic model. No longer were the police to be communicators of the will of a hegemonic party and the enforcers of the state ideology.

---

* This chapter was completed in the final period of Gorbachev's rule and before the demise of the Soviet Union. The piece anticipates many of the problems that made the transformation of the Soviet Union so difficult and its dissolution a possible outcome.

The decline of police authority in the late 1980s and early 1990s and their loss of control contributed to their participation in the coup attempt of August 1991 which accelerated the collapse of the Soviet state. The legacy of the Soviet system still remains in the newly established countries formed out of the former Soviet Union. They are operating with the same law enforcement personnel, often under the same legal codes with the same bureaucracy. The ethnic tensions discussed in this chapter have not disappeared in the post-Soviet state. Rather, in many cases the Soviet legacy and the deliberate policies of the newly independent countries have exacerbated the level of ethnic conflict. The Party apparatus and the Party mandate are gone but the tradition of subservience to authority still prevails among police personnel. Consequently, the obstacles to observing the rule of law are as significant as during the Soviet period, and in many of the new Asian countries, the problems may be more severe than in the period of *perestroika*.

They were, instead, to maintain order and protect the citizenry. The realization of this objective required significant changes both in police leadership and in the line personnel who execute orders.

New reformist leadership was brought in at the top, corrupt officials were prosecuted, and tens of thousands of individuals were expelled from the force in an effort to promote respect for legal norms. Thousands of exposés appeared on television and in the press revealing the consequences of police abuse of power. The revelations even further reduced citizen respect for the police, making it difficult to replace the personnel expelled from the force. A crisis in policing ensued. This crisis resulted both from the collapsing credibility of the law enforcers and, perhaps more importantly, from the declining political authority of the central government whose will the police represented.

Perestroika unleashed many forces within Soviet society. Among the most powerful of these were rising nationalism among the diverse peoples of the Soviet Union and a growing political and legal consciousness. Nationalism and democratization both directly challenged the centrally organized police, and efforts to promote change on the local and republic level promoted a backlash from the center directly contravening the principles of the rule of law.

Citizens of the diverse republics no longer wanted a police force directed by the central government in Moscow and dominated by Russians. Instead, many republics sought autonomous police forces that would be responsive to the needs of their citizenry rather than the directives of the Moscow-based national bureaucracy. The republics' challenge to Soviet authority proved more than the conservative military and Party elite could accept. In a crushing and symbolic blow to the burgeoning independent law enforcement systems of the republics, military and Soviet Ministry of Internal Affairs troops bloodily reasserted authority in January 1991 over the breakaway Latvian and Lithuanian police forces by occupying these republics' ministries of internal affairs (the bodies responsible for Soviet policing) (Schmemann, 1991). A similar but less bloody struggle followed in the capital. In Moscow, in a desperate effort to suppress pro-Yeltsin supporters who challenged the authority of the central government, Gorbachev transferred jurisdiction of the Moscow city police to the Russian national interior ministry to try and avert anti-Gorbachev demonstrations (Clines, 1991).

The violent acts in the Baltic republics and the confrontation over policing authority in Moscow occurred because a coalition of top-ranking officials in the military, the military–industrial complex, the Party, and the secret police successfully reasserted control over the direction of national policy. In December 1990, these political conservatives and reactionaries, the so-called "forces of order" in the Soviet Union, achieved hegemony on the national level. The implications for policing were immediate and highly visible. The reformist Minister of Internal

Affairs, Bakatin, who had tried to make the police subordinate to the law rather than the will of the Party apparatus, was ousted and replaced by Pugo, a hardline KGB (secret police) official. If his ouster were not enough of a signal that the rule of law was no longer an immediate goal of the Soviet state, Gorbachev made this explicitly clear several days later. In mid-December 1990, Gorbachev proclaimed: "Unfortunately, our society is not ready for the procedures of a law-based state. We don't have that level of political culture, those traditions. All that will come in the future" (Remnick, 1990).

The police reforms of the *perestroika* period, in retrospect, appear to be a short deviation from a long historical tradition dating back to the Tsarist period, in which the law enforcers considered themselves above rather than subordinate to the law. The struggle to make the police suddenly abide by the rule of law was difficult in a society with an authoritarian tradition without a well-developed legal consciousness.

The Rule of Law: Comparative Perspectives

Most of the other contributors to this book discuss the move away from the rule of law in U.S. policing. To draw an analogy between the Soviet Union and the United States is difficult. In the United States, the foundations for a legal order remain even though there may be a distinct erosion of individual civil liberties and an augmentation of police powers. But in the Soviet Union, within a matter of weeks the government managed to undo many of the many major reforms in the law enforcement apparatus that had been achieved with such difficulty from 1985 to 1990. This reversal could occur so rapidly because the rule of law was never institutionalized under Gorbachev. Justice institutions remained tools of the state and Party apparatus rather than independent institutions subordinate to a higher legal order. A more appropriate analogy concerning the rapid transition away from the rule of law might be made to Latin American countries. In many of these countries without well-established legal traditions, a political coup quickly erases the gains in civil liberties achieved during a period of democratization.

The United States and the former Soviet Union have divergent legal cultures and different attitudes toward political authority. In the Soviet Union, unlike in the United States, neither the state nor the citizen paid much attention to the law and individuals did not have recourse against state authority. The Constitution and the Bill of Rights lie at the core of American society and values. But in the Soviet Union, law had never been considered fundamental. According to the ideology, law was always considered part of the superstructure. There were no inalienable rights.

The U.S. two-party system has provided a check on the limits of the law. Furthermore, the division in authority among the legislative, judicial, and executive branches has helped ensure that no branch of government has an exclusive ability to enforce its will. But in the Soviet Union, political authority was both centralized and concentrated. Until recently, the Communist Party had a constitutionally recognized monopoly of political power. Without competing political interests, there could be no checks on the authority of the ruling party. In the United States, the courts have served as a check on the administrative apparatus of the state including the police. In contrast, in the Soviet Union, the courts' traditional role was to uphold the interests of the state whether they conflicted with the rule of law or the interests of the citizenry. There were few options for the citizen to contest the exercise of police power.

These circumstances created a different relationship between the citizen and legal authority, particularly with respect to policing. In the United States, there is state commitment to rule based on consensus rather than coercion. During the post-World War II period, individual rights were enhanced by the Supreme Court under Justice Warren. The balance of power between the citizen and the state shifted. Defendants, already enjoying certain protections under the law, saw their rights enhanced often at the expense of police authority. Although police brutality still remains a major problem, defendants enjoy Miranda rights and other protections that are even now unknown in Russia. In the Soviet Union, only under *perestroika* did a shift in the balance between state authority and citizen rights begin to occur. But even as Gorbachev and legal reformers advocated such a shift, there were few governmental mechanisms to ensure that the new legal norms would be respected. The press rather than any institutionalized mechanisms within the established legal structure ensured greater respect for the rule of law.

The police remained outside of citizen control. In the United States, civilian controls exist over the police. The Department of Justice and the courts have taken action against police officials who have exceeded their authority. Although the Commission of Security and Cooperation in Europe Vienna agreements (part of the Helsinki process), of which the Soviet Union was a signatory, requires that the police and military be under civilian control, the Soviet Union failed to abide by this fundamental principle of a law-governed state. In this important respect, the Soviet Union, even failed to conform to the structural requirements deemed necessary by Western democracies for the control of police activity.

United States courts, in the postwar period, have been at the forefront of police reform, establishing clearly defined limits for permissible law enforcement practice. In contrast, Soviet courts traditionally failed to protect the citizens from overzealous law enforcers who violated legal procedures. Rather, until recently, Soviet courts were defenders of the Party rather than the individual.

An adage of Western policing is that the more nasty the reputation of the police, the less nasty they have to be in the field (Ker Muir, 1977). This generalization about policing was not applicable to the Soviet Union because, until Brezhnev's death, the Soviet *militsiia* operated with almost total impunity.[1] Illegal investigative techniques such as unauthorized wiretaps were used as evidence in court, and physical abuse of defendants and witnesses was the rule because it yielded confessions that were accepted without challenge by judges. Citizens rarely had the opportunity to challenge in court police officers who had maimed or killed civilians. Recourse for less serious encroachments on individual rights was nearly precluded.

The courts did not intervene to remedy police misconduct, and no external watchdog required the police to adhere to a certain level of professional conduct. Furthermore, the *militsiia* did not need to police itself because the law enforcers had no accountability to the community or to the law. They were not concerned with representing the will or the values of Soviet citizens. Instead, their exclusive responsibility was to the Party.

The move away from the rule of law is driven by different forces in the United States and the Soviet Union. In the United States, an increasingly conservative electorate has resulted in a judiciary and legislature that seek to limit some of the civil liberties granted in the previous decades. But in the Soviet Union, a reactionary political elite forced the rejection of a still popular legal direction—the enhancement of individual rights. The reason for these differences is that the decisions and policies of U.S. legal institutions cannot be undone merely by a single presidential decree, as in the Soviet Union, but only as the result of numerous court decisions and legislative actions. Attitudes toward the rule of law could be reversed rapidly in the Soviet Union because, unlike in the United States, power was concentrated almost exclusively in the center and legal institutions were weak.

In the United States, the more restrictive interpretation of legal rights is evident in many facets of U.S. society, not only in the area of policing. The police move away from the rule of law discussed by many of the contributors to this book is only part of a shifting political balance that enhances the state's right rather than that of the individual. Conversely, in an authoritarian society like the Soviet Union, police attitudes toward the rule of law constitute a major barometer of state power. Consequently, the first and clearest signs of the dramatic reassertion of authoritarian politics in December 1990 were the visible shift in the police leadership,

---

[1] An exception might be a limited period in the Khrushchev years when some militia misconduct was punished.

the enhancement of police powers, and the greater visibility of law enforcers on the streets in joint police–military patrols.

Advocates of the rule of law in the Soviet Union recognized that the transition toward a state where legal institutions, including the police, abide by the rule of law was going to be much slower than previously recognized in the first euphoric stages of *perestroika*. With the collapse of the Soviet state, any move toward the rule of law that may occur in the newly independent countries will occur against a backdrop of major political change. The movement toward the rule of law in parts of the former Soviet Union will not occur, as in the United States during the postwar period, in an orderly fashion through established legal and civil institutions.

Sources

This chapter is based on a great variety of sources. It draws on interview data, published and unpublished works, as well as legislative sources. Interviews were held with former police personnel in Israel and the United States. Recently, with the greater openness in the Soviet Union, it was possible to conduct interviews with high-level *militsiia* personnel. The Soviet Ministry of the Interior (MVD) and legal publications available in the Soviet Union and abroad were used. Published and unpublished legislation available in the West was reviewed to gain an understanding of the scope of *militsiia* activity. The Smolensk Party archives, seized by the Germans in World War II, were examined for their reports on *militsiia* conduct in the 1920s and 1930s. *Samizdat* (unofficial writings illegally circulated in the Soviet Union) were used to analyze the political dimensions of *militsiia* work.

The *militsiia*, which was once a taboo topic, became a subject of central concern in the Soviet mass media as reformers sought to restructure the regular police. Extensive use was made of Soviet periodicals that carry very explicit accounts of *militsiia* performance. The heavy reliance on Soviet materials has been necessary as there has been neither Western research in the field nor the site access that might accompany such a study on a more open society.

History of Soviet Policing

Police history in the Soviet Union as in Western societies can be divided into different periods. Whereas in the United States complex political and social forces make it difficult to delineate the precise years of a particular period, in the Soviet Union, where the *militsiia* was tied to national politics, the eras of policing can quite naturally be divided by the succession of Party secretaries. Different periods of Soviet policing exist coinciding with the different stages in the development and leadership of the Party.

The first period from the Soviet revolution in 1917 to Stalin's death in 1953 marks the birth of the Soviet *militsiia* under Lenin and its development under Stalin. The first years of the Soviet state were highly unstable. The Bolsheviks, a minority group, defeated internal opposition to consolidate their power. The Soviet Union was again engaged in bloody conflict as they faced the German onslaught during World War II.

The Bolshevik leadership moved quickly in 1917 to abolish the hated Tsarist police. Although only a few prerevolutionary police personnel were permitted to serve the new Soviet state (Eropkin, 1967), the new Bolshevik leadership adopted the local organizational structure and many of the methods of the Tsarist police. The new workers' and peasants' police, entitled the *militsiia*, remained a tool of state policy as in the prerevolutionary period. Furthermore, the police intrusion into politics that prevailed under the Tsar continued under the Bolsheviks.

From the first days after the revolution, the newly constituted *militsiia* worked with the army and the Cheka (the secret police), to which it was subordinate, to ensure Bolshevik control of Soviet society. In the face of massive opposition to Soviet power, the police ignored the few laws that existed. Their primary goals were political. They could not focus on legal rights even for ordinary criminals, because all elements of the society were forced to conform to the will of the state and the Party.

From its formation, the *militsiia* had sweeping social and economic responsibilities (Eropkin, 1967), even though its focus was primarily on ensuring political control. The poorly staffed and trained body was hard put to perform even a delimited number of tasks. In Moscow and the western Slavic regions where the Bolsheviks managed to secure and maintain control without great internal strife, the *militsiia* was able to perform such traditional police tasks as catching criminals and detaining drunks (Shchelokov, 1971). In many parts of the Soviet Union, particularly in Siberia and Central Asia, where the Soviets faced strong opposition, *militsiia* members were civil war participants. Soviet chroniclers of early *militsiia* history describe them as a militarized body no less brutal then the regular army in combatting opposition (Dzalilov, 1968, 1970; Motylev and Lysenko, 1967; Mukhamedov, 1965).

Following the civil war and the suppression of the Central Asian opposition, the *militsiia* turned to other pressing problems of internal order. They aided in the purges of political opponents, but their primary responsibilities were economic and social. They tried to control banditry, embezzlement, *kolkhoz* (collective farm) disorders, and harvesting crimes, as well as the usual array of offenses (Fainsod, 1958). Years of revolution and internal strife created large numbers of homeless youth. Youth bands and armed marauders became primary foci of *militsiia* efforts. The passport system, still one of the strongest *militsiia* controls over the population, was introduced in 1932 to control the mass rural-to-urban migration that accompanied collectivization (Conquest, 1968).

The state was militarized and so were the police. The *militsiia* and the secret police were merged into the nearly omnipotent NKVD (People's Commissariat of Internal Affairs). Social control was subordinate to other police functions as the citizens' protection was not the state's priority. Political and economic control of the Soviet Union was the primary objective of the Soviet police under Lenin and Stalin.

It is this historical legacy that has made the rule of law so difficult to implement. Soviet society never fully and openly confronted the crimes of Stalinism. Furthermore, the generation raised under Stalin lacked a legal consciousness, and members of the legal apparatus quickly learned the costs of legalism over expediency. Citizens still view the law as a tool of repression rather than a vehicle for the expression of rights.

The second period (1953–1963) comprises the years of the post-Stalin transition and of Khrushchev's leadership. Social and economic policy received priority rather than political order. The *militsiia* tried to meet the demands of an increasingly complex industrialized society.

In 1953 the MVD was separated from the KGB (the security police) to de-Stalinize policing. This was an important step in isolating political control from ordinary crime control activity. It reduced the terror instilled by the law enforcement apparatus and helped professionalize the *militsiia*. The ordinary police changed slowly as recruits replaced retirees. More educated individuals were recruited for full-time service and were trained to be responsive to the citizenry. Changes in *militsiia* activity resulted from a policy and training decision to emphasize criminalistics (forensic science and ballistics work) and sophisticated detection methods over brute force.

During the 1950s the *militsiia* turned away from its political functions, focusing instead on social and economic regulation. New laws were introduced to enhance the state agriculture sector at the expense of private domestic activity. These laws became the marching orders of the *militsiia*. The newspapers featured reports of arrests of shippers of fruit and vegetables from private plots in the Caucasian republics and of women who fed bread to animals.[2]

Khrushchev popularized the regular police by enlisting millions of volunteers (*druzhinniki*) to assist in street patrols (Berman, 1982). Some Western scholars have suggested that mass mobilization is associated with totalitarian societies. Khrushchev's effort to popularize the *militsiia*, however, recalled the early revolutionaries' efforts to promote the

---

[2] See "RSFSR Militia Interviewed on Drive Against Using Bread as Livestock Feed," *Survey of the Soviet Press*, No. 278, Oct. 1, 1962:24–25; "RSFSR Ukase Stipulates 3-Year Minimum Sentence for Feeding Bread to Livestock," *Survey of the Soviet Press*, No. 311, May 27, 1963:66–67.

withering away of the state. In this respect it was a move away from the totalitarianism of Stalin. The populism proved problematic because citizens often did not know the laws they were to uphold. Despite this drawback, government and citizen oversight meant that the *militsiia* was subject to much greater scrutiny.

The third period from 1963 to 1982, the Brezhnev years, marks the beginning of the mature Soviet police. *Militsiia* morale recovered from the de-Stalinization and popularization drives. The stagnation of the late Brezhnev era was not evident in its initial years. During the 1960s Brezhnev upgraded the quality and image of the regular police. Increased professionalism and power (Knight, 1984) were the hallmarks of the Brezhnev *militsiia*. New and more qualified personnel were recruited to improve the qualifications of those already on the force. New equipment for *militsiia* operations was purchased. The *militsiia*'s primary function was the maintenance of social and economic order. But its role in the control of dissidents meant that it had a political mandate greater than that known in Western democratic societies.

The rising police star of the 1960s and 1970s eventually proved counterproductive to Brezhnev's own interests. The increasing corruption that accompanied augmented power discredited the *militsiia* and eventually led to the diminution of Brezhnev's influence because family members figured prominently in the police corruption scandals. Andropov, the KGB chief with a reputation for integrity, rather than a Brezhnev protege, assumed the post of Party Secretary after Brezhnev's death.

Brezhnev's death ushered in a new period for Soviet policing whose ultimate result is still unclear. A major anticorruption drive was initiated under Andropov and was sustained by the short-lived Chernenko and subsequently by Gorbachev. Between 1983 and 1985, 161,000 individuals were dismissed from the Ministry of Internal Affairs (Vlasov, 1988:47). Subsequent dismissals raised the figure to nearly 200,000, or approximately 25 percent of the total regular police. New, more mature cadres were directed to police employment. The extent of personnel changes orchestrated since Brezhnev's death proved unsettling to conservative elements of the Party, and the impact of these new cadres is still uncertain.

The police, a taboo topic for many decades, became a prime subject of the *glasnost'* era press, as the mass media made the police accountable for its behavior. Between 1986 and 1988, 2500 vivid revelations of police brutality, violations of individual rights, and endemic corruption appeared in Soviet newspapers and magazines.[3]

The police was forced to respond to the new conditions created by *perestroika*. The reemergence of civil society under *perestroika* changed

---

[3] See "MVD Official Discusses New Structural Measures," *FBIS Daily Report*, April 7, 1988, p. 44.

citizens' attitudes toward the state. Individuals joined religious, social, and political organizations by the millions. Many ceased being passive, isolated individuals, but the powers of the police remained extensive. Citizens still found that the police force established the limits of permissible conduct. Abusive police practices declined because the police was under closer scrutiny, particularly by the media. But structural changes in policing were more limited. Although the national legislature established limits on eavesdropping in the Fall of 1989, the right to stop and search, the right to examine citizens' internal passports, and the right to enter premises to search for offenders all remained legitimate rights of the *militsiia*.[4]

With the collapsing authority of the central government, citizens attacked its most visible symbol—the police. Police fatalities increased dramatically and, by the late 1980s, numbered several hundred annually.[5] The police were not only vulnerable but ineffective. Relaxed controls and economic uncertainty contributed to rising crime rates.[6] In many ways the police failed to respond to the rapidly changing political and economic conditions. The police were criticized in the mass media for their frequently brutal behavior at mass demonstrations (Andrusenko, 1988; Miloslavsky, 1988), their declining clearance rate for offenses, and their acceptance of large bribes from speculators and cooperative owners operating in the new economic environment (Volkhin, 1988).

The dramatic political about-face in December 1990 brought immediate changes to Soviet policing. Paramilitary squads operated in conjunction with regular police personnel to brutally squash peaceful protests in the republics. Joint police–military patrols were established in many cities to enhance order and social control. Furthermore, the *militsiia* acquired the right to inspect " 'without hindrance' the properties, supply stocks, cash accounts and ledger books of all domestic and foreign businesses in the country" (Remnick, 1991).

The regular police became a discredited body within Soviet society. They were no longer able to communicate the ideological objectives of the state because the ideology lost its credence with the population.

---

[4] See "Militsiia" in A. Ia. Sukharev (Ed.), *Iuridicheskii Entsiklopedicheskii Slovar'* ed, Moscow: Sovetskaia Entsiklopedia, 1984, p. 175.

[5] See "Figure for Crime Against Militia Disclosed," *FBIS Daily Report*, March 16, 1990, p. 84.

[6] V. Valer'ev, "Rekordnyi uroven' prestupnosti," *Izvestiia*, February 20, 1991, p. 6. Conversations with Soviet criminal statisticians, *militsiia*, and procuratorial and court personnel, as well as examination of the published crime statistics, suggest that the nearly 40 percent rise in crime rates in the first half of 1989 reported by the Ministry of Internal Affairs was not merely a result of changes in reporting practices or the failure of the antialcohol campaign. It appears to be real and particularly profound in the area of violent crime, suggesting that the anomic circumstances of *perestroika* were having criminogenic consequences.

Without this justification for their existence, they remained an institution out of step with the rapidly changing political and social environment.

The Structure of the *Militsiia*

In the post-Stalin period the *militsiia* was subordinate to both the MVD and local units of government. This dual subordination of the *militsiia* was intended to provide greater checks on law enforcement, thereby avoiding some of the excesses that so characterized both the ordinary and the political police in the Stalinist years. In practice the *militsiia* was controlled by the MVD,[7] but local government commissions kept a watchful eye over law enforcement personnel.[8] The local party organization was supposed to provide a check on the activities of the MVD, but as numerous newspaper accounts revealed,[9] the Party was an unwilling and inefficient watchdog.

The *militsiia* was not a monolithic organization. Rather it was divided into city, regional, and *oblast'* (district) administrations that reported to the Party organizations at the appropriate level. The *militsiia* was organizationally removed from the KGB (Knight, 1988). Only its authorizing legislation required that the ordinary police cooperate with the KGB.[10]

Each police administrative unit was divided into numerous separate divisions with distinct responsibilities and activities (Bakhrakh and Seregin, 1976). In a typical city, each unit of 150 to 200 personnel may have had as many as twenty different subunits (Kutushev, 1983). The urban subunits of the *militsiia* were considered filials and were under the direction of a senior *militsiia* officer. The senior *militsiia* administrator had at a minimum two assistants. They were the deputy chief for operations and the deputy chief for political affairs, who was responsible for relations with the Party apparatus and the KGB. These *militsiia* functions set the Soviet police apart from their democratic counterparts. With this structure the *militsiia* was denied any autonomy from state rules.

---

[7] The MVD also has responsibility for the prison and labor camp system, the *vnutrennaia voiska*, the fire troops, and the guard units (*vedomstvennaia* and *vnevedomstvennaia okhrana*).

[8] A Soviet legal scholar told me that as a member of an oversight committee associated with the *ispolkom*, members of the *militsiia* were interviewed to detect problems of corruption or other factors that might affect appropriate law enforcement.

[9] See D. Likhanov, "Klan," *Strana i Mir*, No. 4, 1987, pp. 43–53; "Battle Against Uzbek 'Mafia' Described," *FBIS Daily Report*, January 28, 1988, p. 58.

[10] See "Polozhenie o sovetskoi militsii," Decree Council of Ministers No. 485, June 8, 1973.

Subordinate to the deputy chief for operations were numerous police divisions responsible for crime and social control within the community. The personnel employed by these branches worked solely for the division to which they were assigned; there was no rotation of assignments.

Administrative and political divisions complemented the operational units at the city level. These units oversaw personnel matters and internal affairs, political education of the *militsiia* force, and propaganda among the citizenry. At the *oblast'* and republic levels, *militsiia* administrative units had additional responsibilities. *Militsiia* units at the higher levels handled more serious offenses, investigations of Party members, and the conduct of the militia personnel and had more contact with the procuracy (a very powerful prosecutor's office) and the KGB. Crime statistics were registered at the first special division of the republic *militsiia*.

The desire for increasing autonomy among the Soviet republics led many areas to set up their own municipal and republic militias. The central authorities sharply criticized the independent police in Georgia and Moldavia but they did not suppress these forces as was done in the Baltic republics in January 1991. The Soviet law on the militia that was enacted in March 1991 allowed local governments to establish their own municipal police forces and allowed republic governments to obtain more control over policing.[11] The decentralization of the police was, however, no guarantee of enhanced rule of law. The Moldavian police chose to receive training from the neighboring Romanian police, a body hardly known for its appreciation of the rule of law. Moreover, in other republics the newly constituted police forces were accused of attacking members of minority groups residing within the republics.

In the absence of a tradition of respect for individual rights, the emergence of new police bodies is no guarantee that individual rights and the law will be any more respected than they were under the centralized government. The only guarantee of higher standards of conduct is institutionalized accountability to the community and civilian authorities, a situation that could not be achieved while the Communist Party had still not relinquished its control over the power structure.

Style and Method of Operation

In the Soviet Union, the *militsiia* remained more encompassing, more intrusive, and freer of legal constraints than would be deemed appropriate in democratic societies. The range of police functions of the regular police was more similar to that of prerevolutionary France than that of a

---

[11] See Zakon Soiuza Sovetskikh Sotsialisticheskoi respublik, "O sovetskoi militsii," *Izvestiia*, March 16, 1991, p. 2.

contemporary Western society. Moreover, the concept that certain conduct should not be subject to police scrutiny was not recognized either culturally or legally. Police still retained the right to search individuals at will and to monitor their travels and even short trips away from home.

Leninist policy, reenforced by Stalin, centralized power and tried to induce uniformity in the culturally heterogeneous Soviet Union. In their efforts to build a unified state, these leaders ignored the essential differences among various nationalities. As a result of their policies, policing was centralized and every attempt was made to standardize law enforcement in regions with different ethnic groups and their own distinct political, social, and religious traditions. The Marxist ideological commitment to equality also meant that policing should be devoid of not only regional but also social differences.

Yet the state's ideological commitment to equal treatment was unattainable in such a diverse society. Moreover, there was a very real discrepancy between the professed goals and the policies implemented. For example, from the first days of the Soviet period, differential treatment was institutionalized by means of special privileges for Party members that, in effect, exempted many Party members from arrest and prosecution.[12]

Despite the centralization of Soviet policing, law enforcement was not uniform throughout the country. There were varieties of police behavior, but these variations were very different from those identified by criminal justice scholar James Q. Wilson in the United States.[13] Two of his three styles of policing, legalistic and service, did not exist in the Soviet Union because there was no interest in upholding legal norms or in serving the community. Rather, the *militsiia* operations were those of his third style, the watchman. But the watchman style assumed different forms in socially and culturally distinct cities, regions, and republics within the country.

Urban policing differed by neighborhood and by the character of the city. Even though Soviet urban life was not as clearly segregated by income level or social class as life in most Western cities, in major cities

---

[12] In accordance with Party police, militia investigators could not investigate a party member unless they first receive party approval. Likewise, arrests of Party members had to be sanctioned by the Party. Investigators who proceeded against well-placed Party members without obtaining party approval found themselves, not the actual criminals, the defendants in criminal trials. Under *glasnost'*, legal critics urged the equal treatment of all citizens and the elimination of Party-sanctioned exemption from prosecution. For a discussion of this see R. Sharlet, "The Communist Party and the Administration of Justice in the USSR," in D.B. Barry, F.J.M. Feldbrugge, and P. Maggs (Eds.), *Soviet Law After Stalin*, Alphen aan den Rijn: Sijthoff and Noordhoff, 1979, Vol. 3, pp. 376–378, and O. Chaikovskaia, "Obizhates' na menia, ne obizhaites'", *Literaturnaia Gazeta*, October 22, 1986, p. 12.

[13] Ibid.

there were neighborhoods that were more clearly identified with workers or intellectuals. Working-class neighborhoods, where fights were more likely to break out, were often policed with less civility than those inhabited by individuals with social status and Party connections.

Legal operations in all regions, although not uniform, were characterized by an absence of respect for legal norms. More violations were, however, observed in the Central Asian republics and the remote Slavic regions than in other areas (Vlasov, 1988). In Central Asia, corruption was particularly pronounced and local party or collective farm leaders literally controlled local law enforcement officials. Individuals seeking justice disappeared.[14]

The variations in law enforcement increased with the emergence of popular front movements and newly elected governments in many republics demanded and obtained greater control over their ministries of internal affairs. This fact was recognized by the adoption of a new police statute. The trend toward diversification of law enforcement continued as the Soviet Union moved away from the centralism it had known.

The Soviet Union, until its collapse, was a more centrally controlled, hierarchical society than most Western democracies. The Party could mandate more citizen participation, could implement more encompassing campaigns against forms of criminality, and could be more intrusive into the lives of its citizens. Encompassing records were kept on the residence and movement of the entire population. The state's rights in relation to its citizenry had a profound effect on the operations of Soviet policing. In the Soviet Union, even with reforms, the law remained on the side of the *militsiia*.[15]

The operating style of the *militsiia* reflected the authoritarian nature of this centrally planned society. Operations of the *militsiia*, like those of all Soviet agencies, functioned according to a plan, often formulated several years in advance. An assigned number of educational lectures had to be given, a certain percentage of reported crimes had to be cleared, and a plan to maintain community order had to be presented every three years.[16] This plan discussed the daily requirements of *militsiia* activity, as well as *militsiia* operations at sports events and mass functions. As difficult as it was, both the expected and the unexpected had to be foreseen.

---

[14] See "Sokolov on Adylov Ruling Uzbek 'Kingdom,'" *Literaturnaia Gazeta*, January 20, 1988, p. 13.

[15] In "'Unusual Situation' After Journalists Attempt to Exchange Records," BBC News Summaries SU/0033, December 23, 1987, p. B/1, the journalist investigating *militsiia* operations came to this general conclusion because the presumption of innocence operated against the accused who was presumed guilty.

The following discussion focuses on some of the distinctive aspects of policing criminality in Soviet society. Although the Soviet Union shared the patrols, safe houses, and vice squads common to police in many societies, these marked similarities should not overshadow the important ways in which Soviet police practices differed from practices in societies that place more emphasis on the rule of law.

A combination of overt and undercover activities were used to deal with deviants and criminals. The Soviet police, however, lacked the sophisticated sting operations that proved so successful for U.S. federal and local law enforcement. The innate suspiciousness of the population, a remnant of the Stalinist period, may have precluded these kinds of police operations. Nonetheless, police in the Soviet Union still enjoyed certain advantages over their Western counterparts, who must operate under the rule of law. Citizens more readily cooperated with the *militsiia*, a consequence of tradition and the degree of coercion represented by the Soviet law enforcement apparatus.

Policing was more formalized in the Soviet Union than in most Western countries. Informants were necessary for all policing; yet in the Soviet Union, contracts were concluded with informants for both the secret police and the regular police. Individuals could not easily resist informing because the state had at its disposal the means to force compliance. Without fundamental procedural guarantees available to the citizen, the *militsiia* could readily impose its will on both the criminal and the law-abiding individual. Citizens could be compelled not only to inform on others but to police their communities. Auxiliary and vigilante groups have arisen in many societies to help the state maintain order. But in the Soviet Union, this state-orchestrated movement became a mass effort resented by many. Only under *perestroika*, did citizens take the law into their own hands and establish neighborhood police groups, which were sometimes out of the Party's or their workplaces' control.

Discussion of Soviet undercover work is necessarily different from much of what has been written about police undercover work in democratic societies. In these societies, "it is a necessary evil" (Marx, 1988) that is an important but not a primary means of combatting crime. In democratic societies, based on the rule of law, undercover work is supposedly closely scrutinized and adequate protections are to be provided the citizen against what might otherwise be arbitrary police authority. Yet in a nondemocratic society like the Soviet Union, undercover work is not perceived as a necessary evil but as a fundamental means of pursuing criminals. Because ensuring an acceptable degree of political and social order is paramount in the Soviet Union, no operational technique or undercover work that controls crime has been subject to close scrutiny.

---

[16] Interview with MVD official in October 1987.

Yet the increasing technology available to law enforcement personnel in developed societies makes undercover work threatening to the citizenry in a way never known previously. Although this problem exists in all societies, it is especially problematic in modern authoritarian societies like the Soviet Union, where there have been few institutionalized legal safeguards to protect the population from the increasingly sophisticated law enforcers. Those restraints on *militsiia* undercover activity that did exist sometimes failed, mainly because the rule of law had not been institutionalized within Soviet society. As the Soviet Union tried to move toward a law-based state, it needed to place greater controls over listening devices, anonymous denunciations, and secret monitoring devices. The Supreme Soviet decision in the Fall of 1989 to prohibit police wiretaps was an indication of a move in that direction, but the legislature was not able to control police conduct in other areas or to ensure the observance of this new legal norm.

Many states mount campaigns against crime. The regular police live from the issuance of one campaign to another. In the Soviet Union, campaigns were initiated in a more formal fashion than in most other societies. Although all police campaigns were launched with publicized addresses of leading politicians, in the Soviet Union, papers had to be signed by line *militsiia* personnel at individual precincts. Orchestrated campaigns against hooliganism, speculation, and alcoholism—formulated at the Politburo and Central Committee level—became the marching orders of the *militsiia*, determining the focus of enforcement even in remote communities. Direction from above was so specific as to preclude misinterpretation from below. The long-term effect of these campaigns on various social problems was minimal, whereas their impact on individual rights was consistently negative.

Analysts of the war on drugs have expressed increasing concern that this struggle has eroded civil liberties. The rule of law has been subordinated to what many law enforcers perceive as the larger goal of society. In the Soviet Union, this erosion of civil liberties occurred whenever a campaign was initiated, whether against drugs, the sale of Western records, or the offense of speculation. Most recently it was evident in the campaign against cooperative operators who had amassed significant funds. While these campaigns continued, Soviet legal analysts addressed their concern about the moral and legal responsibility of *militsiia* personnel who ruthlessly executed these campaigns. In 1987, before the idea of moving to a market economy acquired such currency, a campaign against business activity was initiated.

When the campaign against "unearned incomes" began, it was militiamen and their public order volunteers who pulled down hothouses, trampled down tomato beds, destroyed the fruits of human labour. It was done on instructions from the district Party committee or the district Soviet, and the latter carried out instructions issued by higher authorities.

Can the ruthless actions be justified by these instructions? Those who obeyed them could expect no trouble. A militiaman could be dismissed at worst, while public order volunteers did not need to worry at all. (Feofanov, 1990)

During these campaigns, law enforcers relied ever more heavily on raids to trap offenders. Forays were made, often along with *druzhinniki* (citizen auxiliary police), to locate offenders in locales where criminals and deviants congregated.

All of these differences exist between police operations in the Soviet Union and democratic societies because the Soviet state enjoyed such significant power in relation to its citizens. Defendants had limited protections. Defense attorneys did not have access to clients until a criminal investigation was completed, and almost all cases that went to trial resulted in a conviction. With the state enjoying such power and the citizen so little, there were few checks on the operations of the *militsiia*. Under such conditions, the rule of law could not exist.

Conclusion

During the period of *perestroika*, the Soviet Union seemed to be moving in the opposite direction from the United States. While the United States appeared to be more concerned with crime control and less so with the rule of law, the Soviet Union was trying to restrain police authority, even if it meant losing effectiveness in combatting crime.

Yet the move toward greater emphasis on the rule of law was halted at the end of 1990. In a society long accustomed to a high degree of order, the increasing nationalist conflicts, the rapidly increasing crime rates, and the visible social protests were signs of chaos. To combat these problems, Gorbachev acquired new presidential powers. Steps were taken to move the police away from the rule of law and increasingly under the control of the military and the secret police. Such a rapid reversal in policing could not take place in a democratic country like the United States. But the Soviet Union reverted to its traditional patterns of social control because it was not able to control the forces set loose during *perestroika*.

No change in national policy on *militsiia* operations could occur until the balance of power between the state and the individual was shifted and greater legal safeguards were institutionalized within the system. But the increasing societal disorder and the declining power of the Party made it hard, despite the professed intention, to implement the rule of law throughout the Soviet Union. It can only be hoped that the rule of law will be better implemented with the demise of the Soviet State and the emergence of independent republics.

References

Andrusenko, A. (1988). "Moskva segodniia. Vzgliad s petrovki," 38. *Sovetskaia Kultura*. P. 8.

Bakhrakh, D.N. and A.V. Seregin. (1976). *Otvetsvennost' za narushenie obshchestvennogo poriadka*. Moscow: Iuridicheskaia Literatura.

Berman, H. (1982). *Justice in the USSR*. Rev. ed. Cambridge, MA: Harvard University Press. Pp. 291–298.

Clines, F.X. (1991). Soviet Opposition Defies Ban on Rally. *New York Times*, March, 28, p. A12.

Conquest, R. (1968). *The Soviet Police System*. New York: Praeger. P. 55.

Dzalilov, T.A. (1968). *Vernye Otchizne*. Tashkent: Uzbekistan: Pp. 68–119.

Dzalilov, T.A. (1970). *Stranitsy istorii militsii Khorezma i Bukhary*. Tashkent: Uzbekistan: Pp. 16–70.

Eropkin, M.N. (1967). *Razvitie organov militsii v sovetskom gosudarstve*. Moscow: Vysshaia Shkola MOOP. P. 13.

Fainsod, M. (1958). *Smolensk Under Soviet Rule*. Cambridge, MA: Harvard University Press. Pp. 195–209.

Feofanov, Y. (1990). Ours Not to Reason Why? *New Times*, No. 10:33.

Ker Muir, W., Jr. (1977). *Police: Street Corner Politicians*. Chicago: University of Chicago Press.

Knight, A. (1984). Soviet Politics and the KGB–MVD Relationship. *Soviet Union*, No. 11, Pt. 2:157–181.

Knight, A. (1988). *The KGB Police and Politics in the Soviet Union*. Boston: Unwin Hyman.

Kutushev, V.G. (1983). *Sotsial'noe planirovanie v organakh vnutrennykh del*. Saratov: Izd. Saratovskogo universiteta.

Marx, G.T. (1988). *Undercover: Police Surveillance in America* Berkeley, CA: University of California Press.

Miloslavsky, L. (1988). The Court Disagrees With the Militia. *Moscow News*, No. 41.

Motylev, Ia. and E. Lysenko. (1967). *Soldaty Poriadka*. Dushanbe: Efron. Pp. 37–40.

Mukhamedov, A.M. (1965). *Slavnyi Put'*. Askhabad: Turkmenistan: Pp. 33–71.

Remnick, D. (1990). We Are Already in a State of Chaos. *Washington Post*, December, 13, p. A30.

Remnick, D. (1991). KGB Given Powers Over Businesses. *Washington Post*, January, 27, p. A1.

Schmemann, S. (1991). Soviet Commandos Stage Latvia Raid; 4 Civilians Killed. *New York Times*, January, pp. A1, A13.

Shchelokov, N.A. (1971). *Sovetskaia Militsiia*. Moscow: Znanie.

Vlasov, A. (1988). Na strazhe pravoporiadka. *Kommunist*, No. 5:47–48.

Volkhin, V. (1988). Reket ni pri chem. *Pravda Ukrainy*, No. 4:3.

8
Law Enforcement Innovation and the Rule of Law: Comparative and Historical Perspectives*

WILLIAM F. MCDONALD

Community policing is being hailed as the most important innovation in recent law enforcement history. Reportedly, "community policing is the new philosophy of professional law enforcement in the world's industrial democracies. [It] has emerged as the major strategic alternative to traditional practices that are now widely regarded as having failed" (Bayley, 1988:225).

Assessing the merits of this innovation is, however, not easy. Advocates have distinguished between the vision and the reality, for example, specific programs like foot patrol, team policing, Neighborhood Watch, and property marking (Operation I.D.). Thus none of the evaluations of these programs provides an adequate basis for judging the larger vision.[1] Rather, the vision and its assumptions must be examined. Such an assessment necessarily becomes somewhat speculative and ultimately normative.

What social values are protected by policing as we know it today? What shifts in priorities are likely to result if this new philosophy is substantially implemented? How would it affect the balance among the competing values of democracy, liberty, legality, and security?

The appropriate methodology for answering such fundamental questions is not survey research or the field experiment, but comparative history (Skocpol, 1984:5). Advocates of community policing have partially understood this. Kelling and Moore (1988a) invented a history of U.S.

---

*This paper was supported by the NIJ Fellowship Program via Grant 88-IJ-CX-0026 from the National Institute of Justice, Office of Justice Programs, U.S. Department of Justice, to Georgetown University; sabbatical funding from Georgetown University; and a travel grant from the Institute of Criminal Law and Procedure, Georgetown University Law Center. I thank Robert Bell and Lisa McDonald for reviews of drafts of this paper. Points of view or opinions are those of the author and do not necessarily represent the official position on policies of the U.S. Department of Justice or Georgetown University.

[1] For reviews of these evaluations see Melnicoe (1987), Greene and Mastrofski (1988), and Rosenbaum (1986).

145

police that both defines community policing and implies its compatibility with the values of liberal democracies.

Kelling and Moore's history can be faulted for its distortions and omissions (Walker, 1984; Hartmann, 1988), but more importantly for its foreshortened scope. When reckoning the proper balance among fundamental social values in free societies, the U.S. experience since the 1840s alone provides something less than comprehensive grounds for sound judgment. A longer time frame and a broader sample would be nice. Such a larger scope might help explain why community policing is not emanating from Italy, Germany, and France[2]; and indeed, why those liberal democracies would condemn it as illiberal and as incompatible with their understanding of the rule of law.

This chapter places community policing in comparative and historical contexts. Its thesis is that the important law enforcement innovations lie at the prosecution end of the law enforcement function rather than at the order maintenance end, toward which community policing is primarily directed. Moreover, the prosecution innovations are enhancing the efficiency, legality, and freedom-protecting aspects of law enforcement, whereas community policing represents a threat to legality and liberty.

Although certain features of community policing would be useful, the overall strategy raises high risks for doubtful gains. Such initiatives as democratizing the police internally and externally, allowing police priorities to be influenced by ill-defined and questionably motivated groups, expanding police powers and responsibilities, politicizing the police, and encouraging the police to drop their aloof posture and use their discretion more are dangerous not simply because they may invite corruption. Their threat is far more profound. They compromise the structures by which industrialized liberal societies have only recently managed to approximate the degree of restraint on police power that might be hoped for in societies that value freedom and view police power as an unfortunate necessity, not as a precious resource.

The Western experience suggests that freedom under law is best guaranteed when the police function is narrowly drawn and when the exercise of police power is governed by general principles of law and policy formulated by the duly elected representatives of the people and administered impartially, consistently, and skillfully by disinterested agents who are held accountable for their actions. Proponents of com-

---

[2] It is not that the European police forces have failed to recognize the problem of the police becoming too distant from the police. There has been an ongoing debate over the proper size of police forces. After World War II the Allied High Commission in Germany created small locally controlled police forces. But since then, in Germany and elsewhere, the undeniable trend has been to larger forces, and the fear among police is that this will mean losing touch with the public (see Fowler, 1979:78).

munity policing have dubbed this the "professional crimefighting" strategy, which they reject.

Some support for my argument is mustered in the following. The historical review of the distinctions among liberty, legality, and democracy is offered as groundwork for channeling future assessments of community policing. A description of the truly significant innovations in law enforcement is presented.

Comparative and Historical Perspectives

When addressing the questions "For what social purpose do the police exist?" and "What values do the police serve in a democratic society?" discussions need to be broad-based and clear. The ideas of democracy, liberty, and legality must be distinguished. I do this in this chapter and illustrate the relationships among the concepts using nineteenth-century Prussia as a comparative example. Although this analysis is limited, it suggests several things. The rule of law is neither synonymous with nor a guarantee of liberty or democracy. The rule of law is an alternative to certain forms of democracy as a method for achieving accountability to principle. The rule of law is interpreted far more rigidly in continental than in Anglo-American countries, which reflects the differences among these countries in their respective histories regarding the way in which the rule of law emerged in the struggle against absolute political power. Philosophies like community policing, which call for democratizing the police in the sense of giving them maximum discretion, are incompatible with the rule of law.

Legality, Liberty, and Democracy

The concept of the rule of law is a subtle one that is the harder to reach because of the thicket of slogans and false dichotomies used to popularize it. One such misleading dichotomy is Montesquieu's assertion that "Where law ends, tyranny begins," which has been chipped in stone on the Department of Justice building in Washington, DC. Another is the Anglo-American rallying call, "the rule of law vs. the rule of men."[3]

If it were true that tyranny begins where law ends, societies seeking to live under the rule of law would have to have laws covering every conceivable contingency in human affairs. The laws would have to be so comprehensive and detailed that they would be beyond the capacity of

---

[3] For continentals the phrase is usually, "the rule of law versus the rule of judges," reflecting their bitter experience with the prerevolutionary inquisitorial and patrimonial systems of justice.

even today's supercomputers to administer. Western scholars know this lesson, but for theoretical reasons many have chosen not to admit it. The law is not a closed, gapless, comprehensive system of rules covering all contingencies.

The Emperor Justinian believed that he could make it so. Unhappy with the conflicting interpretations of the law, he had a commission produce an elegant restatement of the code. Satisfied that this had settled matters forever, he ordered that no more commentaries be written (Cappelletti, Merryman, and Perillo, 1967:6). Supposedly, the law now spoke for itself. But the history of the European schools of glossators and the subsequent restatements of the code point to the error of such beliefs. We can imagine that the rewriting of Justinian's code began the day his scholars received the order prohibiting it. The first commentary was probably entitled "Yes, But What Does He Mean?"[4]

Laws cannot rule; only men and women, judges and police officers, and human beings in other roles can rule. The rule of law means that the decisions taken by these individuals will be determined by a set of general principles that have been established in advance by some authorized social group or agent. It means that the legal representatives are not free to choose how to handle matters as they please, nor in general may they handle similar situations differently.

The rule of law has come to be identified with modern, liberal and democratic societies. But, these associations can be misleading. Legality, liberalism, and democracy are not synonymous, nor are they are all fully compatible with each other. In particular, increasing democracy threatens liberty and legality.

In principle, legality refers only to the extent to which the arbitrariness of decision making by legal officials is reduced (Selznick, 1969). The opposite of legality is despotism. Besides increasing predictability, legality may increase the freedom of citizens, but it need not. Rather, it protects against arbitrary official interventions, whatever zone of freedom has already been established. Yet, even Rosseau admitted that the amount of liberty in a society does not depend on law per se. It is determined by other factors (Neumann, 1957:178).

Nineteenth-century British liberalism advocated that the zone of freedom be as large as possible, that government intervention in all aspects of

---

[4] The assumption that laws can be written so clearly that there is no need for commentaries and efforts to prevent such commentaries has a long tradition. Bentham demanded such a code in place of the common law (Neumann, 1957:197, footnote 37). The French enacted such a proposal in 1790. They forbade judges to interpret laws and created the *referee legislatif*, a mandatory of the legislative power, to interpret ambiguous provisions of law. The "enlightened despots" Frederick II of Prussia and Joseph II of Austria strictly forbade legal inter-pretations of laws, as did a Bavarian instruction in 1813 (Neumann, 1957:197, footnote 37).

economic, political, and social life be held to the absolute minimum, laissez-faire all around. Citizens should be free to do anything as long as it did not injure anyone else. In countries with histories of local self-government and the rule of law like England and the United States, the values of legality and liberalism easily blended, and the two have tended to be thought of together.

But, in countries like Prussia, France, and what became Italy, where there had been long traditions of absolutism and centralized, bureaucratic administration, constitutionalism and liberalism made difficult and uneven progress during the nineteenth century. The principle of legality came to be accepted in varying degrees, but reducing the government's penetration of social life and returning the control of governmental decisions to local communities did not fare well, particularly with regard to matters of police and the administration of criminal justice (Chapman, 1970; Davis, 1988; Fried, 1963; Thomason, 1981).

Liberalism is a doctrine concerning the scope and purpose of government (what the law ought to be, which in this case is minimum government and maximum individual liberty) (de Ruggiero, 1959). Its opposite is totalitarianism (maximum government and a derogation of the interests of the individual to those of the state). Democracy, on the other hand, is a doctrine about how political decisions should be arrived at, namely, that the people should decide issues through the election of individuals who assemble and make policy choices. Its opposite is authoritarianism (see, generally, Hayek, 1960; Schumpeter, 1975).

The term *democracy* has become a general term of praise and is used with the almost unquestioned assumption that democratizing anything makes it "better." Currently there is a movement to democratize workplaces of all kinds (Zwerdling, 1978), including the police (Angell, 1971). The antiauthoritarian and egalitarian sentiments that support these efforts blind their advocates to the possibility of conflict between democracy and the ideals of legality and liberty. One hears little concern for the tyranny of the majority that so preoccupied earlier political thinkers like de Tocqueville and Madison.

Prussia: Authoritarian, Illiberal, but Legalistic

The complexities of the relationships among the ideals of legality, liberty, and democracy can be illustrated by examining the Prussian experience. Judging from the sheer size of the Prussian legal code of 1794[5] (17,000 detailed sections) (Merryman, 1985:29) one might conclude that Prussia was governed by the rule of law. Clearly the code represented a substantial degree of legality, which, indeed, was its intention. It was part of

---

[5] *Allgemeines Landrecht.*

Prussian legal developments, which included an effort to import English constitutionalism and eventually resulted in Prussian–German legal theorists' adopting the doctrine of the *Rechtsstaat*—state based on law.[6]

The *Rechtsstaat* sounded like the English concept of the rule of law and to some extent it was[7]; however, it lacked the cultural and structural contexts through which the English rule of law operated to guarantee liberty. Conditions favorable to the full realization of legality did not exist. The king was not subject to the rule of law; the separation of powers was not well established; the legislature did not effectively control the law-making power. Neither the judiciary nor the police were independent of political control. Moreover, the sphere of Prussian freedom was narrow. Government was not minimal. An enormous central bureaucracy and a standing army had been created. Government's purpose was to promote the moral and cultural well-being of the people, not just to maintain public order and security. In short, the rule of law was a feature of an authoritarian state.

The Prussian police were empowered to issue regulations (in the form of ordinances) that forbade certain behaviors and required others. Infractions of these regulations were punished by fines or jail terms of up to fourteen days. The police could enforce compliance with their directives "on the spot." There were legal safeguards intended to protect against arbitrary and abusive police behavior, but they operated ex post facto and were not enforceable in the ordinary courts.

Citizens who felt abused had to register their complaints with the administrative authorities or file suit before the higher courts of administration. But these courts were concerned only with whether the police action was legal, not with whether it was appropriate, and the police were given extensive legal authority (Thomason, 1981).[8]

---

[6] Friedrich Julius Stahl, the founder of the theory of the Prussian monarchy, described the new theory as follows:

The state is to be a Rechtsstaat; that is the watchword, and expresses what is in reality the trend of modern developments. It shall exactly define and inviolably secure the direction and the limits of its operation, as well as the sphere of freedom of its citizens by means of law. . . . It signifies above all not the aims of the state, but merely the method of their realization. (Neumann, 1957:169)

[7] Neumann (1957:169) asserts that "the English rule of law and the German *Rechtsstaat* doctrines really have nothing in common." But, Hayek (1960) strongly disagrees with this (but see Neumann, 1986:179ff.; and Dietze, 1973).

[8] Some of the range of police authority in this Prussian *Rechtsstaat* is described by Anderson (1976:48):

If a person wished to move to another town he had to obtain the approval of the police in the proposed seat of domicile. Once he had moved, he required police permission for entering any one of a large number of occupations. The police power determined whether and how he might use his piece of land; it had to pass on plans to improve his dwelling; it decided whether he might build a factory

As for democratic control of "the police," there was none. When Prussia was on the verge of extinction, Minister Baron von Stein succeeded in convincing the king (Frederick William III) that the only chance for a national renaissance lay in the abolition of the feudal system and the emancipation of the peasantry combined with fundamental reform of local government leading up to the institution of a national parliament. The liberty that had once existed in medieval times had to be restored.

Stein's administrative reforms were intended to create free towns in a free state. He wanted to decentralize state authority and rehabilitate civil authority in local self-government. The first fruit of his efforts was the Municipal Ordinance of November 19, 1808, applying to all the towns of the kingdom. It concentrated power in the hands of the representative authority, providing that "the town councilors as a whole control the entire administration of the municipality in all its branches" (Dawson, 1914:21). There was, however, one important exception. All judicial jurisdiction was withheld from local control. Forced to compromise with political opposition, Stein had agreed that no police functions would be conferred on the local authorities.[9]

It should be noted that the idea of "police" was defined broadly at the time in Prussia, as it had been in France after whom the Prussian police were modeled.[10] Thus, Stein did not want to deplete too much of this power of the central executive. The administration of police in the Prussian state was placed under the control of the minister of the interior, who ruled through a hierarchical chain of command through district government presidents and local officials appointed by the central government (Thomason, 1981; Dawson, 1914:13ff.).

The "Most Objective Authority in the World"

The ironic lessons of the Prussian experience do not end with the failure to democratize the police. They include the creation in the first half of the nineteenth century of the office of the public prosecutor—

---

and, if so, where and according to what plan; it passed on the installation of machinery. It could lay paths and roads, dig ditches and canals across his fields. It penetrated his home, checked on the upbringing of his children, their school attendance, their religious instruction. It watched over his activities in private associations. It entered his house as tax official or as security officer and searched the premises.

[9] The retention of police power was expressed in No. 166 of the *Staedteordnung*: "To the state is reserved the power to erect its own police organization in the cities or to delegate the activities of the police to the magistracy, which then exercises them by way of assignment" (Thomason, 1981:19).

[10] In 1830 the Berlin police had five divisions. Only two of them involved "policing" in the narrow English sense which has developed since the establishment of the Metropolitan Police of London in 1829 (Thomason, 1981:20ff.).

Staatsanwaltschaft—and the liberal reformers' struggle to free law enforcement from political interference by the king. Law enforcement was not to be accountable to any political body but to abstract principle, the rule of law.

This was to be achieved by institutionalizing a rigid form of the rule of law. The *Staatsanwalt* (state attorney) was required to operate according to the so-called legality principle, *Legalitatsprinzip*. Unlike the French *procureur du roi*, after whom it was modeled and who had some discretionary power, the *Staatsanwalt* was strictly denied any discretion regarding either the pursuit of investigations or the decision as to whether the evidence was sufficient to press charges. The highly legalistic new prosecutor was what the Germans to this day refer to as "the most objective authority in the world" (Jescheck, 1970).

To protect his impartiality the *Staatsanwalt* was defined as a judicial agency and lodged in the Ministry of Justice, whereas the police were clearly an executive agency and were located in the Ministry of Interior. To extend the rule of law to the police, however, the reformers gave the *Staatsanwalt* responsibility over the investigative work of the police. Thus, even today in Germany—and Italy and France—the police are functionally subordinated to the public prosecutor but administratively housed in and controlled by a separate ministry.

In his analysis of the fate of democracy in German history, Dahrendorf (1969:131) notes lugubriously that the creation of the *Staatsanwalt* illustrates how a country with an authoritarian past solves its conflicts in an authoritarian way. He says that "wherever opposing interests meet in German society, there is a tendency to seek authoritative and substantive rather than tentative and formal solutions." The *Staatsanwalt* represents the typical way in which Germany still sets up solutions "in such a way as to imply that somebody or some group of people is 'the most objective authority in the world,' and is therefore capable of finding ultimate solutions for all issues and conflicts. In this manner the conflict is not regulated, but 'solved.'"

Community Policing: Progress or Regress

Kelling and Moore (1988a) divide U.S. police history into three eras. During the political era (1840s to early 1900s) the police objective was to control crime and maintain order. They provided social services and had close ties with politicians. Their primary tactic was foot patrol; their organization, decentralized; their technology, limited. Their orientation was to maintain citizen and political satisfaction with police services.

During the reform era (1930s to 1970s) the police were insulated from political influence. The corporate strategy became "professionalism." It emphasized impartial law enforcement and scientific crime control. Social services were divested. The police function was narrowly defined and bureaucratically organized. The principal tactic was preventive patrol. The relationship with the community became professionally remote. Since then, the community policing era has emerged.

The Corporate Strategy of Community Policing

The strategy of "community, problem-oriented policing" cannot be described in one sentence. Advocates with different agendas invoke it, and, like any concept, there is some inherent ambiguity to its meaning. Advocates have stressed the advantages of this. It encourages experimentation and sustains the movement.

There are disadvantages. Without better internal guidance the initiative is like a dangerous weapon launched in a general direction but capable of going astray. The threat of the community policing movement lies in the open-endedness of its ideas. Many of the specific programs, such as foot patrol and property marking, are no cause for alarm. But the larger vision within which they are being packaged and which could carry them well beyond themselves should put us on the alert.

A fix on this larger vision can be had by examining the central ideas and the underlying values involved. There are four clusters of nonmutually exclusive and loosely defined ideas: community-orientedness, problem solving, an expanded police role, and police accountability. Also, the vision is directed more at maximizing certain values than others. Although its value priority cannot be assessed with precision, there are clear indications that it can be ranked in descending order of importance as follows: democratization of policing, order maintenance, crime prevention, legality and liberty.

Departing From "Professional" Policing

It is helpful to know that the proponents of community policing generally agree that the new police should be a departure from the "professional crimefighting" strategy of the past. According to Kelling and Moore (1988b:1), the old professional crimefighting strategy ranks police autonomy (and the values it protects) ahead of effective crimefighting and order maintenance. Community policing, they say, is needed to reorder these priorities.

Moore and Trojanowicz agree and specify some of the values protected by this allegedly anachronistic policing model:

The concept of professional policing encourages distance between the police and the community in the interests of ensuring impartiality and avoiding corruption. That distance, useful as it is in pursuing these values, comes at a price. The police lose their intimate link to the communities. This hurts their crime-fighting capability because it cuts them off from valuable information about the people and conditions that are causing crimes (1988:6).

The price for the community, however, is a curtailment of its liberties.

Community-Orientedness: Multiple Meanings

The community-orientedness idea is as rich in connotations of democratic value as it is ambiguous in its operational implications. It has implications for democratizing the police both internally and externally. The phrase bundles together five distinct but intertwined meanings. Three of them—police accountability, problem-oriented policing, and the expanded new role for the police—are addressed separately later. Two of them—community self-help and the new closeness to the community—are addressed here.

It is easy to get confused as to what is meant by community-orientedness. On the one hand, it refers to something that the police are going to do; namely, the police will literally orient themselves toward and get closer to something variously referred to as the community, the people, the neighborhood, or specific groups in the community.[11] This dimension has a wide range of nuances that go from the significant albeit nonradical proposition that the police should be more sensitive to the public to more problematical ideas like community participation in the setting of police priorities. These latter meanings are wrapped separately under the appealing but operationally vague phrase *police accountability*.

On the other hand, within the idea of community policing is the notion that it is the community—*not* primarily the police—that is going to have to do the changing. Community-orientedness is code for community self-help. The new policing means engaging the community more in protecting itself from crime through such things as Neighborhood Watch, property marking, and home security measures. Also, citizens must be encouraged to staunch the physical and civil decay of their neighborhoods. The police contributions to this are of two kinds. They should promote self-help measures, and they should engage in "aggressive order maintenance" in decaying neighborhoods as a way of reducing the "signs of crime."[12] The community self-help side of the idea is intended to redistribute away from the police the sisyphean burden of blame for the perennial inability to reduce crime.[13] Skolnick and Bayley (1988:3) report that community self-help is the common denominator among examples of community policing from around the world.

---

[11] For criticisms of the conceptualization of community used see Klockars (1988).
[12] For example, vandalism, graffiti, rude behavior, panhandling, public drunkenness, and sleeping vagrants (Wilson and Kelling, 1982).
[13] See, for example, the comments of Chief Davis of Santa Ana, California, whose department Skolnick and Bayley (1988) regard as exemplary, and the Canadian Office of the Solicitor General promotion of community policing (Canada Solicitor General, 1990:20).

As for the police getting closer to the community, the advocates propose to do this in both a literal sense—more personal and frequent contact between the police and the public—and in a far more problematical political sense—wherein the new police will be "more accountable" to the people. Although community police will supposedly increase crime prevention and order maintenance, the highest value here is democracy, that is, police "accountability" to the local community.

Community policing has revitalized the workplace democracy movement in policing.[14] Community policing would radically democratize police organization. The centralized, bureaucratic form of police organization with its reliance on specialization, chain-of-command, and internal supervision is to be replaced. Organization and command are to be decentralized. Police officers are to be innovative problem solvers whose discretion must be increased not decreased. Here (workplace) democracy ranks higher than legality, as Kelling and Moore (1988a:19) make clear when they argue that the "use of discretion is the sine qua non of problem-solving policing."

Problem-Oriented Policing

Goldstein's (1979, 1990) case for problem-oriented policing begins with the proposition that the police should not allow themselves to be driven by calls for service. Instead they should resolve the problems underlying situations that repeatedly produce demands on police. He does not mean the deep, root causes of crime and disorder—things beyond police control—but the just-below-the-surface, epidermal causes.

"Problems"—groups of frequently recurring incidents—rather than the isolated incidents should be the basic units of police work. "Problems" must not be conceived in terms that do not lend themselves to remedial action. They must have time, place, and scope limits set in ways that suggest and permit solutions.

The Expanded Police Role

The troublesome part of Goldstein's idea lies in the proposed expansion of the police role. This expansion is not inherent in the logic of problem-oriented policing. Rather it is a gratuitous addition to an otherwise sound idea. Nonetheless, proponents of community policing have seized upon it with great favor.

Two facets of the police role are to be expanded: the types of problems the police should address and the types of powers they should employ.

---

[14] During the early 1970s team policing experiments dropped the traditional barriers between patrol officer and detective. Team police officers were deemed generalists; however, evaluations of team policing questioned its value (Schwartz and Clarren, 1977; Sherman, Milton, and Kelly, 1973).

Ironically much of the appeal of Goldstein's idea lies in its argument that the police's mistake in the past was their overextension, their failure to limit themselves to discrete units ("problems") of manageable proportions. Yet, the range of problems that he would have the new police address would take them far beyond traditional policework. He knows his idea equates the police role with government as a whole, but he offers no guidance as to where to draw the line (Goldstein, 1987:19).

His criterion for measuring police work, the quality of urban life, suggests that he would not draw the line narrowly. For him the value priorities seem to be order maintenance and social justice over liberty and legality. Goldstein recognizes that "the mere suggestion that police assume the role of an advocate on behalf of community groups is offensive to many citizens" (1987:19). Nevertheless he and others favor it (Goldstein, 1990:47; Kelling and Moore, 1988b).

Organizing the community on behalf of change as "advocate officers" is one of the new forms of police power that community problem solving policing contemplates. In addition, the police are encouraged to make innovative and creative use of their control or influence over licensing, inspectorial, zoning, and any other civil powers with which they might attack epidermal causes like "nuisance bars," where drugs are sold or disorderly behavior originates.

Police Accountability

A hallmark of liberal democratic societies is that police power is both constrained and accountable to the people. Such societies vary in the ways these two things are achieved. The primary means are through law and the political process. These mechanisms are not entirely congruent and tension can exist between them. It is thus appropriate to think of the police as being accountable to two masters that are not always in agreement. The crucial problem for free societies has been to devise ways of resolving the tension that simultaneously upholds these two conflicting principles: the police should be governed by the impartial rule of law, yet they should respond to the demands of the people.

Underlying this tension is the irresolvable conflict between the imperatives of procedural and substantive justice. To be fair and provide for the equal protection of the law, the police must enforce the laws equally. But, to accommodate the needs of specific groups the police must be selective in their enforcement tactics.

In general, when a conflict between the two principles arises liberal democracies have placed their faith in the rule of law over political responsiveness. The greatest variation here lies between those countries influenced by English history, with its adversarial system of criminal justice and its long tradition of local government, and those countries descended from the continental experience, with its civil law tradition, inquisitorial justice, and relative absence of experience with local government.

The Anglo-American countries always and sincerely assert their unswerving devotion to the rule of law. But they are comfortable with the reality of discretion, especially if it is structured, at least in some way, such as by explicit policies. Moreover, they are at ease with local self-government. Thus, the thought of local political units shaping local police policies is not beyond the pale of acceptable forms of governance for them.

The liberal democracies of continental descent also are devoted to the rule of law; however, they are highly suspicious of discretion and of political involvement at any level in the administration of justice. The tyranny of the caesars through the ages has left them with an abiding commitment to insulating the criminal justice system from political influence and to asserting the primacy of law over politics. To the extent that political considerations are allowed to play at all, they must operate through the central government, which can be held accountable in parliament.

In continental countries like Italy, where the police must immediately report every case to the public prosecutor and the public prosecutor has no choice but to prosecute, the mere fact that U.S. public prosecutors and sheriffs are elected local politicians is regarded as a shocking compromise of liberal principles and an open invitation to corruption and tyranny (McDonald, 1990). Little wonder that at a 1988 international course entitled "External and Internal Oversight of the Police," hosted by a United Nations-supported criminological center in Sicily and attended by 150 police officials from 49 countries, "community policing" was not on the agenda and was never mentioned (International Centre, 1988).

Moreover, the idea of police accountability, the crux of the entire meeting, took a distinctively continental twist. Most of the formal presentations were from continental countries. Most stressed the need to strengthen internal mechanisms for ensuring efficiency and legality. They are still seeking to perfect the corporate strategy of professional policing.

The Principal Commissioner of the National Police of Spain, a country in transition from an authoritarian to a democratic regime, focused on internal control, stressing the importance of a code of professional ethics among police officers. Spain has adopted the Code of Conduct for Law Enforcement Officials formulated by the Council of Europe. This, he says, is in keeping with the new philosophy of policing, one that initially sounds identical to the rhetoric of community policing. But it calls for the kind of impartial, legalistic, politically neutral policing that community policing advocates regard as passé.[15]

---

[15] He says that an "active and profound understanding between the community and police officers . . . is the 'raison d'etre' of the [police]," that it is "a determining factor in the success or failure of their action", and that it is a principle that emanates from "the constitutional principle of equality before the law and which

If the continentals are at one end of the extreme of insulating the police from politics and "accountability" to the people, the Anglo-American proponents of community policing are at the other. Their new police are going to be more "democratic," and the distance between police and politics is to be reduced. In their view such distance diminishes police effectiveness, and anyhow, it was just a temporary, historical expedient against conditions that could never happen again (Kelling and Moore, 1988b; Klockars, 1988:243–244).[16]

The community policing advocates are aware that reducing the distance between the police and the community raises the risk of corruption and illegitimate political demands. They recognize the tension between legal impartiality and political responsiveness, but they are not concerned because they believe that times have changed and political interference in policing is gone forever (Kelling and Moore, 1988a:20; Moore and Trojanowicz, 1988:10).

"Police accountability" is one of those favorite but ambiguous phrases in the community policing movement. It is a more palatable way of talking about reducing the distance between police and politics, but it blurs the critical issues of how precisely this is to be done and how it is to be reconciled with the rule of law. It potentially refers to three distinct

---

demands political neutrality, impartiality and the prevention of all arbitrary or discriminatory conduct" (International Centre, 1988:56).

This philosophy is mandated by Spanish law (Organic Law 2/1986 of March 13, 1986, Article 5), which states that the "essential principles of conduct of members of Security Forces and Corps" include "(b) acting, in the exercise of their duty, with political neutrality and absolute impartiality and, consequently, without discrimination with regard to race, religion or ideology; and (c) obedience in their professional tasks to the principles of hierarchy and subordination" (Ibid.:57). Significantly, this is not seen as incompatible with the goal of being more sensitive to the public (Ibid.:58).

[16] Los Angeles Chief of Police Daryl Gates has taken exception to the Kelling–Moore history and their portrayal of the autonomy of today's police.

If anyone . . . believes today that political influence does not prevail in major cities in this country, you are deluding yourselves.

Chiefs today are unfortunately deeply tied to politics and politicians. It's a very sad commentary on local policing. How do chiefs refer to their mayor? "My mayor." "Is your mayor going to win this election? Yes, I think she is going to win. Yes, I think he is going to win." And if they do not that is the last time we see that commissioner or that chief. Gone, because of political whim, not his or her performance as a chief. So, if you do not think politics are tied to policing today, you are being very, very foolish. (Hartmann, 1988:6)

These observations are particularly ironic in light of Chief Gates's bitter and losing effort to prevent the political process from removing him and holding him accountable for his Department's racism and brutality in the wake of the Rodney King incident. Hiding behind the Progressive reform that insulated his office from politics, he became the shining example of the error of that principle (Mathews, 1991a, 1991b, 1991c; Cannon, 1992; Sansweet, 1992).

levels of external democratization of the police. In declining order of radicalness, these are (1) allowing community groups to influence more or less directly police policies and priorities; (2) opening the police up to greater public scrutiny, feedback, and possible sanctioning (e.g., review board sanctions) regarding police operations and behavior; and (3) having the police be more attuned to and solicitous of community needs, fears, and suggestions. In fact there may be less here than meets the eye. Despite the alarming talk about reinjecting police into politics, prominent advocates of community policing seem to intend only the least radical of the three meanings. (Of course, the danger is that regardless of their intentions, the language they use invites much broader interpretations.)

For Goldstein police accountability is merely a synonym for his conception of problem-oriented policing with its expanded responsibility for solving community problems. By canvassing the community for information about its problems and nipping problems in the bud, the police are de facto being more accountable to the community. Representatives of the community will have input into police policy making, although the exact mechanisms for this are not specified (Goldstein, 1987:47–48).

A variety of police–community liaisons are arrayed by Skolnick and Bayley (1988) as examples of how to achieve police accountability. For them that phrase means "listening sympathetically [and] creating new opportunities to do so" (1988:12) and expanding "civilian input into policing" (Ibid:15). But they admit that the devil is in the details of exactly how these arrangements should work. Citing a study of police–community consultation in England and Wales, they identify community policing with the "partner" version of the three (nonmutually exclusive) models.

It stresses the importance of police being in touch with citizen views and emphasizes "the desirability of the police jointly engaging with citizens and other agencies in crime prevention and detection initiatives" (Skolnick and Bayley, 1988:14). They reject the "steward" model, which merely requires the chief constable to publish an annual report that gives an accounting of policing in his area. It does not go far enough. It leaves policy and practice solely in the hands of the police.

Remarkably, Skolnick and Bayley also reject the "directive" model. Their rejection is perplexing for it seems to contradict not only the most salient connotation of the word, accountability, but also much of the talk about bringing the police closer to politics. The directive model "puts police policy in control of democratically elected committees, either parliament or elected local committees" (Idem). It goes too far.

In fact Skolnick and Bayley are caught wriggling on the hook of the underlying problem, that is, democratizing the police without sacrificing liberty and legality. They clearly want police policy and priorities to be influenced by the community. They refer to the community in democratic language like "the will of the majority," and they value this democratic feature higher than mere order maintenance. But, at the brink of radical democratic control over the police, they retreat. Evidently the new police policies must reflect the wishes of the majority but must not be controlled by them. How the line is to be drawn between these two principles, who will decide outcomes when there is no clear majority, who will look out for the minorities—these nagging details go unanswered. If these decisions are not to be made through the political process, then by default they must be made by the police themselves. Perhaps this fact, together with Skolnick and Bayley's hesitation and the fact that the community policing movement is largely a product of propolice forces, means that community policing is more akin to a corporate image makeover than a political takeover.

The Rest of the Story

The crucial innovation in policing in the nineteenth century was not the establishment of the Metropolitan Police of London per se. Rather it was the radical reduction in the scope of the police function that the London Police represented. The concept of police was confined to a narrow set of activities related directly to patrolling the streets, maintaining order, and assisting in the apprehension and prosecution of criminals.

Before 1829 the concept of police was regarded as almost synonymous with government as a whole. Policing in the Ancien Regime can be described in terms strikingly similar to those of proponents of community policing. The powers and responsibilities of the police of the Ancien Regime went far beyond merely fighting crimes. They had direct responsibility for many governmental services and measured their effectiveness in terms of the quality of urban life, not the number of "good pinches."

In 1667 Louis XIV created the Parisian police, which represented a different kind of administrative authority than had existed previously and was equally different from what the English created in London.[17] In the freezing winter of 1783–1784 the Parisian police distributed food and fuel to needy families. Even during the best of times they provided financial assistance to some people. Throughout much of the eighteenth century

---

[17] Bernard (1970:41) writes that the new chief of police of Paris was the equivalent of a modern mayor or urban executive with a sweeping jurisdiction including "the supervision of street cleaning; fire fighting; flood prevention; the provisioning of the city; price control; supervision of butchers stalls; inspection of marketplaces, fairs, hotels, inns, furnished rooms, gaming houses, tobacco shops, and places of ill repute; investigation of illicit assemblies and other disorders; overseeing the guilds; in spections of weights and measures and of regulations pertaining to the book trade; enforcement of the ordinances against carrying weapons; and much more."

they operated an elaborate system for linking peasant wetnurses from the country whose good morals had to be certified by local priests with Parisian orphanages and mothers (Williams, 1979).

They fought urban decay, the "signs of crime," and the physical hazards in the city, especially fire. They protected the public health as well as contemporary knowledge would allow. They used their licensing power (ineffectively) to try to control the practice of medicine and pharmacy. They experimented with the control of venereal disease and epilepsy. They used their inspectorial power to protect the quality of meat and milk. They obtained legislation that controlled the growing stench and pollution created by garbage and waste. Incredibly not only were the Parisian police problem solvers, but this arm of centralized absolutist royal power was also "accountable to the community." They patrolled neighborhoods by foot and consulted with the community (Williams, 1979:142).[18]

The English decision to sharply restrict the police mission to activities directly related to crime control and order maintenance was an essential part of the compromise that made the idea of a police force acceptable to them. It helped make the police compatible with English liberty. They had resisted the establishment of a police force for over a half a century, willingly paying the price in the crime and civil disorder that the absence of a police force cost. Liberty was valued more than order, crime prevention, or social justice (Critchley, 1967).

A Path Not Taken

When examining crossroads it is useful to consider the paths not taken. What alternative trajectories did not develop as visions of the new police and why? It is worth mentioning at least one plausible alternative, depolicing. If nothing worked, then why not reduce the police presence?

There is an inverse relationship between law and self-help. The larger and more intrusive a police force is, the weaker self-help is. Summarizing this literature, Black (1976) has shown that with the growth of law and the police, the citizenry became increasingly dependent on the state to maintain order. As that happened, people increasingly ceased to take responsibility for their own security and dispute settlement and hesitated to become involved in similar problems of others (Black, 1980:195ff.).

A credible argument can be made that the community policing strategy of increasing the police presence in the community as a means of stimulating self-help, empowering citizens, and making them "coproducers" of

---

[18] Williams (1979:142, footnote 107) inspected three lists from 1744 of eminent citizens with whom the police commissioners required local investigators to consult. The most prominent names on them were of notaries, attorneys, and merchants.

crime control (Skolnick and Bayley, 1988:3) will be at best ineffectual and at worst self-defeating. Indeed, the early experience with community police suggests that the new strategy is not succeeding in overcoming the tendency toward citizen inertia (see Goldstein, 1987:22).

Innovations in Prosecution

Community policing is an illusion that has diverted attention away from the truly significant innovations in law enforcement that lie at the prosecution end. In the United States, England, Italy, and West Germany there have been dramatic changes in the prosecution system over the past two decades. The changes in Italy are likely to spread to Spain and eventually to all of Latin America and other countries that administer the inquisitorial form of criminal justice. Although the specifics differ, the general trend of these changes has been in the direction of increasing the legality, liberty, and efficiency of the respective systems.

The United States

In the United States since 1970 there has been a significant reconfiguration of the relationship between the police, the public prosecutor, and the judiciary regarding the operation and control of the front end of the prosecution process—those activities and decisions regarding the disposition of cases after arrest and before trial. Decisions that used to be dominated by the police and the lower judiciary have been taken over by newly expanded and professionalized public prosecutors' offices. Increasingly, the public prosecutor's office has claimed the right to control the charging decision and has come to dominate the front end of the justice system formerly controlled by the police and the judiciary (McDonald, 1979).

The old police practice of stuffing cases of whatever legal merit into the court system is being stopped, and the old arrangement of relying on the judiciary to screen out dubious cases is being replaced by early screening by public prosecutors. This transformation has been fought by the police in Philadelphia, Chicago, Alaska, New Orleans, and other places. They did not want their authority on the street undercut and they did not want to lose their ability to make troublesome offenders "take a ride even if they were going to beat the rap."

Yet in every case they lost the fight, and prosecutors in those places are now dismissing enormous percentages of cases brought to them by the police. In 1982 for thirty-seven major jurisdictions, of every 100 felony arrests brought by the police for prosecution, 23 were rejected at screening, 21 were dismissed in court, and 5 were diverted or referred.

Only 51 were carried forward and 47 of those were disposed by guilty plea (Boland et al., 1988:Figure 1).

The impact of this transformation has been regarded as mostly beneficial, but it has raised new questions as well as the old dilemma of choosing between procedural and substantive justice. As advocates of this reconfiguration had argued as early as the 1920s (Cleveland Crime Survey, 1922), early screening saves the court system and the accused substantial costs. Inasmuch as many cases were dismissed anyway, efficiency could be maximized by getting rid of weak cases as early as possible.

Indubitably, early screening has achieved efficiency for court systems. But whether it is efficient from the larger perspective of deterring recidivism remains to be determined. Meanwhile prosecutors have already confronted the choice between procedural and substantive justice, and they opted for the former. For instance, the famous "no-plea-bargaining" ban inaugurated in 1976 by then Attorney General Avum Gross in Alaska was intended primarily to make the practice of prosecution more professional. Gross insisted that all weak cases brought to them by the police be rejected. He eliminated plea bargaining, which he believed had encouraged poor prosecution work (McDonald, 1985).

The police protested vehemently against the new policy. Ironically they found themselves on the reverse side of their traditional complaint about prosecutors. Formerly they claimed that the high rates of plea bargained cases meant that prosecutors were not supporting the police. Now they argued that the high rate of case rejection meant that prosecutors were not supporting the police. They wanted weak cases accepted so that at least something could be gained from them through plea bargaining.

Subsequent evaluations of the Alaskan no-plea-bargaining policy have shown two findings of special interest here. The early evaluation indicated that the main effect on the disposition of cases was not on those kinds of serious cases (e.g., repeat offenders and/or serious offenses) about which there is general consensus as to the need for severe punishment (Rubinstein and White, 1980). Those cases continued to receive the same degree of severe punishment they had received before the policy. Rather, the new policy with its rigid legalistic stance of prosecuting all cases where the evidence met legal standards had its greatest impact on those cases in which, one might hope, discretion would be exercised and formerly had been, namely, first offenders or less serious crimes or special circumstances.

Remarkably, the no-plea-bargaining policy has survived in somewhat modified form to this day (Carns and Kruse, 1991). Also remarkable is the new attitude of the police toward the policy. Although charge bargaining is now fairly common, the prosecutor's office continues to demand well-prepared cases at initial screening. The police no longer oppose this policy but rather say it has made them more professional, a view that is concurred with by prosecutors and others.

England

The Alaskan experience with the reshaping of the relationship between police and prosecutors is evidently being replayed in England. There a truly dramatic change in law enforcement was the establishment in 1985 of the Crown Prosecution Service. Until then, England had never had a system of public prosecution like those in the United States, Scotland, Ireland, and the continental countries. Although the weaknesses of the English system of prosecution were as much the object of eighteenth- and nineteenth-century reformers as the system of police, an entrenched group of clerks and magistrates successfully resisted efforts to rationalize the system (Kurland and Waters, 1959). The police served as public prosecutors and, where they needed people with legal knowledge, they hired private solicitors to handle their cases (Hay, 1983).

Under the new system the Crown prosecutors are independent of the police, and as might be expected they are holding the police to a higher legal standard of case acceptability than the police were used to in the past. Predictably the police have decried the prosecutors' obsession with legalism and their failure to appreciate how the decision to charge someone formally with a crime (even if subsequently dismissed) has traditionally served to bolster police authority on the street (Wakefield and Hirschel, 1989, 1990). If Alaska serves as a model, these protests should start to fade into hosannas for the newly professionalized English police in a few years.

The Continent

Continental countries have institutions of police and public prosecutors with lineages traceable to the origins of the inquisitorial system with the emergence of Imperial Rome (Esmein, 1913); however, their histories as liberal democracies go back only to the end of World War II. Since that time they have sought to reshape their institutions in ways intended to make them more protective of freedom and more efficient, but not more democratic or accountable to the people in the sense used by the community police movement.

The focus of this effort has been on the institutions of prosecution. The most significant and symbolic change is the extinction of the investigating magistrate. This ancient institution that was so central to law enforcement on the continent and that survived the liberalizing reforms of the French Revolution was finally put to rest in 1975 in West Germany (Herrmann, 1978:192) and in 1989 in Italy (McDonald, 1990:20).

The investigating magistrate had been a combination of judge, prosecutor, and police detective (Ploscowe, 1935). There was no equivalent to it in Anglo-American law, although the United States flirted with the idea of importing it as an alternative to the exclusionary rule as the solution to the problem of police interrogation of suspects (Kauper, 1932). The investigating magistrate supervised the police work or personally conducted the investigation of cases. He interrogated suspects and witnesses, evaluated the evidence, and composed the secret dossier—case file—against the accused. He effectively determined the case because the trial amounted to reviewing the evidence in the dossier. The demise of the investigating magistrate has been accompanied by a more careful separation of judicial and prosecutorial powers. In Italy, for example, the prosecutor used to have the power to detain suspects pretrial. Now he or she lacks any direct coercive powers.

At the same time, the continental countries are trying to achieve the mandate of the Council of Europe (1988), whereby they have imposed on themselves the requirement of making their criminal justice systems more efficient. The most widely heralded feature of Italy's new code of criminal procedure, namely, its "plea bargaining" provision, is there precisely for the same reason it exists in the United States and in England (Baldwin and McConville, 1977), to make the system more efficient.

Conclusion

The significant innovations in law enforcement in the last two decades have been at the prosecution end of the law enforcement function. Those changes have gone uncelebrated but they are tangible, dramatic, and supportive of the values of legality, liberty, and efficiency. In contrast, the widely touted innovation known as community policing is an ill-defined and internally contradictory vision that would sacrifice legality, liberty, and efficiency for democracy and order. Community policing does not enhance the rule of law and, in some versions, may well subvert it.

References

Anderson, E.N. (1976). *The Social and Political Conflict in Prussia: 1858–1864.* New York: Octagon Books.

Angell, J.E. (1971). Toward an Alternative to the Classic Police Organizational Arrangements: A Democratic Model. *Criminology 9*, August/November: 185–206.

Baldwin, J. and M. McConville. (1977). *Negotiated Justice: Pressures to Plead Guilty.* London: Martin Robertson.

Bayley, D.H. (1988). Community Policing: A Report From the Devil's Advocate. In Greene, J.R. and S.D. Mastrofski, (Eds.), *Community Policing: Rhetoric or Reality.* New York: Praeger.

Bernard, L. (1970). *The Emerging City: Paris in the Age of Louis XIV.* Durham, NC: Duke University Press.

Black, D. (1976). *The Behavior of Law.* New York: Academic Press.

Black, D. (1980). *The Manners and Customs of the Police*. New York: Academic Press.

Boland, B., W. Logan, R. Sones, and W. Martin. (1988). *The Prosecution of Felony Arrests, 1982*. NCJ-106990. Washington, DC: Bureau of Justice Statistics.

Canada Solicitor General. (1990). *A Vision of the Future of Policing in Canada: Police-Challenge 2000* [Discussion Paper]. Ottawa, Ontario: Ministry of the Solicitor General.

Cannon, L. (1992). L.A. Taps Philadelphia Police Chief. *The Washington Post*, April 16, 1992, p. A16.

Cappelletti, M., J.H. Merryman, and J.M. Perillo. (1967). *The Italian Legal System*. Stanford, CA: Stanford University Press.

Carns, T. and J. Kruse. (1991). *Alaska's Plea Bargaining Ban Re-evaluated*. Anchorage, AK: Alaska Judicial Council.

Chapman, B. (1970). *Police State*. New York: Praeger.

Cleveland Crime Survey. (1922). *Criminal Justice in Cleveland*. Cleveland, OH: Cleveland Foundation.

Council of Europe. (1988). *The Simplification of Criminal Justice* [Monograph]. Recommendation No. R(87)18. Strasbourg: Council of Europe.

Critchley, T.A. (1967). *A History of the Police in England and Wales: 900–1966*. London: Constable.

Dahrendorf, R. (1969). *Society and Democracy in Germany*. Garden City, NY: Anchor Books.

Davis, J.A. (1988). *Conflict and Control: Law and Order in Nineteenth-Century Italy*. London: MacMillan Education.

Dawson, W.H. (1914). *Municipal Life and Government in Germany*. London: Longmans, Green.

Dietze, G. (1973). *Two Concepts of the Rule of Law*. Indianapolis, IN: Liberty Fund.

Esmein, A. (1913). *Continental Legal History Series*. No. 5: *History of Continental Criminal Procedure* (Simpson, J. Trans.). Boston, MA: Little, Brown.

Fowler, N. (1979). *After the Riots: The Police in Europe*. London: Davis-Poynter.

Fried, R.C. (1963). *The Italian Prefects*. New Haven, CT: Yale University Press.

Goldstein, H. (1979). Improving Policing: A Problem-Oriented Approach. *Crime and Delinquency 25*, April:236–258.

Goldstein, H. (1987). Toward Community-Oriented Policing: Potential, Basic Requirements, and Threshold Questions. *Crime and Delinquency 33*, No. 1:6–30.

Goldstein, H. (1990). *Problem-Oriented Policing*. New York: McGraw-Hill.

Greene J.R. and S.D. Mastrofski. (1988). *Community Policing: Rhetoric or Reality*. New York: Praeger.

Hartmann, F.X. (1988). *Perspectives on Policing*. No. 4: *Debating the Evolution of American Policing*. Washington, DC: National Institute of Justice, U.S. Department of Justice.

Hay, D. (1983). Controlling the English Prosecutor. *Osgood Hall Law Journal 21*, No. 2:165–186.

Hayek, F.A. (1960). *The Constitution of Liberty*. Chicago: University of Chicago Press.

Herrmann, J. (1978). Development and Reform of Criminal Procedure in the Federal Republic of Germany. *Comparative and International Law Journal of Southern Africa 11*:183–197.

International Centre of Sociological Penal and Penitentiary Research and Studies. (1988). *Internal and External Oversight of the Police*. Proceedings of the XI International Course of Higher Specialization for Police Forces, Messina–Milazzo–Rome, October 4–15, 1988. Messina.

Jescheck, H.H. (1970). The Discretionary Powers of the Prosecuting Attorney in West Germany. *American Journal of Comparative Law 18*:508–517.

Kauper, P.G. (1932). Judicial Examination of the Accused—A Remedy for the Third Degree. *Michigan Law Review 30*:1224–1255.

Kelling, G.L. and M.H. Moore. (1988a). From Political to Reform to Community: The Evolving Strategy of Police. In Greene, J.R. and S.D. Mastrofski (Eds.), *Community Policing: Rhetoric or Reality*. New York: Praeger. Pp. 3–25.

Kelling, G.L. and M.H. Moore. (1988b). *Perspectives on Policing*, No. 4: *The Evolving Strategy of Policing*. Washington, DC: National Institute of Justice, U.S. Department of Justice.

Klockars, C.B. (1988). The Rhetoric of Community Policing. In Greene, J.R. and S.D. Mastrofski (Eds.), *Community Policing: Rhetoric or Reality*. New York: Praeger.

Kurland, P.B. and D.W.M. Waters. (1959). Public Prosecutions in England, 1854–79: An Essay in English Legislative History. *Duke Law Journal*, Fall 1959, No. 4.

Mathews, J. (1991a). L.A. Police Chief Commands Respect, Fear From Overseers: 1937 Law, Crime Concerns Are Power Sources. *The Washington Post*, March 25, 1991, Pp. A1–A8.

Mathews, J. (1991b). L.A. Chief Put on Leave: Police Panel Action Offends City Council. *The Washington Post*, April 5, 1991, p. A1.

Mathews, J. (1991c). L.A. Chief to be Reinstated: City Council Overrules Police Commission. *The Washington Post*, April 6, 1991, p. A1.

McDonald, W.F. (1979). The Prosecutor's Domain. In McDonald, W.F. (Ed.), *The Prosecutor*. Beverly Hills, CA: Sage. Pp. 15–52.

McDonald, W.F. (1985). *Plea Bargaining: Critical Issues and Common Practices*. Washington, DC: National Institute of Justice, U.S. Department of Justice.

McDonald, W.F. (Spring 1990). Politics, Criminal Prosecution, and the Rationalization of Justice: Italy and the United States. *International Journal of Comparative and Applied Criminal Justice 14*, No. 1:15–24.

Melnicoe, S. (January 1987). Fear of Crime. *Crime and Delinquency 33*, No. 1:3–154.

Merryman, J.H. (1985). *The Civil Law Tradition*. 2nd ed. Stanford, CA: Stanford University Press.

Moore, M.H. and R.C. Trojanowicz. (1988). *Perspectives on Policing*. No. 6: *Corporate Strategies for Policing*. Washington, DC: National Institute of Justice, U.S. Department of Justice.

Neumann, F. (1957). *The Democratic and the Authoritarian State: Essays in Political and Legal Theory*. Glencoe, IL: Free Press.

Neumann, F. (1986). *The Rule of Law: Political Theory and the Legal System in Modern Society*. Leamington Spa, UK: Berg.

Ploscowe, M. (1935). The Investigating Magistrate (Juge D'Instruction) in European Criminal Procedure. *Michigan Law Review 1935*, No. 2:1010–1036.

Rosenbaum, D.P. (Ed.) (1986). *Sage Criminal Justice System Annuals*. Vol. 22: *Community Crime Prevention: Does It Work?* Beverly Hills, CA: Sage.

Rubinstein, M.L. and T.J. White. (1980). Alaska's Ban on Plea-Bargaining. In McDonald, W.F. and J.A. Cramer, (Eds.), *Plea-Bargaining*. Lexington, MA: D.C. Heath.

de Ruggiero, G. (1959). *The History of European Liberalism*. Boston, MA: Beacon Press.

Sansweet, S.J. (1992). LAPD Officers Are Acquitted in King Beating: Mayor Declares Emergency Amid Rise in Violence: National Guard Is Called. *The Wall Street Journal*, April 30, 1992, p. A14.

Schumpeter, J.A. (1975). *Capitalism, Socialism and Democracy*. New York: Harper and Row.

Schwartz, A.I. and S.N. Clarren. (1977). *The Cincinnati Team Policing Experiment: A Summary Report*. Washington, DC: The Urban Institute and Police Foundation.

Selznick, P. (1969). *Law, Society and Industrial Justice*. New York: Russell Sage Foundation.

Sherman, L., C.H. Milton, and T.V. Kelly. (1973). *Team Policing: Seven Case Studies*. Washington, DC: Police Foundation.

Skocpol, T. (1984). *Vision and Method in Historical Sociology*. New York: Cambridge University Press.

Skolnick, J.H. and D.H. Bayley. (1988). *Community Policing:Issues and Practices Around the World*. Washington, DC: National Institute of Justice, U.S. Department of Justice.

Thomason, F.J. (1981). *The Prussian Police State in Berlin, 1848–1871* [Unpublished Ph.D. dissertation, John Hopkins University]. Ann Arbor, MI: University Microfilms.

de Tocqueville, A. (1969). *Democracy in America* (Lawrence, G., Trans; (Mayer, J. P., Ed.). Garden City, NY: Anchor Books.

Wakefield, B. and D.J. Hirschel. (1989). *Progress or Stalemate?Police Responses to the Independent Prosecution Service for England*. Paper Presented at the Annual Meeting of the Academy of Criminal Justice Sciences, Washington, DC, March 1989.

Wakefield, B. and D.J. Hirschel. (1990). *Public Prosecution in England: Resistance to Change*. Paper presented at the American Society of Criminology Meeting, Baltimore, Maryland, November 8, 1990.

Walker, S. (1984). Broken Windows and Fractured History: The Use and Misuse of History in Recent Police Patrol Analysis. *Justice Quarterly 1*, No. 1:75–90.

Williams, A. (1979). *The Police of Paris: 1718–1789*. Baton Rouge, LA: Louisiana State University Press.

Wilson, J.Q. and G.L. Kelling. (1982). Broken Windows: The Police and Neighborhood Safety. *The Atlantic Monthly*, March:29–38.

Zwerdling, D. (1978). *Workplace Democracy*. New York: Harper and Row.

Part V
Crime Control and Police Control: Future Trends and Problems

9
Why Crime Control is Not Reactionary

LAWRENCE W. SHERMAN

To the intelligent general reader of this book, the title of this chapter may seem quite odd. Although police *methods* can always be debated, is there any thoughtful opposition to the *goal* of controlling crime? Does that goal in itself strike anyone as inherently reactionary or anti-democratic, in a society plagued with substantial violent crime? Does a book about police innovations need to justify an explicit concern with better crime control? Although it may surprise most taxpayers, modern students of American policing will readily answer "yes" to each of these questions. For those students know how much police scholarship has been influenced by the writings of Stanford University Law Professor Herbert Packer and the ethos of the 1960s in which his central treatise was produced.

Professor Packer has a lot to answer for. For a quarter century, he has given the noble police mandate of crime control a bad name. Not that he alone is to blame. But more than anyone else, he has fostered academic disdain for the primary mission of the police. His brilliant 1968 treatise on *The Limits of the Criminal Sanction* (Packer, 1968) presents a model in which crime control values are opposed to the rule of law. The effect of this model, however unintentional, has been to stigmatize an important social task as a reactionary, neofascist quest. It has also led some intelligent social scientists of the police into some extreme and insupportable arguments about the history and nature of policing. Worst of all, it helped to delay for almost fifteen years the development of academically serious work on police innovations for better crime control.

The future of police innovations must certainly be premised on the rule of law. But with equal certainty, it must be premised on efforts to control crime as the primary goal of the police. By "control" I mean keeping the volume and seriousness of crime lower than it would be without such police efforts, including *reactions* to crimes that have already occurred, *prevention* of crime through social engineering of reduced criminal opportunities and motivations, and general *deterrence* of crime through patrol and other legal methods of surveillance.

At the same time, of course, our society must maintain its control of the police, using the same theories and strategies that police use to control nonpolice crime. Renewed public attention to the continuing problems of police brutality and corruption shows a need for innovations in police control that is as great as the need for innovations in crime control. Put another way, the control of police crime is included in a properly broad understanding of crime control. The need for control of police crime is a natural by-product of the adversarial posture we ask police to take against criminals. All contests need good umpires watching the game closely, with strict powers of enforcement. Unfortunately, too many observers have confused the need for good umpires with a preference that the game not be played at all. That is why this chapter is necessary.

The chapter supports that claim with a brief, recent intellectual history of the idea that crime control *is* indeed reactionary, leading necessarily to a loss of due process, civil liberties, or taxpayers' money in a futile effort to do the impossible. The second part of the chapter suggests the flaws in reasoning and scholarship that characterize that idea. The third part develops a prescriptive model of crime control values that can guide further innovations and evaluations of police efforts to control crime, including crime by police.

The Intellectual Assault on Crime Control

Attacks on criminal justice efforts in general have a long tradition in labeling theory and capital punishment research, raising complex and important questions about the capacity of legal punishment to control crime. Attacks on crime control by police in particular are more recent, dating from the 1960s, a time of great ferment in American policing. The decade opened with the "discovery" of police discretion (Goldstein, 1960), based on the field observations of the American Bar Foundation's Survey of the Administration of Criminal Justice. LaFave's (1965) detailed analysis of that Survey's field notes revealed even more about the role of police values and objectives in deciding when and how to invoke the criminal law, rather than in acting as automatically programmed ministers of the legislature. Black and Reiss's (1967) systematic observation field studies of three big-city police departments, especially the evidence on police brutality against prisoners in custody (Reiss, 1968), offered further grim evidence of a deviant police subculture flaunting the rule of law. Police corruption scandals in Chicago, Indianapolis, and other cities (Smith, 1965) made scholars even more distrustful of police efforts to control crime, and race riots ended the decade with police brutality blamed as a major flashpoint.

In this context, the U.S. Supreme Court issued a series of landmark decisions restricting police investigatory powers. The most famous of these was *Miranda v. Arizona* (384, U.S. 486 (1966)), which relied heavily on the Inbau and Reid (1962) text on criminal interrogations as an empirical description of police practices. That text blatantly advocated lying to suspects, treating them as "quarry," tricking them, and placing psychological pressure on them over many hours. Howls of protests from police leadership over being "handcuffed" by the Warren Court confirmed the image of police as crime controllers without regard for due process.

Packer's Crime Control Model

It is little wonder, then, that Packer (1968) chose to place crime control and due process on two opposite poles as models of criminal justice in general and policing in particular. If one supports due process, Packer's essay drives one to being against crime control. His very definition of crime control is the "repression" of criminal conduct (1968:158), a word often associated with dictatorships' stifling of free speech and dissent. The key to the operation of Packer's crime control model is "the presumption of guilt," at least for those not screened out (1968:160). For Packer (1968:163), the crime control model resembles an "assembly line," whereas the due process model resembles an "obstacle course" stressing the possibility of error. The due process model's values are "anti-authoritarian" (1968:166); the crime control model's values, by implication, must therefore be authoritarian, an intellectual codeword for the values of Nazi Germany (Adorno et al., 1950).

The authoritarian values are clearly spelled out. Packer's crime control model (1968:168) "cannot tolerate . . . the exclusion of evidence illegally obtained or . . . the reversal of convictions in cases where the criminal process has breached the rules laid down for its observance." The due process model is then shown to be concerned about equality of legal representation for the poor; by implication, again, crime control values either lack that concern or oppose it. Finally, Packer claims (1968:170) that due process values offer a "mood of skepticism about the morality and utility of the criminal sanction." By implication, the crime control model must therefore have no reservations on those points.

In short, Packer makes an oxymoron out of a civil libertarian interested in crime control. He closely identifies crime control with the criminal process, rather than the many other aspects of police practices. He implicitly identifies crime control, even as an *ideal type*, with the discredited values of the American police subculture of the 1960s. He shows that the biggest threat to our freedom is not crime itself, but crime control, which in 1968 may well have been the case. It seems natural, then, that scholars like Sheldon Messinger (personal communication,

1990) fume that "a crime control perspective" for research on policing is a concept that just "sticks in my craw."

The lasting intellectual impact of these models and the era that produced them, however, often includes blindness to the effect that they had on the police institution. The period of 1965 to 1985 witnessed a revolution in police culture, at least at the administrative level. Under the political pressure generated by the social movements of the 1960s, police leadership in big cities was transformed from a profile of largely uneducated white males opposed to due process to a highly educated, racially (but not sexually) diverse group, publicly and privately committed to constitutional criminal procedure. Institutional oversight of local police misconduct by federal investigators and prosecutors increased substantially, and the press became far more vigilant in investigating police misdeeds (Sherman, 1983).

All of this notwithstanding, there is still a strong academic bias, especially among sociologists and many criminologists, against police even *trying* to control crime. This "politically correct" orthodoxy has been used to reward some scholarly careers and punish others (Bernstein, 1990). With a few exceptions like Morris and Hawkins (1970), the central thrust of police scholarship for almost two decades was anti-crime control. This approach took two forms in empirical research: (1) demonstrating that the police mission was not historically, and is not currently, concerned primarily with crime control, and (2) debunking police assumptions about the effectiveness of their crime control strategies, such as preventive patrol and rapid response. Although the second approach was valuable, the first created nothing but confusion, even among police themselves.

Anti-Crime Control Scholarship: Police Mission Studies

The 1960s saw repeated empirical conclusions that the central task of the police was social service, not crime control. The first was the Cumming, Cumming, and Edell (1965) analysis of telephoned calls for service received at a police department. Divorced from any historical perspective on the rise of telephones as the primary means of public communication with the police, the authors concluded that the "public" (or at least that small fraction of it who call) expects the police to serve as "philosophers, guides and friends," helping them with the crises of everyday life.

Perhaps the most influential work making this point, ironically, is by James Q. Wilson (1968), whose other writings (e.g., Wilson, 1980) show strong philosophical support for police efforts to control crime. To be sure, his actual point was widely misunderstood: that police spent more time in *order maintenance* without invoking the law than they did in actual *law enforcement* through arrest. His analysis (1968:18) of one week's patrol dispatches in Syracuse showed police spending 22 percent of their calls on gathering information (usually taking crime reports, a clear crime control function), 10 percent of the calls on enforcing the law, 30 percent of the calls on maintaining order, and 37 percent of the calls on such services as responding to medical emergencies or handling public intoxication, which at that time accounted for almost half of all arrests nationwide each year. This analysis was intended to show the diversity of tasks police are asked to perform, rather than to prove that policing has little to do with crime. Yet it is the latter view that many readers have drawn from the work.

Foremost among those readers have been many police executives, who cite Wilson's findings in concluding that their primary job is not to control crime, but to "serve the community." This may reassure some audiences concerned with police oppression, by "softening" the police image as helpers, not punishers. But it surely confuses other audiences, who want to know whose job it is to control crime. The answer that crime control is "up to the community," no matter how theoretically sound (Braithwaite, 1989), is not satisfactory. The argument that policing has little or nothing to do with crime has caused massive confusion.

The confusion has been compounded by historical claims that the police were founded for manifest purposes other than crime control. Klockars, for example, advances the astonishing argument that the intended purpose of police patrol was not the deterrence of street crime but the control of police misconduct:

What is of cardinal importance to remember about patrol is that in both England and the United States it was created primarily as a means of controlling police abuses ... To anyone familiar with the origins of patrol it is nothing short of astounding to realize that what was once clearly understood as a means of controlling police could grow to acquire a front-line role in a war on crime. (Klockars, 1985:310–311)

Samuel Walker, in his excellent history of police reform, takes a less extreme view, acknowledging that the manifest purpose of policing and patrol was the control of crime and disorder. He goes on, however, to lend historical credence to the misreading of the Wilson analysis:

As contemporary sociologists have adequately documented, the police maintain a law enforcement image but in reality spend little of their time actually fighting crime. Most of their time is devoted to miscellaneous social services. Although in a somewhat different form, a similar contradiction characterized the nineteenth-century American police. (Walker, 1977:8)

Walker goes on to cite evidence that nineteenth-century police actually spent a great deal of time inside saloons, relaxing in the midst of a boring job but definitely not fighting crime. He also cites scattered evidence from police strikes and other suspensions of patrol to argue that nineteenth-century policing was just as ineffective at crime control as twentieth-century policing, if not more so, as demonstrated by the modern evaluations of the effectiveness of police methods, such as the Kansas City Preventive Patrol Experiment (Kelling et al., 1974).

Police Methods Evaluations

For many sociologists, both theory and ideology suggest that the police (and other systems of formal sanctions) are ineffective in fighting crime. Sociological theory of crime is heavily committed to variables other than punishment, such as family structure, economic opportunity, social networks and neighborhood ecology, learning theory, values, and shame (Braithwaite, 1989). A prevailing ideology of sociologists appears to be distaste for coercion of any sort, with a moderate animus toward figures of authority (Lipset, 1969). More generally, Reiss argues that "American society is more inhospitable toward its police than most societies, and this is most evident in the virulent forms this inhospitability can take in the university" (1971:185).

It was with great joy, then, that many academics welcomed the results of the Kansas City Preventive Patrol Experiment (Kelling et al., 1974). Here, at last, was a carefully designed and executed evaluation that showed police did not do much good anyway. Its findings have not only been widely accepted, but widely overgeneralized to conclusions that nothing police do can deter crime. Klockars, for example, concludes from the study that "it makes about as much sense to have police patrol routinely in cars to fight crime as it does to have firemen patrol routinely in fire trucks to fight fire" (1983:130). Skolnick and Bayley conclude more modestly, but still well beyond the data, that "random motorized patrolling neither reduces crime nor improves chances of catching suspects" (1986:4). Gottfredson and Hirschi generalize from this and other research that "no evidence exists that augmentation of police forces or equipment, differential patrol strategies, or differential intensities of surveillance will have an effect on crime rates" (1990:270). Klockars finds that the Kansas City experiment offers "real possibilities for saving lots of money," presumably through drastic reductions in the numbers of police officers (1983:130).

Similar satisfaction greeted the findings that adding foot patrol to a small number of beats in Newark had no measurable impact on official crime statistics or victimization survey results (Police Foundation, 1981). The same was true of the Kansas City (MO) Police Department's (1977) finding that response time was unrelated to the odds of apprehending suspects, as well as the replication of the key component of response time, citizen delay, as being very long in several other cities as well (Spelman and Brown, 1981). In the initial era of rigorous evaluations of police methods, James Hackler's iron law of evaluation held true: "the more carefully you evaluate [a] program, the greater the probability that it will show little effect" (quoted in Empey, 1979:10). Whether the evaluations were rigorous enough for the claims being made from them, however, is a matter considered later.

Distinctly less academic enthusiasm greeted two major studies in the early 1980s suggesting that criminal justice could be effective in controlling crime: the Greenwood and Abrahamse (1982) analysis of selective incapacitation and the Sherman and Berk (1984) experiment in misdemeanor domestic violence arrests. Although both studies have stimulated further work that helps to limit and clarify their policy implications (Blumstein et al., 1986; Dunford, Huizinga, and Elliot, 1990; Hirschel et al., 1990; Sherman et al., 1991; Sherman, 1992b), they also clearly rubbed against a strong ideological bias against crime control. The ideological position is clearly evident, for example, in the Binder and Meeker (1988) criticism of the Minneapolis experiment. To be sure, opinions about the virtues of research influencing policy for better crime control are divided (e.g., Petersilia, 1987). But there seems to be a clear preference by many scholars for research influencing policy when it shows crime control is ineffective, rather than the converse. Part of it derives from the posture of skepticism which rightly pervades science; part of it derives from social scientists' particular pleasure in exposing hypocrisy and puffery by public officials; and part of it derives from a healthy distaste for any society in which the police command too much power.

An additional factor was academic reaction to the general "get-tough" climate of the Reagan–Bush 1980s, in which prison populations soared while concern for control of police misconduct almost disappeared, even on the Supreme Court. Studies finding crime control benefits from policing, at least in that climate, merely contributed to the national preference for repression over prevention. While Head Start remained underfunded, police budgets began to grow. The war on drugs at the end of the decade created even more academic debate about the limits of the criminal sanction and, by implication, policing.

Ironically, the crime control focus of federally funded research in the 1980s helped spawn more alternatives to the use of criminal sanctions. The "problem-oriented" revolution in policing spawned by Goldstein (1979, 1990) and others (Eck and Spelman, 1987) has fostered a rich body of research on innovations in police crime control methods, many of which focus on opportunity reduction rather than arrests. The Newport News effort to control burglary in a high-crime apartment complex, for example, focused on improving the physical condition and occupancy patterns of the buildings, culminating in their demolition and location of alternative housing for residents happy to move out. Although many police officers still favor vast increases in "warehousing" of serious criminals, police managers are increasingly seeking crime prevention strategies other than incarceration.

Police agencies have been quite open to testing innovations since at least the mid-1970s, and limited funding for academic support was available. But academic efforts to help test new crime control strategies were few and far between, delaying what has since become a major period of police research and development. The subcultural academic preference for debunking, rather than developing, crime control theories was arguably no small part in the delay.

Flaws in the Anti-Crime Control Literature

The intellectual history of the assault on crime control is one thing. The logical and factual strength of its arguments is quite another. This section considers the flaws of Packer's models, the police mission studies, and the conclusions drawn from the police evaluation studies.

Packer's Model

Packer's crime control model cannot be faulted at its face value. It does exactly what Packer intended—demonstrate important tensions in the criminal process. The problem is that it also does much more, associating the extreme version of *some* values in crime control with *all* models of crime control. The result is guilt by association with an admittedly hypothetical ideal type. Packer would probably agree with each of the following propositions, and clearly thought it unnecessary to state them. But their absence leaves the clear impression that crime control is a reactionary threat to freedom.

1. *Crime control embraces many police activities that have nothing to do with criminal investigations, arrests, and prosecution.* Uniformed patrol, inspection of licensed premises, mediation of disputes, and (recently) more systematic attempts at "problem solving" (Goldstein, 1979, 1990) often have nothing to do with law enforcement, but can have much to do with crime control. Just as the Centers for Disease Control evaluate many strategies besides medical treatments of people who are already sick, police crime control strategies have always reached way beyond the case-by-case processing of past crimes to other tasks.

2. *Crime control includes the prevention of crime as well as reaction to it.* The word *control* may have a particularly harsh ring to it, given its associations with financial accounting and engineering. But it is just those associations that demonstrate its primarily preventive definition and its merely secondary concern with the management of breakdowns of prevention mechanisms. Auto traffic control, for example, is accomplished primarily by stoplights, by signs, and, sometimes, by police direction of traffic. Traffic enforcement, through the arrest of violators, is only a tiny fraction of all traffic control systems. In the typical tour of duty, patrol officers in big U.S. cities make no arrests at

all (Reiss, 1971:19). Packer thus builds an elaborate model on a tiny fraction of all police work, ignoring most of what police do to prevent crime.

3. *Crime control has no logically necessary opposition to the presumption of innocence, the exclusionary rule, subsidized legal counsel for the poor, or other protections of suspects' rights.* To claim that these things harm crime control is to make two grave errors. One is to vastly overstate the role of criminal sanctions in the control of crime, so that if some guilty people go free on "technicalities" the crime rate will rise; this seems most unlikely. The other error is to assume that the only way to be in favor of crime control is to oppose due process, which denies a perfectly valid philosophical position: seek the maximum crime control possible in the context of maximum due process. Even if due process does limit crime control, there is no reason why crime control cannot happily accept those limits. Surgeons are required to "first, do no harm." The same ethical obligation sits well, if not easily (Klockars, 1980), on the shoulders of crime controllers. Even a police officer can be a civil libertarian, without betraying his or her professional duty to control crime.

4. *Crime control needs to take no a priori position on the empirical utility of the criminal sanction and opposes sanctions when they are found to be criminogenic.* A utilitarian approach to crime control, as distinct from a just desserts philosophy, welcomes good evidence of sanctions failing to deter or causing more crime; it all helps rationally determine the right penalties to impose or not to impose on the right people for the right crimes (Braithwaite, 1989:6). If the criminal sanction were found, across the board, to be criminogenic, then a practical crime control model would oppose the use of criminal sanctions at all, quite unlike Packer's implications. In this sense, it is crime control, and not Packer's "due process," that is more profoundly skeptical of the utility, and hence the morality, of the criminal sanction.

Perhaps the reason Packer did not make these four points is that a long theoretical tradition assumes a necessary empirical trade-off between crime control and individual rights. This assumption appears to be the foundation of Packer's argument. But as Braithwaite (1989:158–159) points out, the empirical evidence from cross-national and interregional studies is just the opposite: societies with *greater* protection of individual rights generally have less predatory crime. Noting this fact requires no assumptions about cause and effect; it simply contradicts the premise of Packer's model. Similarly, Treiman's (1977:153) analysis of occupational prestige of police across 39 societies finds a moderately strong ($R = .39$) positive correlation with the index of freedom of the press.

In sum, Packer's use of crime control in opposition to due process is a straw man that serves well his analytic purposes. But as a basis for attacking crime control as a public policy mission for police—something he probably never intended—it is woefully inadequate.

Police Mission Studies

Wilson's conclusion that police spend little time on law enforcement is important for placing police in proper relation to the criminal justice process. But many readers jumped from a finding of little *law enforcement* to little crime *control*, assuming that the two concepts were identical (e.g., Walker, 1977:6, as quoted above; Klockars, 1983:133, paragraph 2). This is a major error. Even when police are not making arrests or not intending to do anything about crime, they still may be contributing to the prevention or deterrence of crime. How much they are contributing may be revealed only by carefully evaluating police methods, not by merely classifying police activities at their face value.

Wilson (1968), for example, draws the important empirical distinction between order maintenance and law enforcement. But from a crime control perspective, it is a distinction without a difference. A fight requires order maintenance; a fatal knife wound during a fight requires law enforcement (an arrest for murder). The police respond to both types of incidents, but the former more often than the latter, with the clear goal of *crime prevention* or minimization of injury. How they accomplish this was Wilson's distinction; the crime control objective is the same for both responses.

This point was emphasized by the Wilson and Boland (1978) analysis of robbery rates and traffic enforcement. Although a simple descriptive analysis of police tasks would classify traffic enforcement as unrelated to crime control, Wilson and Boland hypothesized, and found, just the opposite. Traffic enforcement clearly provides opportunities to detect other kinds of crime and provides a constitutional basis for police to monitor and inspect suspicious persons. The fact that higher traffic enforcement rates should be associated (cross-sectionally) with lower robbery rates makes sense. An even more powerful test of the hypothesis by Sampson and Cohen (1988) found the same result. It also found that higher levels of disorderly conduct arrests—"order maintenance"—were associated with lower robbery rates.

The handling of drunks is a case in point. Classified by Wilson's Syracuse analysis as "service," this task has clear crime control implications. Drunks appear to be at greater risk than sober people of both committing crimes (Collins, 1980) and being victimized by them. By enforcing laws against public intoxication, police may have provided a "service," but they also were controlling the potential effects of a criminogenic substance. Thinking of drunk control as a service comparable to getting cats out of trees grossly misrepresents the contribution of intoxication to crime and the contribution of police management of public intoxication to crime control.

Walker's (1977:10) implication that nineteenth-century police who spent time in bars were not fighting crime also misses the link between alcohol and crime. Although it is true that a drunken policemen may be of little use in deterring bar fights, it is likely that many police spent time in bars in reasonable states of sobriety, even if they were breaking the rules to be there. And by being there, they effectively performed preventive patrol at the "hot spots" of crime (Sherman and Weisburd, 1988), which likely accounted for a large portion of serious violence. Taverns have been demonstrated, for example, to occupy less than 1 percent of all addresses in most cities, but to have accounted for 2 percent of 1368 homicides in parts of thirteenth-century England (Given, 1977:193), 8.2 percent of homicides in Philadelphia in 1948–1952 (Wolfgang, 1958:123), 11.2 percent of aggravated assaults in St. Louis in 1961 (Pittman and Handy, 1964:Table 3.3), 13.6 percent of a sample of homicides in Houston in 1958–1961 (Pokorny, 1965:Table 2.4), and 10 percent of homicides in Milwaukee in 1989.

If the report taking, order maintenance, and law enforcement categories of Wilson's (1968) Syracuse analysis are combined, 62 percent of police dispatches are clearly related to crime control. Reiss's (1971:71) analysis of 6712 calls to Chicago police in 1966 also classifies about two thirds as related to criminal matters. Greene and Klockars (1991:273) used more precise measurement of time police spend on calls to attack a common police textbook claim that only 10 percent of policing is "crime related"; they show that 50 percent of active police time in Wilmington, Delaware, in 1985–1986 was spent on "crime" and another 16 percent was spent on "order maintenance."

Moreover, as Reiss makes clear, there has always been more to police work than answering calls. His 1967 studies in three cities found that (Reiss, 1971:11) although 87 percent of police encounters were initiated by citizens (and 13 percent were proactive), 13 percent of those were initiated by citizens on foot. Only 75 percent of all police encounters in the Reiss data, then, were mobilized over the phone, with the other 25 percent possibly more prone to be "crime related."

There is a more fundamental flaw in using telephoned calls for service as an empirical indicator of the police mandate. Even if calls did reveal a majority of demands to be for services unrelated to crime control, that would still fail to prove that "service" is the true police mandate. That conclusion would be true only if all sectors of "the public" are represented by those who make specific requests for police action. Although all taxpayers support police costs, these analyses imply that only those who call the police define their mission. Recent research suggests that the majority of all police calls for service are dispatched to a small proportion of all addresses (Sherman, Gartin, and Buerger, 1989); future work may show that a small oligarchy of chronic callers generate the majority of all calls to police. Callers are a biased sample of the general public. Using calls to define the police mandate is no more reliable than using letters to a member of Congress to indicate majority opinions in her district. Congress has long been using public opinion polls with probability sampling techniques; it is remarkable that academic students of the police do not draw the same lesson in measuring the police mandate.

The history of the police mandate has also been misrepresented. Klockars' novel argument, for example, that patrol was intended for police control rather than crime control, clearly distorts the facts. It is true that there was great reluctance to create the first police forces in London and New York. It is also true that uniformed patrol was more politically acceptable than a detective force, as a uniformed force was easier to control. But to describe the primary public mandate of patrol as anything other than crime control is to ignore the facts.

Why the English people, in 1829, would want to create a brand new force of over 3000 officers just to prevent them from being abusive is not at all clear. Nor is the thesis consistent with the overwhelming weight of historical scholarship on the development of the theory that patrol would deter crime. This scholarship begins with Fielding's (1754/1964) own memoir in *The Journal of a Voyage to Lisbon*, in which he recounts how the British government in 1753 first decided to pay stipends for police patrol out of concern with a summer crime wave of robberies and murders (1754/1964:191–192). It continues with Colquhoun's (1795/1969) treatise, which lays out a Benthamite theory of the general deterrent effects of police patrol. It is bolstered by Miller's judgment, in a highly respected history, that

In both London and New York the growing intolerance of riots in a complex economy was an important prod toward police reorganization, although the growth of more ordinary crime and disorder seemed to be the factor which finally caused legislators to subordinate their fears of police power to the need for order. (Miller, 1977:8)

The evidence for the crime control mandate includes the finding of Home Secretary Robert Peel's 1828 parliamentary commission that "it was absolutely necessary to devise some means to give greater security to persons and property" (Lee, 1901/1971:230), as well as Peel's own aim "to teach people that liberty does not consist in having your house robbed by organized gangs of thieves" (quoted in Pringle, 1955:206). The crime control mandate is even accepted by more balanced accounts, such as Manning's judgment that "It is by no means clear that Peel and others were *solely* concerned with providing an answer to the 'crime problem'" (1977:79).

To claim that most police activity is unrelated to crime control merely confuses our thinking about how crime can be prevented. To say that the inventors of modern policing were uninterested in crime control virtually constitutes disinformation.

Evaluation of Police Methods

The ready acceptance of the Kansas City experiment (Kelling, et al., 1974) was fortunately not universal. Larson (1975) quickly pointed out major questions about the extent of differences in patrol dosage across areas, if any; Farrington (1982) pointed out that the experimental areas had not been selected at random; Feinberg, Larntz, and Reiss (1976) showed that the sample sizes were too small for adequate statistical power. Identical problems can be raised with the Newark Foot Patrol Experiment (Police Foundation, 1981). These problems are severe enough so that scholarly caution would prohibit reaching any general conclusions about the crime control effectiveness of patrol, at least from these studies. But it appears that some scholars find less need for caution when they are "debunking" police crime control than when they are attacking those providing evidence for its support.

Gottfredson and Hirschi (1990:270), for example, in claiming "no evidence" for police effects on crime, fail to even mention a substantial body of literature that reports such effects (e.g., Boydstun, 1975; Wilson and Boland, 1978; Sampson and Cohen, 1988; Sherman, 1986; see also Sherman, 1990, 1992a). Klockars and Mastrofski (1991:137), in claiming that the *only* tool police have to prevent crime is the "threat of punishment," ignore a wide body of research on situational crime prevention (Clarke, 1983) and crime problem solving by means other than threats of punishment (Goldstein, 1990).

Crime control research, and its interpretation, can only suffer from true believers committed to their hypotheses. Both evangelists convinced that community policing is best and Puritans convinced that crime control is the devil shed more heat than light. A truly empirical stance towards crime control would be agnostic about its possibility and even about the potential crime control value of more research. It may well be, as Gary T. Marx claims, that police evaluation research is merely "rearranging the deck chairs on the Titanic," as America's inner-city crime problems escalate (personal communication, 1990). But the long-term benefits of testing the effects of police methods cannot be easily foreseen. The only way to test Marx's hypothesis is to continue to approach the task with open minds and better ideas about innovations worth developing. A commitment to rigorous research methods, equally applied to any innovation, is far more scientific than any pessimistic dogma about what "cannot be" or the inherent limits of police capacity to control crime.

A New Model of Crime Control Values

Perhaps the best way for crime control to resist the stigmatizing label of "repression" is to replace Packer's model of its values with a viable alternative. Neither space nor clarity permits an exposition as detailed as Packer's. Five succinct value statements of a new crime control model should suffice for guiding further research and development on police innovations.

1. *The control of predatory crime is valued more highly than any other police mission.* Taxpayers do not want to be harmed by other people, either strangers or acquaintances. Whether or not taxpayers ever call the police in their entire lives, they still expect police to do everything possible to reduce the risks of predatory crime in their communities. Everything else police do is secondary, at least for routine management of police resources. It is up to police leadership to resist pressures from special interest groups or individuals to divert resources from the primary police mission.

2. *Obedience to the law and due process rules is valued more highly than punishment of any or all offenders.* Whatever the temptation to make moral judgments that ends justify means, any police actions violating constitutional rights can be just as predatory as the crimes police attempt to control. Police must be ever conscious of not becoming additional predators the community must fear, even when some segments of the community or the police subculture itself may demand it. This is especially important in order maintenance, where the most efficient response—sometimes described as "kicking ass" or making arrests solely for "contempt of cop"—is illegal. In restating the Golden Rule, police should never act in ways they do not want citizens to act. Even better, police should treat every suspect the way they would want the FBI to treat them if they were falsely accused of police corruption or brutality.

3. *Criminal sanctions for minor offenses are valued only for their demonstrated crime prevention effects, and are to be used with great caution until such effects are shown.* The war on drugs, the war on drunk driving, and the war on domestic violence have all prompted rapid increases in arrests for misdemeanor offenses, many of which have been routinely dropped by the courts. As a plausible case can be made that these arrests merely encourage more offending, and some experimental evidence supports it (Sherman, 1992b), the principle of doing no harm suggests great caution in mass arrest crackdowns. If crime control is directed primarily at the overall crime rate, rather than just desserts for individual offenders, alternatives to arrest become quite attractive: seizing illegal weapons (without arrests), blocking traffic in open-air drug markets, regulating the location of twenty-four-hour bank cash machines.

4. *High-frequency repeated patterns of crime are more valued than single crime incidents as targets for inventing new tactics and strategies of crime prevention.* Detecting the "top 20" locations, victims, relationships, offenders, and co-offenders involved in serious and not-so-serious crime on a quantitative basis is now easily done with microcomputer systems. Once these targets are identified and their causes are diagnosed, new policies, legislation, patrol patterns, or decoys can be developed for crime control by specific objectives. This quantitative approach to target selection will help to reduce any potential for arbitrariness and discrimination in proactive police problem solving. It also helps to focus on police and public concern about *crime*, as distinct from the adversarial focus on individual *criminals*.

5. *Police ethical sensitivity in creating innovative tactics is equal in value to the innovations themselves.* The new directions for police tactics often lead to waters uncharted by case law or legislation. When the Minneapolis Repeat Call Address Policing (RECAP) officers began to assist landlords in evicting tenants causing repeated police calls for such matters as fights and noise, for example, there was extensive discussion with the chief of police, openly reported in the news media, about the propriety of police officers' using this tactic. This kind of thoughtful reflection, so unusual in traditional police work, is a highly valued standard procedure for planning crime control innovations.

These five principles should clearly establish crime control as a legal, humane, careful, civil libertarian, and ethically sensitive endeavor. Some readers may believe the police to be incapable of adhering to these principles. In the short run, that skepticism will clearly be more justified in some police departments than in others. In the long run, that skepticism simply challenges the police institution to be morally stronger than it has ever been.

Other readers, however, may consider these principles and still conclude that crime control is a reactionary enterprise. They may see danger in suggesting that police should even try to control crime. They may prefer to see police departments greatly shrink in size and spend far less money in attempting to control minor public disorder. They may even be willing to accept the likely consequences of such a trend: more private security, more vigilantism, and greater private ownership of weapons. They might think that a return to the policing system of eighteenth-century London, for that is what this scenario amounts to, is less reactionary than crime control through innovative public policing.

If we use the term *reactionary* properly, it is hard to link it to constitutional innovations under the rule of law. "Depolicing" society of its public police, combined with increasing the use of private guards, is the truly reactionary direction. More rational choices of public and private police methods based on more comprehensive evaluation research move in the opposite direction: uncharted and unprecedented waters. Whether it constitutes "progress" will be for future generations to judge.

At the very least, the dispassionate scientific spirit of the search for better crime control alternatives is consistent with the dispassionate spirit of due process and the rule of law. The passions of policing will always be with us, and must be ever kept under control. It is the goal, if not always the achievement, of both law and science to take passions out of major decisions, such as choices of police strategy and tactics. Perhaps that is the best reason for claiming that the goal of policing for crime control is not reactionary.

References

Adorno, T.W., et al. (1950). *The Authoritarian Personality*. New York: Harper and Row.

Bernstein, R. (1990). Academia's Fashionable Orthodoxy: The Rising Hegemony of the Politically Correct. *The New York Times, The Week in Review*, October 28, 1990, p. 1.

Binder, A. and J. Meeker. (1988). Experiments as Reforms. *Journal of Criminal Justice 16*:347–358.

Black, D.L. and A.J. Reiss. (1967). Patterns of Behavior in Police and Citizen Transactions. In *U.S. President's Commission on Law Enforcement and Administration of Justice, Studies in Crime and Law Enforcement in Major Metropolitan Areas, Field Surveys III*. Washington, DC: U.S. Government Printing Office. Vol. 2, pp. 1–139.

Blumstein, A., J. Cohen, J. Roth, and C.A. Visher. (1986). *Criminal Careers and "Career Criminals."* Washington, DC: National Academy of Sciences.

Boydstun, J. (1975). *The San Diego Field Interrogation Experiment*. Washington, DC: Police Foundation.

Braithwaite, J. (1989). *Crime, Shame and Reintegration*. Cambridge, UK: Cambridge University Press.

Clarke, R.V. (1983). Situational Crime Prevention: Its Theoretical Basis and Practical Scope. In Tonry, M. and N. Morris (Eds.), *Crime and Justice: An Annual Review of Research*. Chicago: University of Chicago Press. Vol. 4.

Collins, J.J., Jr. (1980). Alcohol Use and Criminal Behavior: An Empirical, Theoretical and Methodological Overview. In Collins, J.J. (Ed.), *Drinking and Crime*. New York: Gilford Press. Pp. 288–316.

Colquhoun, P. (1795). *Treatise on the Police of the Metropolis*. London. [Reprinted in 1969 at Montclair, NJ, by Patterson-Smith.]

Cumming, E., I. Cumming, and L. Edell. (1965). Policeman as Philosopher, Guide and Friend. *Social Problems*, 12.

Dunford, F., D. Huizinga, and D.S. Elliott. (1990). The Role of Arrest in Domestic Assault: The Omaha Police Experiment. *Criminology 28*, No. 2:183–206.

Eck, J. and W. Spelman. (1987). *Problem-Oriented Policing in Newport News*. Washington, DC: National Institute of Justice.

Empey, L.T. (1979). From Optimism to Despair: New Doctrines in Juvenile Justice. Foreword to Murray, C.A. and L.A. Cox (Eds.), *Beyond Probation: Juvenile Corrections and the Chronic Delinquent*. Beverly Hills, CA: Sage.

Farrington, D. (1982). Randomized Experiments on Crime and Justice. In Tonry M. and N. Morris (Eds.), *Crime and Justice: An Annual Review of Research*. Chicago: University of Chicago Press. Vol. 4.

Feinberg, S., K. Larntz, and A.J. Reiss. (1976). Redesigning the Kansas City Prevention Patrol Experiment. *Evaluation 3*:124–131.

Fielding, H. (1754/1964). *The Journal of a Voyage to Lisbon*. London: Dent.

Given, J.B. (1977). *Society and Homicide in Thirteenth Century England*. Stanford, CA: Stanford University Press.

Goldstein, H. (1979). Improving Policing: A Problem-Oriented Approach. *Crime and Delinquency 25*:236–258.

Goldstein, H. (1990). *Problem-Oriented Policing*. New York: McGraw-Hill.

Goldstein, J. (1960). Police Discretion Not to Invoke the Criminal Process: Low-Visibility Decisions in the Administration of Justice. *Yale Law Journal, 69*:543–588.

Gottfredson, M. and T. Hirschi. (1990). *A General Theory of Crime*. Stanford, CA: Stanford University Press.

Greene, J. and C.B. Klockars. (1991). What Police Do. In Klockars, C.B. and S.D. Mastrofski (Eds.), *Thinking About Police*. 2nd ed. New York: McGraw-Hill. Pp. 273–285.

Greenwood, P. and A. Abrahamse. (1982). *Selective Incapacitation*. Santa Monica, Ca.: The RAND Corporation.

Hirschel, D.J., I.W. Hutchinson, III, C.W. Dean, J.J. Kelley, and C.E. Peasckis. (1990). *Charlotte Spouse Assault Replication Project: Final Report*. Washington, DC: National Institute of Justice.

Inbau, F. and J.E. Reid. (1962). *Criminal Interrogation and Confessions*. Baltimore, MD: Williams and Wilkins.

Kansas City (MO) Police Department. (1977). *Response Time Analysis*. Washington, DC: National Institute of Law Enforcement and Criminal Justice.

Kelling, G., T. Pate, D. Dieckman, and C. Brown. (1974). *The Kansas City Preventive Patrol Experiment: A Summary Report*. Washington, DC: Police Foundation.

Klockars, C.B. (1980). The Dirty Harry Problem. *Annals AAPSS 452*:33–47.

Klockars, C.B. (1983). *Thinking About Police*. New York: McGraw-Hill.

Klockars, C.B. (1985). Order Maintenance, the Quality of Urban Life, and Police: A Different Line of Argument. In Geller, W. (Ed.), *Police Leadership in America: Crisis and Opportunity*. New York: Praeger. Pp. 309–321.

Klockars, C.B. and S.D. Mastrofski. (1991). *Thinking About Police*. 2nd ed. New York: McGraw-Hill.

LaFave, W. (1965). *Arrest: The Decision to Take a Suspect Into Custody*. Boston: Little, Brown.

Larson, R. (1975). What Happened to Patrol Operations in Kansas City? *Evaluation 3*:117–123.

Lee, M.W.L. (1901). *A History of Police in England*. London: Methuen. [Reprinted in 1971 at Montclair, NJ, by Patterson-Smith.]

Lipset, S.M. (1969). Why Cops Hate Liberals—And Vice Versa. *Atlantic Monthly*, March:76–83.

Manning, P.K. (1977). *Police Work: The Social Organization of Policing.* Cambridge, MA: MIT Press.

Miller, W. (1977). *Cops and Bobbies.* Chicago: University of Chicago Press.

Morris, N. and G. Hawkins. (1970). *The Honest Politician's Guide to Crime Control.* Chicago: University of Chicago Press.

Packer, H.L. (1968). *The Limits of the Criminal Sanction.* Stanford, CA: Stanford University Press. [Reprinted in 1969 at London by Oxford University Press.]

Petersilia, J. (1987). *The Influence of Criminal Justice Research.* Santa Monica, CA: RAND Corp.

Pittman, D.J. and W. Handy. (1964). Patterns in Criminal Aggravated Assault. *Journal of Criminal Law, Criminology and Police Science 55*, No. 4.

Pokorny, A.D. (1965). A Comparison of Homicides in Two Cities. *Journal of Criminal Law, Criminology and Police Science 56*, No. 4.

Police Foundation. (1981). *The Newark Foot Patrol Experiment.* Washington, DC: Police Foundation.

Pringle, P. (1955). *Hue and Cry: The Birth of the British Police.* London: Museum Press.

Reiss, A.J., Jr. (1968). Police Brutality: Answers to Key Questions. *Trans-Action 5*, July–August.

Reiss, A.J., Jr. (1971). *The Police and the Public.* New Haven, CT: Yale University Press.

Sampson, R. and J. Cohen. (1988). Deterrent Effects of Police on Crime: A Replication and Theoretical Extension. *Law and Society Review 22*, No. 1:163–189.

Sherman, L.W. (1983). After the Riots: Police and Minorities in the United States, 1970–1980. In Glazer, N., and K. Young (Eds.), *Ethnic Pluralism and Public Policy.* Lexington, MA: D.C. Heath. Pp. 212–235.

Sherman, L.W. (1986). Policing Communities: What Works? In Reiss, A.J., Jr. and M. Tonry (Eds.), *Community and Crime.* Vol. 8: *Crime and Justice: An Annual Review of Research.* Chicago: University of Chicago Press.

Sherman, L.W. (1990). Police Crackdowns: Initial and Residual Deterrence. In Tonry, M. and N. Morris (Eds.), *Crime and Justice.* Chicago: University of Chicago Press. Vol. 12.

Sherman, L.W. (1992a). Attacking Crime: Police and Crime Control. In Morris, N. and M. Tonry (Eds.), *Modern Policing.* Chicago: University of Chicago Press.

Sherman, L.W. (1992b). *Policing Domestic Violence: Experiments and Dilemmas.* N.Y.: Free Press.

Sherman, L.W. and R. Berk. (1984). Specific Deterrent Effects of Arrest for Domestic Assault. *American Sociological Review 49*, No. 2:261–272.

Sherman, L.W., P.R. Gartin, and M.E. Buerger. (1989). Hot Spots of Predatory Crime: Routine Activities and the Criminology of Place. *Criminology 27*:27–55.

Sherman, L.W., J.D. Schmidt, D.P. Rogan, P.R. Gartin, E.G. Cohn, D.J. Collins, and A. Bacich. (1991). From Initial Deterrence to Long-Term Escalation: The Effects of Short Custody Arrest for Underclass Domestic Violence. *Criminology. 29*:821–50.

Sherman, L.W. and D. Weisburd. (1988). *Policing the Hot Spots of Crime: A Redesign of the Kansas City Preventive Patrol Experiment.* Washington, DC: Crime Control Institute.

Skolnick, J. and D. Bayley. (1986). *The New Blue Line: Police Innovation in Six American Cities*. New York: Free Press.

Smith, R.L. (1965). *The Tarnished Badge*. New York: Thomas Y. Crowell.

Spelman, W. and D.K. Brown. (1981). *Calling the Police: A Replication of the Citizen Reporting Component of the Kansas City Response Time Analyses*. Washington, DC: Police Executive Research Forum.

Treiman, D.J. (1977). *Occupational Prestige in Comparative Perspective*. New York: Academic Press.

Walker, S. (1977). *A Critical History of Police Reform*. Lexington, MA: D.C. Heath.

Wilson, J.Q. (1968). *Varieties of Police Behavior: The Management of Law and Order in Eight Communities*. Cambridge, MA: Harvard University Press.

Wilson, J.Q. (1980). What Can the Police Do About Violence? *Annals of the American Academy of Political and Social Science 542*:13–21.

Wilson, J.Q. and B. Boland. (1978). The Effect of the Police on Crime. *Law and Society Review, 12*:367–390.

Wolfgang, M. (1958). *Patterns in Criminal Homicide*. Philadelphia: University of Pennsylvania Press.

10
Justice Without Trial Revisited

JEROME H. SKOLNICK

My opening argument in *Justice Without Trial* (Skolnick, 1966) was that "law and order" was a misleading cliche. The concept of "order" reflected ideas about how citizens should conduct themselves. Thus, the substantive criminal law sets penalties for misbehavior ranging from homicide to the illegal possession of marijuana. The procedural law sets limits on what police can do in enforcing the substantive law. The conflict between "order" and "law," I argued, posed a fundamental dilemma for police in a democratic society.

The 1960s were unquestionably the pinnacle of constitutional reform in procedural law. Those accused of homicide and other crimes, whom the police wished to interrogate, were required under *Miranda v. Arizona* (384 U.S. 436 (1966)) to be informed by police of their constitutional right to remain silent and to have a lawyer appointed to represent them. Under *Mapp v. Ohio* (367 U.S. 643 (1961)) the Supreme Court extended the exclusionary rule to the states. In this chapter, I argue, for reasons I develop later, that the exclusionary rule has been an important contribution to the development of police professionalism. For various reasons, including the rise in crime in the past twenty-five years and especially the rise in drug crime, the Supreme Court has diluted the gains made during the 1960s. The gains, I suggest, began to have a powerful and positive institutional impact on police during the 1970s and 1980s, and are now being threatened by the war on drugs. At the same time, I argue later, it is neither fair nor realistic to rely on law enforcement as our solution to the United States' drug problem.

Drugs and Crime

When I began field research on *Justice Without Trial* illegal drug trafficking was a significant but not primary concern of criminal justice professionals—police, prosecutors, and courts—in the United States. Today that has entirely changed. Although disagreements over how to

190

control the crime and drug problem in the United States may occur, there is scarce disagreement that drug trafficking and use take up most of the energy of police, prosecutors, courts, prisons, probation, and parole. From a practical perspective, traditional criminal law concerns—degrees of homicide, robbery, theft, fraud, justification, and excuse, the nuts and bolts of the common law and courses in criminal law—pale by comparison.

The prevalence of drug selling, itself a felony in every jurisdiction in the United States, surely undermines the accuracy of estimates of the amounts of felonious crime in this country. Criminologists have traditionally identified two sources of error in crime statistics. One, the so-called "dark figure" of crime, addresses the limitations of the Uniform Crime Reports and refers to crimes undisclosed to police. As many victimizations are not divulged to the police, these statistics, gathered in the Uniform Crime Reporting System, substantially underestimate the kinds and amounts of criminal victimization. The National Crime Survey attempts to correct for this distortion by asking people to report their victimizations to survey researchers rather than the police. Crimes that are underreported to the survey researchers are sometimes said to constitute the "double dark" figure of crime (Kadish, 1983).

There is also, however, a "triple dark" figure involving consensual but felonious crime. At the white collar level, this may include bribes and kickbacks. Still, drug sales must far outnumber these, and by how much we can only guess. The triple dark figure of crime may be our most elusive crime statistic. Its magnitude can be suggested only indirectly by the huge amounts of illegal drugs confiscated by law enforcement authorities[1] and the complaints of local citizens reporting a sharp rise in neighborhood drug selling.

In sum, although burglaries and robberies appear to have declined in the past decade the public has not become less concerned about crime. Why not? Obviously, it is because both the actual and perceived criminality, and especially violence associated with drugs and gangs, has become a major area of public concern.

Drugs and Procedural Justice

As drug enforcement has escalated, the issue of procedural justice, especially of the scope of the exclusionary rule, has become increasingly salient. In a series of decisions meant to curb the rule, the Supreme Court

---

[1] On September 29, 1989, twenty tons of cocaine were seized in a San Fernando Valley warehouse by local and federal drug enforcement officials. And on November 4, 1989, eight tons of cocaine were seized by officials in New York City.

has rendered its legitimacy open to question. In *United States v. Leon* (468 U.S. 897 (1984)) and *Massachusetts v. Sheppard* (468 U.S. 981 (1984)) the Court announced a "good faith" exception to the exclusionary rule. It also announced that the exclusionary rule is not constitutionally mandated, but is rather a judge-made rule that can be changed depending on how well it is working. This reasoning has offered an invitation to judges to cut back on the application of the rule.

The exclusionary rule was initially imposed on grounds that it was required by the confluence of the Fourth and Fifth amendments.[2] The warrantless seizure of records was analogized to a forced confession. Several decades later the rule was mandated in federal criminal cases on grounds that government officials should act with integrity. If the government's agents acted "without sanction of law" as they did in *Weeks v. United States* (232 U.S. 383 (1914)), they should not be permitted to benefit from using the evidence so obtained.

Opponents of the rule, perhaps the most influential of whom was Benjamin Cardozo, argued in 1926, when he was Chief Judge of New York's Court of Appeals, that the states should not adopt the federal rule because on balance it made no sense that "the criminal should go free . . . because the constable has blundered." In *Wolf v. Colorado* (338 U.S. 25 (1954)) the Supreme Court held that the Fourth Amendment was binding on the states through incorporation in the Fourteenth Amendment. But the court found that the exclusionary rule was not incorporated and should be imposed only on a case-by-case basis in state criminal cases where police conduct was so egregious as to violate fundamental fairness.

Many commentators thought that the exclusionary rule might be introduced through the doctrine of substantive due process. This was especially true after the decision in *Rochin v. California* (342 U.S. 165 (1952)). In this case police had the stomach of a drug dealer pumped to bring up illegally seized evidence. Justice Frankfurter wrote that this conduct "shocked the conscience." But in *Irvine v. People* (347 U.S. 128 (1954)) the Los Angeles police three times broke into the home of a suspected bookmaker. They bugged every part of the premises, from the bedroom to the garage. Justice Jackson, writing for the majority, wrote that "Few police measures have come to our attention that more flagrantly, deliberately, and persistently violated the fundamental principle declared by the Fourth Amendment" (*Irvine v. People*, 1954).

But, relying on the *Wolf v. Colorado* principle that illegally seized evidence need not be barred from state criminal proceedings, the conviction was to stand. However flagrant the *Irvine* violations, they did not compare to the "violence" and "physical brutality" of *Rochin*. Thus, the

---

[2] 347 U.S. at 132.

Irvine ruling substantially limited the theory of substantive due process as grounds for remedying flagrant but nonviolent police misconduct.

Mapp v. Ohio (1961), where the Court reached out to hold that tainted evidence must be excluded from state criminal trials, should be seen as a response to *Irvine*. That case made it clear that absent an exclusionary rule, state and local police could engage in violations of the Fourth Amendment, no matter how flagrant and deliberate, so long as they were nonviolent.

With the exception of its early phase as a rule of evidence for the federal courts, the exclusionary rule has been linked to a legal framework of individual rights. Some legal scholars, however, like Anthony Amsterdam, have for a long time sought a more social systemic understanding of the purposes of exclusionary rule. Amsterdam compared the Supreme Court to the Pythian oracle, occasionally reviewing ill-smelling cases wafted up by litigation, but with little concern for the ooze of the U.S. criminal justice system. Amsterdam argued that the real good achieved by the exclusionary rule and other protections of supposedly individual rights was in improving the quality of police practices.

The goal is not to deter the individual police officer but to mediate that deterrence through the lessons exclusion will bring to the crime control system, particularly to prosecutors and management police. From this perspective, the relevant question is whether the exclusionary rule helps maintain organizational pressure to comply with the Fourth Amendment that would be less strong in its absence (Wasserstrom and Mertens, 1984).

In *United States v. Leon* (1984) the Supreme Court diluted the exclusionary rule, and, I believe, its contribution to a developing police professionalism. The Court examined a narrow band of cases where the police had obtained a warrant from a California lower court judge who had misread whether the police had "probable cause" based on the facts. The *United States v. Leon* investigation began when an informant—of unproven reliability—told a police officer that two people were selling quantities of narcotics from their residence. The informant said he had seen a sale take place five months earlier. The police watched the residence, as well as a couple of other residences. They observed people going in and out of the residences in a way that suggested drug trafficking was occurring. On the basis of their observations, plus the informant's tip, they applied for a search warrant, which was granted. The police searched and found large quantities of narcotics.

On appeal, a federal district court judge ruled that the police had acted in good faith by applying for a warrant, but that the facts did not establish "probable cause." The government appealed the case to the U.S. Supreme Court. In this landmark case, the Court recognized a "good faith" exception to the exclusionary rule. The reason? Even though the police did not have probable cause to make the search, the constitutional violation lay with the magistrate. Thus, the exclusion of such illegally obtained evidence should scarcely influence future police conduct.[3]

That reasoning makes sense if the focus of the exclusionary rule is the individual officer. But the reasoning is flawed if the significance of the exclusionary rule is not to deter the individual officer, but to reform the police as an organization operating within a larger criminal justice system. If the exclusionary rule generates pressure throughout the system to devote more attention and resources to achieving compliance, it does not much matter whether fault lies with the magistrate or the police officer. If illegal evidence is excluded when a magistrate *wrongly* determines that probable cause exists, police will be motivated to learn to better judge the adequacy of their affidavits and to have these affidavits reviewed by more competent magistrates, rather than "rubber-stamped" by magistrates who will be inclined to make mistakes about whether the police have probable cause to search.

My observations of police over the years since *Justice Without Trial* convinces me that most narcotics detectives are intelligent, resourceful, and often as knowledgeable about Fourth Amendment law as the magistrates to whom they are applying for a warrant. A police officer who applies for a warrant with less than probable cause may know exactly what he or she is doing, and can scarcely be assumed to be acting in "good faith."

To this observation I would add four further points. First, opponents of the rule traditionally argue that it is wrong for the criminal to go free, "because the constable has blundered." But the real point is that if the constable had complied with the constitution, the suspect would not have been convicted.

Second, prior to *Mapp v. Ohio*, in states where the exclusionary rule did not apply, constables did not "blunder." On the contrary, they *systematically* ignored the requirements of the Fourth Amendment because there was no reason to pay attention to it.[4]

Third, the absence or presence of an exclusionary rule significantly impacts police subculture and associated values. Without an exclusionary

---

[3] One can question how adequate the cost–benefit analysis is in the majority opinion. There is no effort to quantify the actual loss of cases in "good faith" cases.

[4] The phase originates in Judge Cardozo's opinion in *People v. Defore*, 150 N.E. 585 (N.Y. 1926). Despite Cardozo's emphasis on blunder there continued to be an utter absence of warrants in New York prior to *Mapp v. Ohio*. Also, the outrageous police conduct in *Mapp* itself, where police broke into a house without a warrant, forcibly detained Dolree Mapp, and eventually seized evidence for a crime totally different from the one on which their search was based. That kind of disregard for the Fourth Amendment speaks to an institution's priorities, not the ineptness of individual police officers.

rule, the Fourth Amendment has little meaning to police. The average cop has no incentive to believe that due process values are salient.

Fourth, the police are a bureaucratic organization. Those who head police departments, so-called "management cops" (Reuss-Ianni, 1983), become hard pressed to inculcate Fourth Amendment values if these are merely an abstraction. These points are critical to our understanding of how to control police in a democratic society.

Police Professionalism and Bureaucratic Control

Thirty years ago, when I was collecting observations of the Oakland police department for *Justice Without Trial*, California had adopted the exclusionary rule seven years earlier, whereas New York and Ohio did not (*People v. Cahan* 44 Cal. 2d 434 (1955)). As the research demonstrated, violations of the Fourth Amendment were commonplace in the department. This important fact can be explained in several different ways. It may have been that simply not enough time had elapsed to achieve changes in organizational structure or motivation. It may be that the Supreme Court had not reviewed enough cases to supply detailed, working rules. It is also likely that political factors generated police responsiveness to the communities they were policing. Part of that responsiveness consisted of reducing some of the blatant racism of police in places like Detroit, Newark, and Oakland,[5] especially by increasing the numbers of minority and female officers and supervisors.

During the 1950s and 1960s, in Oakland as in most urban police forces, arrest figures and clearance rates were the primary device for ensuring compliance with organizational imperatives. As I reported in *Justice Without Trial*, however, these measures were both inadequate and even self-defeating. Because police officers enjoy discretionary control over arrests, only field sergeants supervise whether arrests are made for the right reasons or whether arrests will hold up as cases move through the criminal process. Detectives similarly control clearance rates. Thus, the agents supposedly evaluated by the device of arrest and clearance figures were in the best position to manipulate the results. So long as police commanders focused on the these statistics, they had little means of knowing whether the organization was accomplishing its aims.

Even more importantly, the police organizational goals were obscured by the use of these measures which valued clearances and arrests. The clearance rate as a "quality control" measure of police competence sends a message about the organizations's goals: "we care more about arrests and clearances than about conviction." The orienting hypothesis of

---

[5] David Bayley and I describe much of this change in *The New Blue Line: Police Innovation in Six American Cities* (Skolnick and Bayley, 1986).

Justice Without Trial was that the police are bureaucratic workers who respond to the organizational reward structure. When conviction is a goal, especially in the context of drug enforcement, police concerns for Fourth Amendment compliance are heightened. That is as true today as it was thirty years ago.

Between 1984 and 1988, Jonathan Simon and I observed drug enforcement in Oakland (Westville). We believed that adherence to the Fourth Amendment improved significantly from the 1960s to the 1980s.[6] It is, of course, difficult to verify this conclusion. We have not collected statistics, nor could we devise a statistical test of legal compliance. But we can present evidence to back up our claim. Our sense that improvement is real stems in major part from two observed patterns.

First, we saw procedures designed to enforce the Fourth Amendment integrated into almost every sector of the policing enterprise. In an earlier version of this paper we called this a "legal archipelago," because it seemed as if sets of islands of legal values had been distributed throughout the broad experience of policing. We have come to see this as central to maintaining control over the police in a democratic society.

The second pattern was in the difference in discourse and behavior of the police officers themselves. The idea of enforcing the Fourth Amendment has become normalized far more that it was in the early 1960s. It is not that police will no longer disparage the exclusionary rule and lawyers in general. What is striking is how, underneath the veneer of "prime time" cop talk, one discovers that police at all levels demonstrate a routine awareness of procedural tasks that have become as much a part of the job as using the radio or completing paper work. Four factors can be cited as central to the shift:

1. *Training in legal and departmental rules.* This training, to which only a minimal amount of time was devoted in the early 1960s, has become a significant rite of passage through which police cadets must pass on

---

[6] Research for this chapter has taken place in fits and starts. Both Simon and Skolnick conducted observations and interviews with the Oakland Police Department, the Alameda County District Attorney's Office, and the Alameda County Public Defender's Office, during the spring of 1984. During the summer of 1984 Simon worked as a law clerk in the Public Defender's Office doing motions to suppress evidence. During this time he observed suppression motions in Superior Court on a weekly basis. During 1985 Skolnick conducted observations and interviews with the Oakland Police Department in the course of writing *The New Blue Line* (with David Bayley). During the winter of 1987 Simon and Skolnick both conducted observations of antinarcotic operations by the police, including arrests, warrant writing and executing, and warrantless searches. The collection of qualitative data in relatively small samplings over a period raises methodological problems. It also, however, provided both authors with the opportunity to look at the same processes from the point of view of several different agencies in the criminal process, and to reexamine the perceptions formed early in the project.

their way to official status, and to which veterans are resubjected on a regular basis (Slocum, 1986). Furthermore, training may be conducted with minorities and women who tend to infuse police recruits with more positive notions of legal and community responsibility.

2. *The office of the prosecutor.* Once a distant and mistrusted institution, the prosecutor has become more regularly involved with the Oakland Police Department through the production of legal update materials, contact during pretrial motions, and regular interaction in the production of warrants and the evaluation of cases. This latter contact has been particularly significant because the police have developed their own legal specialists who carry norms of the legal process into the department, particularly in the area of drug enforcement.

3. *Visibility of police practices.* When evaluations of police are made on convictions rather than arrests, they become more visible to higher-level police management and to prosecutors. Convictions, especially in drug possession cases, imply procedural knowledge. Police actions in the field are subject to higher-level criticism when they deviate from procedural requirements.

4. *The suppression motion.* Although the motion to suppress evidence occupies a relatively small place in the working lives of most police officers, it is an integral part of those who engage in searches and seizures—the essence of drug enforcement. The structure of the hearing inverts the normal criminal process. Here, the officer is charged with violating the constitutional rights of the accused, the prosecutor is transformed into a defense attorney, and the defense attorney is transformed into a prosecutor. It can be interpreted as a ritual to powerfully reinforce the idea that the rule of law has meaning. Just as the criminal trial can be characterized as a "degradation ceremony," it is possible to view the suppression hearing as a kind of legal identity reinforcing ceremony for the police officer.

In short, the operation of the exclusionary sanction justifies the existence of a set of practices that have reshaped the organizational structure of policing. That dense wall of values that we often call "the police subculture" (Skolnick, 1966:Chap. 3) has not disappeared but it has been modified by legal process norms, not only norms of procedure but also norms of fairness. Thus, equal protection norms, which have resulted in the presence of increased numbers of minorities and women, may well serve to reinforce adherence to Fourth and Fifth amendment procedural norms, all of which embody what Sociologist Max Weber referred to as "legal rationality." This idea includes, above all else, that bureaucratic action be linked to the articulation of reasons that justify those actions.

The "war on drugs" escalated during the 1980s just as constitutional values were beginning to take hold in many police departments. The "war on drugs" offers an illustration of how a metaphor generates and reenforces attitudes. If we put the war on drugs in political perspective, we know how to rid ourselves of the drug problem. As a society we could institute a rule that anyone caught selling or possessing illegal drugs will be summarily executed by a special police narcotics unit. Few of us, however, would choose to live in such a society.

More importantly, that society's narcotics police would not constitute what we in this society ordinarily mean by the concept of police. For although it is true that we invest the police with awesome powers—to arrest, to detain, to search, to use force including deadly force—all of these are monitored and constrained by our constitution. And although execution is currently permitted, other extreme punishments—drawing and quartering, for example—are prohibited by the cruel and unusual punishment clause of the Eighth Amendment.

That our conception of police and punishment implies fealty to the constitution and the rule of law could be considered a platitude. But it is a commonplace worth repeating when measures such as the removal of bail for drug dealers, deployment of the National Guard, curfews for teenagers, street sweeps of supposed gang members, shooting down of civilian planes, random drug testing, crop eradication, and zero tolerance are put forward as a first line in the war against drugs. Not all of these measures are actually being implemented, but they can support a climate for diluting constitutional constraints on detention, search, and interrogation.

Recent Supreme Court decisions limiting the scope of the procedural protections of the Fourth and Fifth amendments cannot be comprehended except as a response to the urgencies of drug trafficking in what law professor Steven Wisotsky has called "The Emerging Drug Exception to the Bill of Rights":

Since the early 1980s, the prevailing attitude has been that cracking down on drugs is imperative. As a result, the three branches of government have deferred very little to constitutional and non-constitutional limits on the exercise of governmental power in the domain of drug enforcement. What Laurence Tribe describes as the Constitution's "pivotal, even mythological place in our national consciousness" is rapidly being eroded by a positivist, bureaucratic attitude that we can—must—do whatever is deemed necessary or expedient in waging the war on drugs" (Wisotsky, 1987:890)

The drug exception continues to prevail. How else could the court conclude that police helicopter surveillance at 400 feet above a private home is not a "search" because any member of the public could legally have been flying at an altitude of 400 feet over the home (*Florida v. Riley* 109 S. Ct. 693 (1989))? Or that one who wraps his trash in opaque plastic bags, which the garbage collector was expected to pick up and deposit at the garbage dump, has "knowingly exposed it to the public" (*California v. Greenwood* 486 U.S. 35, 41 (1988))? Such decisions must be understood as part of a larger war on drugs psychology which has influenced every level of the criminal justice system, although the area most directly affected has, understandably, been the law of search and seizure. It is also my belief that it will set back the development of police professionalism that we saw emerging in the late 1970s and early 1980s.

The Limits of Law Enforcement

Will the "war on drugs" solve the drug problem? It is neither fair nor reasonable to ask law enforcement to take major responsibility for solving the nation's drug problem. Clearly, our civil liberties will be jeopardized by the "war on drugs." The issue is not whether law enforcement can win the war, but what its limitations are (1) in a democratic, free society; (2) against crimes based on a market economy, and; (3) with respect to entrepreneurs who sell products that are popular and illegal. I suggest that these limitations are powerful, and will more effectively erode the gains we have made in police professionalism than they will abate the drug problem.

Moreover, economic imperatives will likely impose equal or greater limits on the efficiency of law enforcement than constitutional norms. In evaluating our law enforcement efforts we must be sensitive to the relationship between demand and supply in the illegal drug market. The *National Drug Control Strategy*, published in September 1989, acknowledges that "[d]espite interdiction's successful disruptions of trafficking patterns, the supply of illegal drugs entering the United States has, by all estimates, continued to grow" (p. 73). Why should that have happened? One part of the reason is that demand generates supply, for drugs just as for video cassette recorders. This results in price reduction, which further stimulates demand.

Closely related is what might be termed the *Darwinian trafficker dilemma.* "As we have expanded our interdiction efforts," the *Strategy* continues, "we have seized increasing amounts of illegal drugs. Stepped up interdiction has also forced drug traffickers to make significant operational changes. Every time we disrupt or close a particular trafficking route, we have found that traffickers resort to other smuggling tactics that are even more difficult to detect" (p. 73). So as we develop increasingly sophisticated tactics for reducing both narcotics production and smuggling, only the stronger and more efficient producers and smugglers survive. This, in turn, heightens supply and lowers cost. As this occurs suppliers seek wider markets, particularly in distressed populations, just as segments of the alcohol and tobacco industries do.

It is difficult to achieve successful interdiction for another reason as well. According to Rand Corporation economist Peter Reuter, who studied whether our borders can be sealed against illegal drugs for the Department of Defense, our Mexican border is especially permeable. There are few barriers from the south to bringing drugs into that country, and the drugs can be "brought across by small plane, private vehicle, or even by boat" (Reuter, 1988:51, 55). A Mexican-American California narcotics agent made a similar observation to me in an interview in 1989: "Four hundred thousand of my people cross the border every year. How can you stop a much smaller number who are carrying a kilo or two of cocaine on their back?"

A related issue discussed by Reuter is the limited costs that interdiction can impose. Interdiction is supposed to reduce street sales by increasing production and smuggling costs—in effect, taxing these—and thus raising the street price. This assumes that production and smuggling costs constitute a significant percentage of street price. But it is relatively cheap to produce and refine a kilo of cocaine, perhaps around $1000 for a kilo that might eventually, when broken down into quarter- or even eight- gram units, retail for $250,000. Smuggling costs might amount to an additional few percent of the retail price.

During the summer of 1989, police reported that gangs (and others) were marketing primarily crack cocaine, although other illegal drugs were available as well. In any event, crack cocaine was the marketing preference of the Los Angeles street gangs, on whom our attention was focused, as well as the Dominican and Jamaican gangs in New York City. From a longer-range policy perspective, however, we should not assume the stability of drug preference among those who enjoy faster living through chemistry. We know from history that drug preference, the epidemiology of drug use, is less related to the intrinsic properties of a drug than to the social definition of a particular substance as the drug of choice. Twenty or thirty years ago, heroin was the "problem" drug in American society (Kaplan, 1983). Today it is crack cocaine. Tomorrow it may be another drug.

Moreover, as we attempt to put pressure on foreign producers we will have to work with authorities in such countries as Columbia, Bolivia, Panama, Peru, and Mexico. The bribe is a familiar part of law enforcement in these countries. Thus, the State Department's Bureau of International Narcotics Matters found that Jorge Luis Ochoa, a major Columbian drug trafficker, "was able to buy his freedom through the intimidated and vulnerable Columbian judicial system" (U.S. Department of State, 1988:86). No matter how honest U.S. drug enforcement agents are, they may find themselves operating in a climate of official corruption.

What of our urban police? Unfortunately, we are all too familiar with the legendary narcotics scandals that have bedeviled the police in various cities. For a recent example, deputies in the Los Angeles County Sheriff's Department were involved in what *The Los Angeles Times* called "one of the worst corruption cases" in the Department's history. Videotape shows one deputy hurriedly taking three $10,000 bundles of $100 bills from a dealer's shoulder bag and putting them into his partner's leather briefcase.[7] Although the possibilities of corruption obtain in any form of vice enforcement, only in drug enforcement do we encounter large sums of cash and drugs held by perpetrators who are in no position to complain against being ripped off by police.

By no means am I suggesting that all narcotics police are corrupt. On the contrary, any number of aware police managers struggle with the potential problem. The Los Angeles Deputies were caught in a sting operation instituted by Sheriff Sherman Block. High-level New York City narcotics officials, whom I interviewed, stressed that integrity and police safety were the two paramount features of narcotics enforcement in New York City.

I am suggesting that it is difficult to uncover narcotics corruption, particularly when a small number of individuals are involved; that whatever is discovered is likely to be the tip of the corruption iceberg; and that corruption needs to be counted as one of the unanticipated costs to police professionalism and constitutional values of drug law enforcement. A cop who will steal drugs and drug money will also lie on the witness stand.

Prison overcrowding offers an additional limitation on the capacity of law enforcement to incarcerate drug offenders. State and federal prison populations expanded in unprecedented numbers during the 1980s. The Bureau of Justice statistics reported at the end of 1988 that the number of U.S. prisoners set a new record for the fourteenth consecutive year. The Bureau counted 329,821 inmates in 1980. By 1988, that figure had risen to 627,402. Projected from Department of Justice figures by The Sentencing Project of Washington, DC, the total for 1989 will include 731,978 in federal and state prisons and 341,851 in local jails—1,055,829 prisoners altogether.[8] Jails and prisons are overcrowded partly by newly convicted criminals, but also by criminals whose probation and parole were revoked largely because they failed their drugs tests when released to the community. California, for example, had a 3200 percent increase in parole violators who returned to prison between 1978 and 1988.[9]

As our advanced drug testing technology consigns more parolees and probationers to prison, we find we cannot continue to convict and impose longer sentences without building new prisons. The need for prison and jail capacity is widely recognized. *The National Drug Strategy* thus recognizes the critical lack of prison space as we expand law enforcement.

---

[7] *The Los Angeles Times*, October 24, 1989.

[8] T. Wicker, *The New York Times*, October 13, 1989.

[9] In 1988, about 47 percent of the admissions to California state prisons were of parole violators returned to prison by the Parole Board without a conviction for a new charge. See Messinger et al. (1988).

It observes that "Most state prisons are already operating far above their designed capacity," and also that "many states have been forced under court order to release prisoners before their terms have been served whenever a court-established prison population limit has been exceeded" (1989:26). In recognition of the shortage of prison space to house convicted offenders and probation and parole violators, *The Strategy* states governments must persuade their citizens to support new prisons. "The task of building prisons remains with state governments, who poorly serve their constituents when prison construction is stalled or resisted" (1989:26). Unfortunately, such exhortation may not prove to be practical. Even those citizens who demand longer and more certain sentences are reluctant to pay for prisons and sometimes even more reluctant to live next door to them. Thus, highly publicized plans for a 700-bed federal prison to house convicted Washington, DC drug dealers at Fort Meade, Maryland, were withdrawn the day after they were announced, *The New York Times* reported, because "there was too much public resistance."[10]

Even if we could build new prisons, imprisonment is not necessarily stigmatic, nor entirely foreboding for those who sell drugs. In our interviews with imprisoned California drug dealers (Skolnick, 1989) we found that imprisonment may offer a kind of "homeboy" status, especially for gang youth, for whom the prison can become an alternative neighborhood. Moreover, imprisonment often motivates prisoners in their troublesome ways. Consigned to the margins of society anyhow, in prison they join gangs, use drugs, and make useful connections for buying and selling drugs. The penitentiary was perhaps once a place for experiencing penance. Today's correctional institutions, overcrowded as they are with short-term parole violators (many of whom have failed their court-mandated drug tests), often serve functions similar to those conventions performed for academics and business people—an opportunity for networking.

When we incarcerate drug dealers in prisons, we also encounter what might be termed the Felix Mitchell Paradox, in honor of the West Coast's formerly most infamous drug distributor. In the mid-1980s, a federal strike force, with considerable assistance and dogged investigation by an incorruptible Oakland Police vice squad, succeeded in convicting and imprisoning the East Bay's three leading drug dealers. Among these was the legendary Felix Mitchell, who was later killed in Leavenworth federal prison and was a hero to the thousands who turned out for his funeral.[11] Theoretically, Oakland's streets should have been cleansed of drugs.

---

[10] April 18, 1989. *The Wall Street Journal* reported on October 20, 1989, that Mr. Bennett has attributed the halting progress of the Washington, DC war on drugs to "local officials" whose "politics" has blocked new prison construction.
[11] The story of Felix Mitchell and his drug operation is told by Covino (1985).

Did that happen? Hardly. The main results were a drop in price and a rise in street homicides and felonious assaults by gang members as they challenged each other for market share. As territorial arrangements have stabilized, so has the homicide rate, but the street price of crack has remained about the same or declined.

Reuter makes a similar observation concerning the District of Columbia's soaring homicide rate. Reuter argues that when the supply of drug dealers exceeds the demand for drugs, "one obvious way to raise earnings is to eliminate the competition through violence." Inactivity by the District's police during the 1980s might be an alternative explanation. But the arrest data show the opposite, that is, a sharp rise in activity. Only 58 juveniles had been arrested for dealing offenses in 1981; by 1987 that figure had reached 1550. In 1981 adult arrests, usually of men in their early twenties, totaled 408; by 1987 the total was 5297 (Reuter, 1989).

Similarly, the escalation in drug selling and violence in Oakland, California, persuaded the legislature and the governor to provide four million dollars from 1985 to 1987 to bolster and expand prosecution, probation, and the courts. The Center for the Study of Law and Society at the University of California, Berkeley, was contracted to evaluate the initiative. Malcolm Feeley, Richard Berk, Roseann Greenspan, and I formed a research team to undertake the evaluation. Following an ethnographic and statistical study, we concluded that all of the law enforcement agencies carried out their mandate thoroughly and professionally and that the intermediate goals of more prosecutions, more convictions, and more probation violations were met. Unfortunately, crime, and narcotics crime in particular, continued to increase. So we concluded that, contrary to popular mythology, the rise in narcotics crime in Alameda County cannot be attributed to inefficient courts, prosecutors, probation officers, or police (Greenspan et al., 1988).

Of all the enforcement initiatives, the least effective will be those aimed at military interdiction; the most satisfying, at least initially, are those involving the community and local police. In a recent National Institute of Justice publication, Mark Kleiman (1988), a proponent of street-level drug enforcement, points to two special threats street drug dealing poses: children may become users, and street dealing may become disruptive or violent.

There is much disagreement, however, about the effectiveness of neighborhood police crackdown.[12] In the same publication, prosecutor Kevin Burke favors street-level enforcement, arguing that "[W]hen balanced against the environment of an open drug market, a visible,

---

[12] See the critiques of Kleiman's article by Arnold Barnett and Anthony V. Bouza in Chaiken (1988).

active police presence is not a tremendous intrusion and therefore not a significant cost of a street-level operation" (Burke, 1988:53).

At the same time, some law enforcement officials are skeptical about the positive effects of crackdowns. Minneapolis police chief Anthony Bouza writes:

Focused, saturation street enforcement will clean up an area, but it is costly and inefficient. It robs others areas of their fair share of scarce resources and it does not eliminate the intractable problem of drug dealing, merely displaces it. It also focuses, inefficiently, on the lowest level of the criminal chain and is sure to lead to abuses and repression, with sweeps and round-ups. (Bouza, 1988:47, 49)

So it is not clear how law enforcement will be able to repair the damage drug dealing imposes on local communities and what the larger social costs are of an expanded police effort in this direction. Everywhere police are seeking counsel and support from private citizens and community organizations, both for identifying the problem and for taking steps within the community to resolve at least a portion of it. Everywhere police departments are, with greater or lesser success, trying to organize community-based crime prevention activities, ranging from organized public surveillance such as Neighborhood Watch, to informational newsletters, to groups that wipe out graffiti. In addition, most police departments have reoriented a portion of traditional patrol activities in favor of proactive anti-drug and anti-gang enforcement.

Yet the narcotics chief of a major East Coast city recently summarized a theme I have heard increasingly from police and prosecutors whom I have interviewed in connection with current research: "The easiest thing to do is make an arrest for drugs. The hardest thing is to stop the drug trafficking." Increasingly, it would seem, police are coming to see the drug problem as a social, economic, and educational issue, rather than primarily a law enforcement responsibility.

Conclusion

Let me conclude by saying that I have continued to study police for the roughly thirty years since I undertook the research for *Justice Without Trial*. During that time there has been a gratifying movement toward police professionalism, especially by higher-ranking officers who benefited from the educational opportunities offered by the Law Enforcement Assistance Administration. Police carry out drug enforcement but they also understand how very limited they are in this enterprise. They are also aware of the ultimate paradox of policing in a democratic society that I wrote of in *Justice Without Trial*:

Appellate decisions upholding the integrity of procedural requirements may well move large segments of the community to greater concern for the security of the substantive ends of criminal law. Especially when the police are burdened with the responsibility of enforcing unenforceable laws, thereby raising the spectre of a "crime-ridden" community, decisions that specifically protect individual liberty may increase pressure from an anxious community to soften these, and thus contain the seeds of a more "order oriented" redefinition of procedural requirements.

During the tenure of the Warren Court, the US Supreme Court was increasingly indulgent of the rights of the accused. Whether this trend will continue, or whether the courts will redefine "due process of law" to offer legitimacy to what is presently considered unlawful official behavior may be contingent on the disposition of the civil community. (Skolnick, 1966)

Clearly, the civil community's response to the drug problem, the "war on drugs," has influenced the Supreme Court's interpretation of due process in ways that can only undermine the "legal professionalism" of police. Appellate court decisions that move away from "bright lines" into doctrinal murkiness such as "good faith" or "totality of the circumstances" may offer police larger discretion but at what cost. They will not solve the drug problem, but they may well undermine the positive social systemic impact of appellate court decisions on police appreciation of due process values.

References

Bouza, A.V. (August 1988). Comments on Street Level Drug Enforcement. In Chaiken, M.R. (Ed.), *Street Level Enforcement: Examining the Issues*. Washington, DC: National Institue of Justice, August.

Burke, K.M. (August 1988). Comments on Street Level Enforcement Activity. In Chaiken, M.R. (Ed.), *Street Level Enforcement: Examining the Issues*. Washington, DC: National Institue of Justice.

Chaiken, M.R. (Ed.) (August 1988). *Street Level Enforcement: Examining the Issues*. Washington, DC: National Institute of Justice.

Covino, M. (1985). How the 69th Mob Maximized Earnings in East Oakland. *California*, November:83.

Greenspan, R., R.A. Berk, M.M. Feeley, and J.H. Skolnick. (1988). *Courts, Probation and Street Drug Crime*. Barkeley, CA: Center for the Study of Law and Society.

Kadish, S.H. (Ed.) (1983). Crime Statistics. In *Encyclopedia of Crime and Justice*. New York: MacMillan and Free Press. Vol. 1.

Kaplan, J. (1983). *The Hardest Drug: Heroin and Public Policy*. Chicago: University of Chicago Press.

Kleiman, M.A.R. (August 1988). Crackdowns: The Effects of Intensive Enforcement on Retail Heroin Dealing. In Chaiken, M.R. (Ed.), *Street Level Enforcement: Examining the Issues*. Washington, DC: National Institute of Justice.

Messinger, S., et al. (1988). *Parolees Returned to Prison and the California Prison Population*. Sacramento, CA: California Bureau of Criminal Statistics.

National Drug Control Strategy. (1989). *National Drug Control Strategy*. September, Washington, DC.: U.S. Government Printing Office.

Reuss-Ianni, E. (1983). *The Two Cultures of Policing: Street Cops and Management Cops*. New Brunswick, NJ: Transaction Books.

Reuter, P. (1988). Can the Borders Be Sealed? *The Public Interest*. Santa Monica, CA: Rand Corp.

Reuter, P. (1989). The D.C. Crime Surge. *Washington Post*, March 26, 1989.

Skolnick, J.H. (1966). *Justice Without Trial*. New York: John Wiley and Sons.

Skolnick, J.H. (1989). *The Social Structure of Street Drug Dealing*. Sacramento, CA: California Bureau of Criminal Statistics and Special Services.

Skolnick, J.H. and D. Bayley. (1986). *The New Blue Line: Police Innovation in Six American Cities*. New York: Free Press.

Slocum, P. (1986) *Police Training and the Exclusionary Rule*. Unpublished doctoral dissertation, UCLA Department of Sociology.

U.S. Department of State, Bureau of International Narcotics Matters. (1988). *International Narcotics Control Strategy Report*, March:86.

Wasserstrom, S. and W.J. Mertens. (1984). The Exclusionary Rule on the Scaffold: But Was It a Fair Trial? *American Criminal Law Review 22*:85.

Weber, Max. (1958). *The Protestant Ethic and the Spirit of Capitalism*. New York: Scribner.

Wisotsky, S. (1987). *Crackdown: The Emerging "Drug Exception to the Bill of Rights. Hastings Law Journal 38*:889.

Author Index

Subject Index

Gross, Avum and no plea bargaining
 ban in Alaska, 163
Guilty plea
 legal theory of, 24
 uses of, 23

H
Habeas corpus
 and martial law, 18
 writ of, 18
Hands off doctrine, 34
Hawthorne effect and police behavior,
 116
Head start project and police budgets,
 177
Homicides, 181

I
Illegally seized evidence
 Irvine v. People (1954), 192
 Mapp v. Ohio (1961), 193
 Rochin v. California (1952), 192
Imprisonment and networking, 202
Industrial revolution and crime, 14
Internal affairs units, 4
International Association of Chiefs of
 Police, 42
Interrogation, 15
 Escobedo v. Illinois (1964), 17
Investigating magistrate activities, 165
Irvine v. People (1954), 192
Italy, corruption and tyranny, 157

J
Judge-made law, procedural
 requirements, 19

K
Kansas City, MO Police Department,
 and response time, 176
Kansas City, MO Preventive
 Patrol Experiment evaluation of, 183
 and police methods, 176
 and police work, 176
KGB, 134
King Louis XIV (1667), 160
King, Rodney, 34, 113
Kolender v. Lawson (1983), and
 constitutional rights, 113

L
Law
 and adjudicatory process, 19
 and arrests, 18
 and communism, 28
 and conduct of officials, 18
 and due process, 19, 84
 and economy, 25
 elements of crime, 18
 as an enterprise, 25
 and forbidden actions, 84
 as an instrument of order, 18
 and internal morality, 24
 and legal controls, 32
 and politics, 25
 and power structure, 25
 and Protestant ethic, 25
 and public opinion, 25
 as social order, 18–19
 in society, 29
 sociology of, 25
 in a total state, 29
Law enforcement
 and community policing, 64
 and crime control, 180
 and crime prevention, 180
 and order maintenance, 180
 and prison crowding, 201–202
 rule implementation, 48
Law Enforcement Assistance
 Administration, and educational
 opportunities, 204
Legal controls
 absence of, 36
 administrative policies, 32
 countertrends, 33
 court decisions, 32
 development of, 36
 statutes, 32
 and U.S. Supreme Court, 37
Legal controls of police and political
 pressure, 49
Legality
 and despotism, 148
 and justice, 24
Liberal democracies and rule of law, 157
Liberalism
 definition of, 149
 and totalitarianism, 149